In Sickness and In Health

The **ANU Indonesia Project**, a leading international centre of research and graduate training on the Indonesian economy and society, is housed in the **Arndt-Corden Department of Economics, Crawford School of Public Policy, ANU College of Asia and the Pacific** at the **Australian National University (ANU)**. Established in 1965 in response to profound changes in the Indonesian economic and political landscapes, the ANU Indonesia Project has grown from a small group of Indonesia-focused economists into an interdisciplinary research centre well known and respected across the world. Funded by ANU and the Australian Government Department of Foreign Affairs and Trade, the ANU Indonesia Project monitors and analyses recent developments in Indonesia; informs the Australian and Indonesian governments, business and the wider community about those developments and about future prospects; stimulates research on the Indonesian economy; and publishes the respected *Bulletin of Indonesian Economic Studies*.

ANU College of Asia and the Pacific's **Department of Political and Social Change** focuses on domestic politics, social processes and state–society relationships in Asia and the Pacific, and has a long-established interest in Indonesia.

Together with the Department of Political and Social Change, the ANU Indonesia Project holds the annual Indonesia Update conference, which offers an overview of recent economic and political developments and devotes attention to a significant theme in Indonesia's development. The *Bulletin of Indonesian Economic Studies* publishes the conference's economic and political overviews, while the edited papers related to the conference theme are published in the Indonesia Update Series.

The **ISEAS – Yusof Ishak Institute** (formerly Institute of Southeast Asian Studies) is an autonomous organisation established in 1968. It is a regional centre dedicated to the study of sociopolitical, security, and economic trends and developments in Southeast Asia and its wider geostrategic and economic environment. The Institute's research programs are grouped under Regional Economic Studies (RES), Regional Strategic and Political Studies (RSPS), and Regional Social and Cultural Studies (RSCS). The Institute is also home to the ASEAN Studies Centre (ASC), the Singapore APEC Study Centre, and the Temasek History Research Centre (THRC).

ISEAS Publishing, an established academic press, has issued more than 2,000 books and journals. It is the largest scholarly publisher of research about Southeast Asia from within the region. ISEAS Publishing works with many other academic and trade publishers and distributors to disseminate important research and analyses from and about Southeast Asia to the rest of the world.

Indonesia Update Series

In Sickness and In Health

Diagnosing Indonesia

EDITED BY

FIRMAN WITOELAR · ARIANE UTOMO

YUSOF ISHAK INSTITUTE

First published in Singapore in 2022 by
ISEAS Publishing
30 Heng Mui Keng Terrace
Singapore 119614

E-mail: publish@iseas.edu.sg
Website: http://bookshop.iseas.edu.sg

All rights reserved. No part of this publication may be reproduced, translated, stored in a retrieval system, or transmitted in any form or by any means, electronic, mechanical, photocopying, recording or otherwise, without the prior permission of the ISEAS – Yusof Ishak Institute.

© 2022 ISEAS – Yusof Ishak Institute, Singapore

The responsibility for facts and opinions in this publication rests exclusively with the authors and their interpretations do not necessarily reflect the views or the policy of the Institute or its supporters.

ISEAS Library Cataloguing-in-Publication Data

Name(s): Witoelar, Firman, editor. | Utomo, Ariane, editor.
Title: In sickness and in health : diagnosing Indonesia / edited by Firman Witoelar and Ariane Utomo.
Description: Singapore : ISEAS – Yusof Ishak Institute, 2022. | Series: Indonesia Update Series | Chapters mostly '... based on the papers written by the contributors to the 38th annual Indonesia Update conference held on 15–17 September 2021.' | Includes bibliographical references and index.
Identifiers: ISBN 9789815011845 (paperback) | ISBN 9789815011876 (hard cover) | ISBN 9789815011852 (ebook PDF) | ISBN 9789815011869 (epub)
Subjects: LCSH: Public health—Indonesia.
Classification: LCC DS644.4 I41 2021

Cover photo credit: Husniati Salma on Unsplash
Edited, typeset and indexed by Tracy Harwood, Canberra
Printed in Singapore by Mainland Press Pte Ltd

Contents

Tables		vii
Figures		viii
Contributors		x
Acknowledgements		xii
Glossary		xiv
1	Introduction: Diagnosing Indonesia *Firman Witoelar and Ariane Utomo*	1

PART 1 THE INDONESIAN HEALTH SYSTEM: CHALLENGES AND OPPORTUNITIES

2	Post-pandemic trajectory of health-reform financing in Indonesia *Laksono Trisnantoro*	17
3	The right to health and the politics of health policy reform in post–New Order Indonesia *Andrew Rosser and Luky Djani*	37
4	The importance of the 2020 Population Census for health data *Terence H. Hull*	56
5	Addressing regional disparities in access to medical specialists in Indonesia *Andreasta Meliala and Srimurni Rarasati*	71

6   Pill pushers: Politics, money and the quality of medicine
     in Indonesia   88
     *Elizabeth Pisani, Relmbuss Biljers Fanda, Amalia Hasnida,
     Mawaddati Rahmi, Yunita Nugrahani, Bachtiar Rifai Pratita
     Ihsan, Ayuk Lawuningtyas Hariadini, Diana Lyrawati and
     Aksari Dewi*

PART 2 HEALTH FOR ALL: LESSONS AND STRATEGIES

7   Navigating access to health care in Indonesia:
     A sociostructural analysis   113
     I Nyoman Sutarsa

8   Impact of COVID-19 on maternal, neonatal and child health
     programs: A case study for health systems strengthening   132
     Tiara Marthias and Yodi Mahendradhata

9   Maternal health: Past, present and moving forward   148
     Salut Muhidin and Jerico F. Pardosi

10   Disability in Indonesia: What can we learn from the
     available data?   172
     Diana Contreras Suárez and Lisa Cameron

11   Out of the shadows: A brief introduction to mental health
     in Indonesia   201
     Aliza Hunt, Sandersan Onie and Hans Pols

12   Dengue control in Yogyakarta, Indonesia: Lessons learned
     from public health innovation using *Wolbachia*-infected
     Aedes aegypti mosquitoes   222
     Adi Utarini

Index   242

Tables

2.1	Projection of Indonesia's economy	29
2.2	State budgets, 2019–2022	29
3.1	Health policy case studies: Outcomes and politics	43
4.1a	2020 census age structure, preliminary release 2021	64
4.1b	2020 census age structure, final release 2021	65
4.2	Provincial total fertility rates (TFRs) from the 2013 official population projection assumptions compared to the 2020 census indirect estimates of fertility	67
4.3	Ratio of age cohort surviving for 10 years from the 2010 census to the 2020 census	69
5.1	Institutions and human resources for health planning in Indonesia	76
5.2	The numbers and ratios of registered health workers per 1,000 population in 2018 and the targeted ratio by 2025	79
5.3	The share of public and private hospitals with internal medical specialists, by category	81
6.1	Estimated demand for products in areas where no company bid successfully to supply e-catalogue products, 2018	94
6.2	Ratio of median maximum retail price (HET) to average public procurement price, 2020	96
6.3	Sales data for different brands of amlodipine 5 mg, from a single pharmacy that serves JKN and non-JKN patients, Nusa Tenggara Timur, 2021	102
9.1	Causes of maternal deaths by province, 2020	154
9.2	Distribution of birth attendants by province, 2020	160
9.3	Percentage of health facility births and maternal deaths in East Nusa Tenggara by district, 2009 and 2016	164

Figures

2.1	Number of daily COVID-19 cases in Indonesia, March 2020 to May 2022	19
2.2	Number of daily deaths caused by COVID-19 in Indonesia, March 2020 to April 2022	19
2.3	GDP growth in Indonesia before the pandemic and in 2020 (%)	21
2.4	Countries' fiscal response packages, 2020 (% of GDP)	22
2.5	The number of hospitals in five regions in Indonesia, 2012–2020	24
2.6	Distribution of surgical oncology specialists in Indonesia, 2022	25
2.7	GDP and tax revenue, 2007–2019 (rupiah trillions)	27
2.8	National health budget, 2017–2022 (rupiah trillions)	31
2.9	Indonesia's national health transformation, 2021–2024	32
4.1	Population pyramid (millions)	66
5.1	The decentralised health service in Indonesia	73
5.2	Number of private and public hospitals by province, 2020	74
5.3	Medical specialists ratio per 1,000 population, 2020	80
5.4	The growth of private hospitals in Indonesia, 2012–2018	82
5.5	Foreign direct investment in Indonesian health care, by country (US$ millions)	83
6.1	Proportion of different brands of furosemide dispensed by Malang district hospital by volume and revenue, January–October 2021	98
6.2	Variation in prices of amlodipine 5 mg: Malang and Nusa Tenggara Timur, 2021 (rupiah)	103
6.3	Maximum permitted retail price (HET), amlodipine and amoxicillin, 2021 (rupiah)	104
8.1	Daily new confirmed COVID-19 cases in Indonesia (thousands)	133
8.2	Trends in antenatal care and facility delivery, and COVID-19 confirmed cases	137

8.3	Trends in postnatal and neonatal care visits, and COVID-19 confirmed cases	138
8.4	Trends in child growth monitoring and immunisation visits for children aged under 5 years, and COVID-19 confirmed cases	139
8.5	Distribution of physicians, 2020	142
9.1	Maternal mortality rate by province (per 100,000 live births)	152
9.2	Proportion of four or more antenatal care visits (ANC4+) by province, 2020	156
9.3	Proportion of health facility births by province, 2020	158
9.4	Maternity care and referral system (Revolusi KIA) in East Nusa Tenggara province	163
9.5	Three delays model for maternal care	165
9.6	Proportion of health facility births in East Nusa Tenggara by district, 2012	167
10.1	Representation of the International Classification of Functioning, Disability and Health	174
10.2	Prevalence of disability in different surveys (%)	179
10.3	Prevalence of people with disability, by province	181
10.4	Number of people with disability, by province	182
10.5	Types of disability as a share of total disabilities (%)	184
10.6	Causes of disability (%)	184
10.7	Total population distribution by age range and disability status (%)	185
10.8	Access to health insurance (bars) and health complaints last month (lines) by age group (%)	190
11.1	A resident at the home of Mbah Marsiyo	203
11.2	Mental health treatment pathways	206
12.1	The study phases of the World Mosquito Program Yogyakarta	229
12.2	Photos posted on social media illustrating WMP Yogyakarta activities in Yogyakarta City	234
12.3	Mapping of government stakeholders in the World Mosquito Program Yogyakarta	236

Contributors

Lisa Cameron, Professorial Research Fellow, Melbourne Institute of Applied Economic and Social Research, University of Melbourne

Diana Contreras Suárez, Senior Research Fellow, Melbourne Institute of Applied Economic and Social Research, University of Melbourne

Aksari Dewi, Researcher, George Institute for Global Health, Sydney

Luky Djani, Lecturer, Department of Political Science, Pembangunan Nasional Veteran University, Jakarta

Relmbuss Biljers Fanda, Researcher, Center for Health Policy and Management, Gadjah Mada University, Yogyakarta

Ayuk Lawuningtyas Hariadini, Lecturer, Department of Pharmacy, Faculty of Medicine, Brawijaya University, Malang

Amalia Hasnida, PhD Researcher, Erasmus School of Health Policy & Management, Erasmus University, Rotterdam, The Netherlands

Terence H. Hull, Emeritus Professor, School of Demography, Australian National University, Canberra

Aliza Hunt, Visiting Fellow, Centre for Mental Health Research, National Centre of Epidemiology and Population Health, Australian National University, Canberra

Bachtiar Rifai Pratita Ihsan, Lecturer, Department of Pharmacy, Faculty of Medicine, Brawijaya University, Malang

Diana Lyrawati, Lecturer, Department of Pharmacy, Faculty of Medicine, Brawijaya University, Malang

Yodi Mahendradhata, Dean, Faculty of Medicine, Public Health and Nursing, Gadjah Mada University, Yogyakarta

Tiara Marthias, Senior Technical Adviser, Nossal Institute for Global Health, Melbourne School of Population and Global Health, University of Melbourne

Andreasta Meliala, Director, Centre for Health Policy and Management, Faculty of Medicine, Public Health and Nursing, Gadjah Mada University, Yogyakarta

Salut Muhidin, Senior Lecturer, Department of Management, Macquarie University, Sydney

Yunita Nugrahani, Researcher, Faculty of Pharmacy, Pancasila University, Jakarta

Sandersan Onie, Post-doctoral Fellow, Black Dog Institute, Australia; and Founder, Emotional Health for All, Indonesia

Jerico Pardosi, Lecturer, School of Public Health and Social Work, Queensland University of Technology, Brisbane

Elizabeth Pisani, Visiting Professor, Faculty of Pharmacy, Pancasila University, Jakarta

Hans Pols, Professor, School of History and Philosophy of Science, University of Sydney

Mawaddati Rahmi, Researcher, Faculty of Pharmacy, Pancasila University, Jakarta

Srimurni Rarasati, Researcher, Centre for Health Policy and Management, Faculty of Medicine, Public Health and Nursing, Gadjah Mada University, Yogyakarta

Andrew Rosser, Professor of Southeast Asian Studies, Asia Institute, University of Melbourne

I Nyoman Sutarsa, Senior Lecturer, College of Health and Medicine, Australian National University; and Department of Public Health and Preventive Medicine, Faculty of Medicine, Udayana University, Denpasar

Laksono Trisnantoro, Director, Graduate Program in Health Policy and Management, Faculty of Medicine, Public Health and Nursing, Gadjah Mada University, Yogyakarta; and Special Adviser to Indonesia's Minister of Health for Resilience of Pharmaceutical and Medical Device Industries

Adi Utarini, Project Leader, World Mosquito Program Yogyakarta, Centre for Tropical Medicine; and Department of Health Policy and Management, Faculty of Medicine, Public Health and Nursing, Gadjah Mada University, Yogyakarta

Ariane Utomo, Senior Lecturer in Demography, School of Geography, Earth and Atmospheric Sciences, University of Melbourne

Firman Witoelar, Fellow, Indonesia Project, Crawford School of Public Policy, College of Asia and the Pacific, Australian National University, Canberra

Acknowledgements

The chapters in this volume, except for the chapter by Hunt, Onie and Pols, were based on the papers written by the contributors to the 38th annual Indonesia Update conference held on 15–17 September 2021. It was the first Indonesia Update conference to be held fully online since the first Update in 1983, usually held at the Australian National University (ANU). The COVID-19 pandemic has unleashed unprecedented public health, social and economic crises with prolonged impacts and consequences. Our conference took place shortly after the onset of the devastating Delta wave, during which many lives were lost in Indonesia, Australia and beyond. We extend our deepest appreciation and gratitude to the contributors, participants, volunteers and organisers of the ANU Indonesia Update 2021 for their work, support, contributions, patience and forbearance during these challenging times.

The Indonesia Update conference is hosted jointly by the ANU Indonesia Project and the Department of Political and Social Change. We are grateful for the support of Blane D. Lewis, Head of the ANU Indonesia Project, for his guidance from the early planning of the conference. We would like to thank Kate McLinton, Cut Nurkemala Muliani, Lydia Napitupulu and Gema Satria Mayang Sedyadi, who organised the conference under much uncertainty and without whom the event would not have run smoothly. We would also like to thank Riandy Laksono, Charlie Barnes and Ginanjar Panggalih, who lent their support during the days of the event, and the Australia-Indonesia Youth Association (AIYA), Perhimpunan Pelajar Indonesia Australia (PPI Australia) and Perhimpunan Pelajar Indonesia se-Dunia (PPI Dunia) for their support in promoting the event to their respective networks and on social media.

We would like to thank Brian Schmidt, Vice Chancellor of the ANU, for his opening address, and Senator the Hon Zed Seselja, HE Penny Williams and HE Y. Kristianto S. Legowo, for their welcoming remarks in the three days of the conference. We thank the conference speakers: Charlotte Setijadi, Nava Nuraniyah, Asep Suryahadi, Ridho Al Izzati, Athia Yumna, James P. Villafuerte, Laksono Trisnantoro, Azad Singh Bali, Adi Utarini, I Nyoman Sutarsa, Diah Saminarsih, Terry Hull, Iqbal Elyazar, Irma Hidayana, Lenny Ekawati, Ahmad Arif, Ahmad Nurhasim, Tiara Marthias, Yodi Mahendradhata, Andrew Rosser, Luky Djani, Diana Contreras Suárez, Lisa Cameron, Ade W. Prastyani, Salut Muhidin, Jerico Pardosi, Andreasta Meliala, Elizabeth Pisani, Aksari Dewi, Relmbuss Biljers Fanda, Amalia Hasnida and Ines Atmosukarto, and the chairs: Greg Fealy, Arianto Patunru, Liza Munira, Kirsten Bishop, Sharyn Graham Davies, Diahhadi Setyonaluri and Hellena Souisa for their contributions.

Our thanks also go to our academic colleagues for their valuable inputs: Arianto Patunru, Budy Resosudarmo, Hal Hill, Peter McCawley, Anne Booth, Chris Manning, Terry Hull, Sarah Dong, Ed Aspinall, Greg Fealy, Marcus Mietzner, John F. McCarthy, Ross Tapsell, Eva Nisa, Liza Munira and last but not least, Ross McLeod, who suggested the title for this Update and the book.

We acknowledge the strong support of the ANU College of Asia and the Pacific. We would also like to express our gratitude to the Australian Government Department of Foreign Affairs and Trade for their support for the 2021 Indonesia Update conference and their continuing support for the Indonesia Project.

Finally, we would like to express our profound gratitude to Tracy Harwood, who provided her invaluable contribution as the copyeditor of this volume. We wish to thank the team at ISEAS – Yusof Ishak Institute in Singapore, which has published the Indonesia Update series since 1994, particularly to Ng Kok Kiong and Rahilah Yusuf for their excellent work.

Firman Witoelar and Ariane Utomo
Canberra, August 2022

In memory of Emeritus Professor Gavin Jones—our mentor, colleague, friend and supporter of the ANU Indonesia Project and the ANU Indonesia Update

Glossary

Adminduk	Administrasi Kependudukan (Population Administration)
ANC	antenatal care
ANC4+	four or more antenatal care visits
ART	antiretroviral treatment
Askes	Asuransi Kesehatan untuk Pegawai Negeri Sipil dan Pensiunan TNI/POLRI (Health Insurance for Civil Servants and Veterans)
Askeskin	Asuransi Kesehatan Masyarakat Miskin (Health Insurance for Poor Communities)
AWED	applying Wolbachia to eliminate dengue
Banglitbangkes	Badan Penelitian dan Pengembangan Kesehatan (National Institute of Health Research and Development, Ministry of Health)
Bappenas	Badan Perencanaan Pembangunan Nasional (National Development Planning Agency)
bidan	midwife
BKKBN	Badan Koordinasi Keluarga Berencana Nasional (National Board of Family Planning)
BP Jamsostek	Badan Penyelenggara Jaminan Sosial Ketenagakerjaan (precursor to BPJS Ketenagakerjaan/BPJS Labour)
BPJS	Badan Penyelenggara Jaminan Sosial (Social Security Agency)
BPJS Kesehatan or BPJS-K	Badan Penyelenggara Jaminan Sosial Kesehatan (Healthcare and Social Security Agency)
BPK	Badan Pemeriksa Keuangan (National Audit Agency)
BPNT	Bantuan Pangan Non-Tunai (Non-Cash Food Subsidy Program; now Kartu Sembako)

BPPSDMK	Board for Development and Empowerment of Human Health Resources, Ministry of Health
BPS	Badan Pusat Statistik (Statistics Indonesia), the central statistics agency
COVID-19	coronavirus disease (COVID-19), an infectious disease caused by the SARS-CoV-2 virus
DALY	disability-adjusted life year
Dana PEN	National Economic Recovery Program Fund
DaSK	Dashboard Sistem Kesehatan (Health System Dashboard)
Desa Siaga Sehat Jiwa	integrated mental health programming
Dinkes	Dinas Kesehatan (local/provincial health office)
Direktorat Keswa dan Napza	Directorate of Mental Health and Illegal Drugs
DJSN	Dewan Jaminan Sosial Nasional (National Social Security Council)
DPR	Dewan Perwakilan Rakyat (People's Representative Council, also known as House of Representatives or parliament)
Dukcapil	Direktorat Jendral Kependudukan dan Catatan Sipil (Population and Civil Registry)
dukun beranak	traditional birth attendant/midwife
EHFA	Emotional Health for All
GAPPRI	Indonesian Cigarette Manufacturers Association
GAPRINDO	Gabungan Produsen Rokok Putih Indonesia (White Cigarette Producers Association)
GDP	gross domestic product
HET	harga eceran tertinggi (maximum retail price)
HRH	human resources for health
IAKMI	Ikatan Ahli Kesehatan Masyarakat Indonesia (Indonesian Public Health Association)
ICF	International Classification of Functioning, Disability and Health
IDHS	Indonesia Demographic and Health Survey
IDI	Ikatan Dokter Indonesia (Indonesian Medical Association)
IFLS	Indonesia Family Life Survey
IHR	International Health Regulations
ILO	International Labour Organization
INN generics	international non-proprietary name generics

IPDS	Institusi Pendidikan Dokter Spesialis (Medical Specialist Education Institution)
Jamkesda	Jaminan Kesehatan Daerah (Local Health Insurance for the Poor)
Jamkesmas	Jaminan Kesehatan Masyarakat (National Health Insurance for the Poor and Near Poor)
Jampersal	Jaminan Persalinan (Maternity Health Insurance)
Jamsostek	Jaminan Sosial Tenaga Kerja (Workers' Social Insurance scheme)
jamu	traditional medicine
JKN	Jaminan Kesehatan Nasional (National Health Insurance scheme)
JPS-BK	Jaringan Pengaman Sosial – Bidang Kesehatan (Social Safety Net – Health)
JPS-Gakin	Jaringan Pengaman Sosial – Keluarga Miskin (Health Safety Net for Poor Families)
kabupaten	district
kader jiwa	community mental health advocate
Kartu Keluarga	Family Card
Kemenkes	Kementerian Kesehatan (Ministry of Health)
KJS	Kartu Jakarta Sehat (Jakarta Health Card)
KKI	Konsil Kedokteran Indonesia (Indonesian Medical Council)
Kopigawa	Komunitas Peduli Kesehatan Jiwa (Mental Health Care Community)
kotamadya	municipality
KPSI	Komunitas Peduli Skizofrenia Indonesia (Indonesian Schizophrenia Support Community)
LAMPTKES	Lembaga Akreditasi Mandiri Pendidikan Tinggi Kesehatan Indonesia (Indonesian Accreditation Agency for Higher Education)
LKPP	Lembaga Kebijakan Pengadaan Barang dan Jasa Pemerintah (Public Procurement Policy Board)
LMICs	low- and middle-income countries
MNCH	maternal, neonatal and child health
MoH	Ministry of Health
MUI	Majelis Ulama Indonesia (Council of Indonesian Ulama)
NGO	non-government organisation
NTT	Nusa Tenggara Timur (East Nusa Tenggara province)

Glossary xvii

NU	Nahdlatul Ulama (traditionalist Islamic organisation)
panti	social rehabilitation centre
Panti Sosial Dosaraso	government-run residential care facility
pasung	the practice of physically restraining people, using stocks, chains or cages
PBI	Penerima Bantuan Iuran (government health subsidy for the poor)
PBPU	Peserta Bukan Penerima Upah (voluntary contribution to JKN by informal sector workers)
PDI-P	Partai Demokrasi Indonesia-Perjuangan (Indonesian Democratic Party of Struggle)
PDSKJI	Penhimpunan Dokter Spesialis Kedokteran Jiwa Indonesia (Indonesian Psychiatric Association)
PEN	Program Pemulihan Ekonomi Nasional (National Economic Recovery Program)
Perpres	Peraturan Presiden (Presidential Regulation)
PERSI	Perhimpunan Rumah Sakit Seluruh Indonesia (Indonesian Hospital Association)
PES	Post Enumeration Survey
PIP	Program Indonesia Pintar (Smart Indonesia Program)
PJS	Perhimpunan Jiwa Sehat (mental health advocacy organisation)
PKH	Program Keluarga Harapan (Family Hope Program, conditional cash transfers)
Potensi Desa	Village Potential Statistics
PPKM	*pemberlakuan pembatasan kegiatan masyarakat* (enforced restrictions on community activities)
PPU	Pekerja Penerima Upah (compulsory contribution to JKN by employees and employers in the formal sector)
PSBB	*pembatasan sosial berskala besar* (large-scale social restrictions)
puskesmas	*pusat kesehatan masyarakat* (community health centre)
Pw/oD	people without disability
PwD	people with disability
Rastra program	Rice Program (from *beras sejahtera*, 'rice for the prosperous')
Revolusi KIA	Revolusi Kesehatan Ibu dan Anak (Mother and Child Health Revolution)
Riskesdas	Riset Kesehatan Dasar (Basic Health Survey)

Rp	rupiah
rumah sakit	hospital
Sakernas	Survei Angkatan Kerja Nasional (National Labour Force Survey)
SARS	severe acute respiratory syndrome
SDH	social determinants of health
Sensus Penduduk	Population Census
Simkeswa	Sistem Kesehatan Jiwa (national mental health reporting system)
SIRS	Sistem Informasi Rumah Sakit (Hospital Information System)
SLK	*sekolah luar biasa* (special school)
STI	sexually transmissible infection
Supas	Survei Penduduk antar Sensus (Intercensal Population Survey)
Susenas	Survei Sosio-Ekonomi Nasional (National Socioeconomic Survey)
tagana	volunteer mental health crisis worker
TFR	total fertility rate
TKSK	*tenaga kesejahteraan sosial kecamatan* (district social welfare worker)
TPKJM	Tim Pelaksana Kesehatan Jiwa Masyarakat (Community Mental Health Implementation Team)
TTS	Timor Tengah Selatan (South Central Timor)
UN	United Nations
UNFPA	United Nations Population Fund
UNICEF	United Nations Children's Fund
WG	Washington Group on Disability Statistics
WHO	World Health Organization
WMP	World Mosquito Program

1 Introduction: Diagnosing Indonesia

Firman Witoelar and Ariane Utomo

Canvassing health transition in Indonesia

In 1950, about 189 out of 1,000 babies born alive in Indonesia would not have survived past their first birthday. Such a high infant mortality rate overwhelmingly contributed to the population's low life expectancy for the newly independent nation at the time. Assuming the prevailing age-specific patterns of deaths, for the same year, life expectancy at birth was estimated to be 39.4 years. By 2022, Indonesia's infant mortality rate has fallen to 17.7 deaths per 1,000 live births, and life expectancy at birth has risen to 68.25 years.[1]

If we go by these trends in infant mortality rate and life expectancy, the future trajectory for the general health and wellbeing of the average Indonesian is looking rosy. After all, the two indicators are meant to capture the underlying factors and contexts that shape the health of the nation. At the outset, gains in life expectancy—and correspondingly, the reduction in infant mortality rate—reflect a narrative of improvements in income per capita, living conditions, nutritional intake and education, as well as access to and quality of health care in recent decades. But focusing only on these two broad indicators may also obfuscate the complex history of Indonesia's health transition, where wins are often coupled with setbacks, and where health-related innovations regularly intersect with novel conundrums.

What do we mean by health transition, and why do we often hear that Indonesia's health transition has been marked by increasing complexity over time? The term health transition is often used interchangeably with

---

1 United Nations Data Portal Population Division, https://population.un.org/DataPortal/, accessed 31 August 2022.

epidemiologic transition. The latter was first conceptualised by Abdel Omran in 1971 to refer to the long-term shifts in the mix of diseases as people live longer through the course of economic development and social change. More specifically, Omran coined the term epidemiologic transition to describe 'the complex change in patterns of health and disease and on the interactions between these patterns and their demographic, economic and sociological determinants and consequences' (1971: 510). In the first iteration of the epidemiologic transition theory, Omran proposed that there are three distinct stages in the transition: the age of pestilence and famine, the age of receding pandemics, and the age of degenerative and man-made diseases. Herein lies the basic premise of the epidemiologic transition theory: along with development and social change, the mortality and disease patterns in a particular geographic location would gradually shift from being dominated by infectious diseases (afflicting predominantly infants and young children) to chronic, non-communicable and degenerative diseases that tend to occur in older ages.

Over the years, there have been many critiques, iterations and challenges to the epidemiologic transition theory (Mackenbach 2022; Omran 1998; Santosa et al. 2014; Vallin and Meslé 2004). The re-emergence of infectious diseases, and emergence of new infectious diseases such as HIV/AIDS, and now COVID-19, is one of the more obvious challenges. Another glaring limitation is to do with how the original epidemiologic transition theory—like many other concepts in social science and public health—was largely drawn from a characterisation of what had happened in Western Europe and North America in the past (Mackenbach 2022).

In this book, we adopt a wider definition of health transition whereby the epidemiologic transition is a component in the overall transformation of the health profile of Indonesia as a nation. Frenk et al. (1991) conceptualised two broad components in health transition. The first is to do with the long-term shifts in the 'patterns of diseases, disability and death', and the second component refers to the shift in the 'organized social response to health conditions' (p. 23). The second component, for example, relates to factors such as transformations in health care infrastructure and provisions.

Like the experiences of many other middle- and lower-middle-income countries, Indonesia's health transition is governed by multiple challenges, the first of which is to do with inequality. The history and nature of economic development in many developing countries is marked by deep socioeconomic inequalities, making patterns of health transitions across their diverse subpopulations incredibly complex (Frenk et al. 1991). In the case of Indonesia, inequalities in access to and quality of health care are shaped not only by wealth inequalities, but also by longstanding regional inequalities. As shown in the chapter by Andre Meliala and Srimurni Rarasati in this book, Indonesia continues to struggle to address the unequal access to health infrastructure and health care professionals across its vast archipelago. Another challenge is the double burden of mortality and morbidity from infectious and non-communicable diseases (Mackenbach 2022). In Indonesia, and in other countries of similar economic standing, before the decline in mortality attributed to infectious diseases has reached low levels (see Chapter 12 by Utarini on dengue eradication, for example), mortality from non-communicable diseases is already on the rise (Bloom et al. 2015; Kusuma et al. 2019; Mboi et al. 2018; Witoelar and Miranti 2021).

This book aims to capture a slice of the complex story of how Indonesia's quest for longer and healthier lives of its people has unfolded to date. The contributors of this edited collection are scholars, policymakers and expert practitioners who were invited to speak at the 2021 Indonesia Update—an annual conference hosted by the Indonesia Project of the Australian National University in Canberra, Australia, usually timed to take place during the southern hemisphere's early spring. In the first quarter of 2021, we were optimistic that the pandemic would turn a corner, and that it was possible to hold a hybrid event by September 2021. We were wrong.

By July 2021, Indonesia had become the epicentre of the pandemic, and two large states in eastern Australia were deep in lockdown. The Delta variant drove record numbers of new COVID-19 cases and deaths in Indonesia. The health system was on the verge of collapse and cemeteries were overwhelmed with the sudden and excess demands for burials (Abdurachman et al. 2021). This book came at a time where we—and the contributors of this volume—were ironically traversing the very setbacks and novel conundrums of a health transition. As we navigated our personal and collective grief and losses through the pandemic, the statistics, theories and challenges of health transition became all-consuming and too close for comfort. Indeed, the heavy toll from the COVID-19 pandemic has now been reflected in the estimated loss of roughly three years in the estimated life expectancy at birth in Indonesia, from 70.52 in 2019 to 67.57 in 2021. After the largest loss in life expectancy being recorded during the mass 'anti-communist' killings in the 1960s (estimated decline from 49.23 in 1964 to 42.60 years in 1965), this was the second-largest dip in life expectancy in the country's post-independence demographic history.[2]

---

2 United Nations Data Portal Population Division, https://population.un.org/DataPortal/, accessed 31 August 2022.

An assessment of Indonesia's health transition has been long overdue, even before COVID-19 came into the picture. The last time health transition was a major theme for the Update series was in 1996. The late Professor Gavin Jones and Professor Terry Hull—the convenors of the Update at the time—wrote in their introduction:

> While the New Order government has given single-minded attention to reducing rates of population growth by reducing fertility, it has been less single-minded about reducing mortality. Vaccination campaigns have certainly been conducted with some enthusiasm, but budgetary figures reveal very low proportion of government budgets devoted to health by regional standards and an overemphasis on expensive curative facilities in the large cities at the expense of an effective system of primary health care and efficient referral. The results are clear in Indonesia's greater success in reducing fertility than in reducing mortality. There is an urgent need to allocate more resources to health and improve the effectiveness in the health sector. (Jones and Hull 1997: 3)

How has Indonesia traversed the path of health transition since then? Clearly much has changed, with some promising trends and new challenges emerging prior to COVID-19. Using estimates from the Global Burden of Disease Study, Mboi et al. (2018) found that Indonesia's life expectancy at birth had risen by about 8 years between 1990 and 2016. Such gain in life expectancy was higher than the average of 6.6 across comparable countries. In the same period, they further estimated that the total disability adjusted life years (DALYs) lost to communicable, maternal, neonatal and nutritional causes had significantly declined by 58.6 per cent. In contrast, total DALYs due to non-communicable diseases had risen. Six of the top ten causes of DALYs in 2016 were non-communicable diseases, up from three in 1990. In 2019, seven of the top ten diseases—including the top three of cardiovascular disease, cancer, and diabetes and chronic kidney disease—were non-communicable diseases (Witoelar and Miranti 2021). While the increasing share and number of people with chronic non-communicable diseases in the population's health profile is straining health system financing, Indonesia still faces serious problems associated more with countries at a lower level of development, such as child underweight and stunting, and neglected tropical diseases such as dengue (see Chapter 12 by Utarini). Furthermore, underneath the indicators of health outcomes that reflect progress at the aggregate level, the issues of geographical disparities persist. And it is only recently that disability and mental health have become national health priorities (see Chapter 10 by Contreras Suárez and Cameron and Chapter 11 by Hunt, Onie and Pols).

Assessing the vulnerabilities of the health system

An observation frequently made since the COVID-19 pandemic is how the pandemic unmasked the vulnerabilities of a country's health system. For Indonesia, and perhaps for some other countries, that observation may be misleading. Despite much progress in the health sector in the past few decades, the vulnerabilities of Indonesia's health system were apparent even before the pandemic. For example, indicators of availability of physical infrastructure for health, such as the number of health facilities, remain below the World Health Organization standards, and the growth in the number of human resources for health (HRH) at all levels has not kept up with increasing need (Booth et al. 2019; Mahendradhata et al. 2017). There are large disparities between regions in terms of both quantity and quality of health infrastructure (Wulandari et al. 2022) as well as HRH (Meliala et al. 2013; Chapter 5 by Meliala, this volume). One of the main reasons for this is the continuing underinvestment in health. In the past two decades, government expenditure on health as a percentage of government budget—indicating prioritisation—was around 3 per cent per year until it increased to about 5 per cent from 2016. This stands in contrast with central government expenditure on education, which since 2008 has been around 20 per cent of the budget. Health expenditure per capita in purchasing power parity in 2019 is US$358, below the Philippines (US$380), Vietnam (US$559), and less than half of Thailand's expenditure (US$731).[3]

The national health insurance program, Jaminan Kesejahteraan Nasional (JKN), was launched in 2014 with the ambitious aim to have universal coverage within just five years. Badan Penyelenggara Jaminan Sosial Kesehatan (BPJS-K, Healthcare and Social Security Agency) was established to administer the mandatory health insurance, making it the operator of the largest single-payment health insurance scheme in the world. The JKN is mandatory and enrolment is paid through contribution schemes either by individuals, employers, or, in the case of the eligible poor, by the government. The early participants came from the recipients of the existing health insurance schemes that are mostly subsidised by the government (e.g. Askes, Jamkesmas, Jamsostek and Jamkesda), and the fully subsidised health insurance for the eligible poor. The membership was then expanded to include formal employees from small, medium and large corporations, and informal and self-employed workers (Agustina et al. 2019). As in other countries with a large share of informal workers,

---

3 World Health Organization Global Health Expenditure Database, accessed 10 May 2022, https://apps.who.int/nha/database/Select/Indicators/en

there is a sizeable 'missing middle', the uninsured informal sector workers who are unwilling to enrol in the program. By January 2022, BPJS-K claims to have covered 86 per cent of the population, of which around 42 per cent are under the subsidised scheme (BPJS-K 2022). The JKN has been running a deficit since its inception, and the central government is mandated to pay the deficit (Agustina et al. 2019; Pratiwi et al. 2021; Chapter 2 by Trisnantoro, this volume). The deficit is partly due to the low amount of contributions relative to total health expenditure. The system is considered to be generous: many advanced and expensive treatments are fully covered, including for non-communicable diseases that lead to catastrophic health expenditure (Pratiwi et al. 2021). At the hospital level, chronic diseases such as cardiovascular disease, kidney disease and cancer account for the largest case-based payment from BPJS-K (Prabhakaran et al. 2019). The double burden of morbidity and mortality from infectious and non-communicable diseases means that the financial strain on the JKN will only get worse.

On the supply side, in addition to the shortage and uneven distribution of HRH including medical specialists, there is also the issue of availability of medical equipment and affordable drugs and vaccines. While the increase in demand spurred by the expansion of the health insurance system has impelled private sector expansion in the markets for medicines, medical devices and hospitals, until 2018 much of the growth was still concentrated in more urbanised Java and Sumatra (Britton et al. 2018). Regulations governing the production, procurement and licensing of pharmaceuticals and medical devices may need to be reformed in order for the market to be more responsive to the increase in demand.

Decentralisation adds to the complexity of health system governance where, on one hand, some outcomes have turned out to be positive, such as an increase in health utilisation by the poor and, in some regions, development of health initiatives to address local challenges. On the other hand, significant discrepancies in fiscal capacities between local governments have led to uneven distribution of health services. Decentralisation has also weakened the link between the national health information system and the district-level health information system (Mahendradhata et al. 2017).

It was under these straitened circumstances that Indonesia was hit by the COVID-19 pandemic. One question that emerged was how the health crisis would affect the trajectory of health reform: whether it will change the trajectory, accelerate the reform or derail the reform together. In Chapter 2, Laksono Trisnantoro examines how the trajectory of health-reform financing will likely be affected by the COVID-19 pandemic. He begins by reviewing the early health sector fiscal responses to the pandemic and the pre-existing health system challenges. The high and increasing proportion of payments for advanced treatment services from BPJS-K continue to threaten the financial sustainability of the JKN. In the second part of the chapter Trisnantoro describes a road map of post-pandemic health reform that reflects a shift to a health system that puts more weight on primary care screening and prevention.

In Chapter 3, Andrew Rosser and Luky Djani investigate the political dynamics that have shaped health policy reforms in post–New Order Indonesia, and how these have resulted in uneven reform. The authors focus on the key actors who play the major roles in shaping health policy reforms and set forth in detail each actor's often conflicting interests and agendas: the technocrats who support state investment in provision of health services and a robust social safety net, paying attention to affordability and cost-effectiveness, while encouraging high levels of private sector involvement; the political, military and bureaucratic officials who more strongly support health investment that is central to their own interests; the progressive element of civil society with only limited access to pockets of health policymaking; and finally the politicians, national and local, who seek to mobilise political support. Using this framework, Rosser and Djani then examine the political dynamics between the actors and the outcomes that emerge by focusing on three cases of health reform: health insurance, tobacco control and health security. They show how the nature of the reforms—whether they are access-enhancing or address underlying preconditions of health—and the political dynamics between the actors explain the uneven outcomes. They conclude by discussing whether the shocks to the health system brought about by COVID-19 will shift the power alignment and alter the future trajectory of reforms.

In Chapter 4, Terry Hull assesses the results of the 2020 Population Census, which was disrupted by the COVID-19 pandemic. He begins by describing the role of the census in building the strength and capacity in the Indonesian government to produce and make data available for research and policy, and the importance of high-quality data in shaping demographic-informed health policy. The 2020 census was supposed to be groundbreaking in several ways. First, it was supposed to resolve the longstanding tensions between Statistics Indonesia (BPS) and the Ministry of Home Affairs on the 'official' estimate of the population numbers. Second, it would be the first Indonesian population census conducted with in-person interviews and digital data collections, a truly ambitious innovation. The COVID-19 pandemic derailed parts of the plan. Most importantly, the post-enumeration survey in 2021 that was originally designed to collect detailed information of a sample of the households did not take place. The quality of the 2020 Population Census is likely to be compromised as a result. Hull presents and assesses the population numbers, total fertility rate and survivorship numbers based on the available results, with a stern warning about the quality.

The JKN program has increased the demand for high-quality health services, such as access to medical specialists, at affordable costs. To meet this increase in demand it was expected that the supply side, whether government or private sector, would respond. In Chapter 5, Andre Meliala and Srimurni Rarasati investigate the supply barriers that allow regional disparities in access to medical specialists to persist. The archipelagic nature of the country, the complexity of HRH planning and management under decentralisation, and the multitude of stakeholders with conflicting interests are among some of the factors behind the disparities. The authors highlight the regulatory barriers in producing and licensing medical specialists and some signs of private sector responses motivated by the expansion of the JKN.

In Chapter 6, another chapter focusing on the supply side of health services, Elizabeth Pisani and co-authors investigate how the establishment of the JKN program has changed the landscape of medicine production and distribution in Indonesia. The move to mandatory universal health insurance has meant that most of the drugs that were paid for by patients are now paid for by the insurance system. The government has created incentives to push prices of medicines down, through a set of regulations governing medicine procurement. The authors seek to learn how the quest to provide affordable medicines—a quest misaligned with the incentives of pharmaceutical companies to maximise profit and health providers' interests for cost recovery—affects the availability and quality of medicines in the market. The authors built on their extensive work on this topic and used an array of secondary data from national institutions and primary data collected through in-depth interviews, price and stocks data, and mystery shopper surveys. What they found was an intricate description of an equilibrium with segmented markets where medicines of different quality are offered at different price points, targeted to different groups of patients.

Health for all: Lessons and strategies

The strengths and weaknesses of health systems shape people's health-seeking behaviour and outcomes. In the next five chapters of this volume, the contributors explore everyday challenges faced by Indonesians in accessing essential health services for mothers and children, and for those living with disability, discrimination and mental illness.

In Chapter 7, Nyoman Sutarsa analyses inequities to health services access in an approach that uses multiple lenses beyond the individual-level analysis. Sutarsa draws on two case studies of transgender people navigating HIV services. He employs an intersectionality approach and demonstrates how this method can be helpful in providing insights into the underlying causes of health access inequities. In one of the case studies, he shows how mainstreaming HIV services into health community centres may end up missing those on the margins. The approach not only helps to better understand health and health inequity outcomes, it will also help to improve ways to formulate policies.

At the onset of the COVID-19 pandemic, essential health services in many countries around the world were severely disrupted. Understanding the ways in which pandemic-induced disruptions have derailed ongoing efforts to achieve equitable health transition in Indonesia is particularly important given the novel risks posed by future shocks associated with climate change and emerging pandemics. In Chapter 8, Tiara Marthias and Yodi Mahendradhata present a case study on how the pandemic has caused disruptions in the provision of routine maternal, neonatal and child health (MNCH) services. They use an integrated database, from the Ministry of Health, that collects monthly reporting of reproductive, maternal and child health services from 514 districts, and combine that information with COVID-19 data from Our World in Data. The trends in selected key MNCH services are plotted against COVID-19 confirmed cases to show the impact of the disruptions. In their investigation they also find how the pandemic has exacerbated the existing health system challenges in Indonesia: the uneven distribution of HRH, the limited health information system and quality of data, and the underinvestment in health.

The longstanding issue of maternal health in Indonesia continues to be the focus of Chapter 9 by Salut Muhidin and Jerico Pardosi. At present, various estimates suggest that Indonesia's maternal mortality ratio is unacceptably high, ranging from 200 to 350 maternal deaths per 100,000 live births in 2015 (Utomo et al. 2021). More conservative estimates still put Indonesia's maternal mortality ratio at an unacceptably high level, particularly when compared to other countries in the region. For example, the United Nations Population Fund estimated that the maternal mortality ratio in Indonesia was 177 deaths per 100,000 live births in 2017, compared to Thailand (37), Vietnam (43), Malaysia (29), the Philippines (121), Cambodia (160) and India (145).[4] Muhidin and Pardosi

---

4 UNFPA World Population Dashboard, www.unfpa.org/data/world-population, accessed 31 August 2022.

begin their chapter with a comprehensive overview of the trends and determinants of maternal mortality in Indonesia. They include a detailed discussion canvassing various policy initiatives and issues surrounding maternal health provision around the country which, again, underline the ever-present problem of regional disparities. Here, they look deeper beyond the statistics and drew upon their recent fieldwork in East Nusa Tenggara to examine the three pressing drivers of maternal mortality in regional Indonesia: (1) delay in decision-making to seek care, (2) delay in reaching a health facility and (3) delay in receiving adequate care.

The challenge with high maternal mortality is one that is longstanding, but arguably it has received more policy attention than other facets of serious health challenges in the country, including that of disability. It was only roughly ten years ago—in 2011—that the Indonesian government ratified the United Nations Convention on the Rights of Persons with Disabilities. In 2016, a new law on disabilities (Law No. 8/2016) was passed, promising equal rights for people with disabilities, including protection of their rights to employment. Indeed, Diana Contreras Suárez and Lisa Cameron begin Chapter 10 with a strong statement: 'For many of us, the concept of disability is at once familiar and unknown'. Data on disability prevalence and needs in Indonesia remain limited, hindering programmatic development and reach to promote disability inclusion. Drawing on various data sources, including the Indonesian Census, the National Socioeconomic Survey (Susenas), the National Labour Force Survey (Sakernas), and the Indonesia Family Life Survey, Contreras Suárez and Cameron provide a baseline of disability indicators. These include disability prevalence and its regional variation, profiles of disability status by age group, causes of disability, unmet demands for assistive devices and services, comparative indicators on access to education, employment and public services among people with and without disabilities, and a profile of families and carers of people with disabilities. Overall, this comprehensive snapshot provides a useful starting point to canvas disability-related challenges facing Indonesia. Moreover, these data can potentially serve to track the progress of disability inclusion over time.

Apart from disability, mental health is another serious health challenge that tends to be forgotten in national policy discourse. Starting with two vignettes of individuals living with mental illness, in Chapter 11, Aliza Hunt, Sanderson Onie and Hans Pols call for urgent action to make mental health a priority in Indonesia's national health agenda. Drawing upon their collective expertise and long experience of field-based research in the country, the authors complement the vignettes with a comprehensive mapping of the prevailing mental health system, mental health data, existing challenges to do with treatment gaps, and the strategies employed by various civil society, consumer groups and for-profit organisations to overcome such challenges. They further provide a nuanced discussion on the impact of COVID-19, juxtaposing the rising demands for mental health services with a welcome rise in awareness of mental health issues more broadly.

The final chapter in this volume describes the remarkable 10-year journey of an innovation in public health policy that may help solve a persistent health problem in Indonesia. In Chapter 12, Adi Utarini discusses the public health intervention that was conducted by her and her colleagues from the World Mosquito Program Yogyakarta to control dengue, a viral infection transmitted by the *Aedes* mosquito. The intervention involves injecting *Aedes* mosquitoes with a *Wolbachia* bacterium, which inhibits replication of the dengue virus inside the mosquitoes. As part of a randomised control trial, the *Wolbachia*-infected mosquitoes were released into communities in parts of Yogyakarta. The prevalence of mosquitoes in the treatment area was quickly dominated by the *Wolbachia*-infected mosquitoes. By comparing the treatment and control areas, Utarini and her team found that the intervention reduced the incidence of dengue by 77 per cent, a result that was celebrated by the international scientific community. The chapter recounts the long path taken by the project and offers valuable lessons on the challenges in applying innovative research as a public health intervention, which include the efforts to earn buy-in from the government and other stakeholders, and the somewhat unorthodox ways that were used to gain public trust and acceptance.

Conclusion

This book explores questions of how Indonesia's quest for longer and healthier lives of its people has unfolded in the past and present, and what this means for the future. Drawing on the interdisciplinary expertise of our contributors, the chapters in this volume examine longstanding and emerging health challenges, and identify lessons learnt and opportunities for health system strengthening in the country. All contributors stress the immediate need for reliable and accessible data on health services, health financing, HRH, health supplies and health surveillance data for formulating health policy and research. With several chapters examining the political dynamics that shape health policies and affect the supply side of the health system, we show how health transition is intrinsically situated within broader socioeconomic and political contexts. Discussions on how Indonesians navigate the barriers to access services as they come into contact with the health system underline the enduring problems of regional and socioeconomic inequalities, as well as persistent stigma and discrimination afflicting marginalised populations.

On 15 July 2019, in his first speech at the beginning of his second term, President Joko Widodo stated that human capital development is the key to Indonesia's future. There is evidence that in terms of some important health outcomes, Indonesia has been moving in the right direction. The COVID-19 pandemic has disrupted the trajectory, exposing the existing vulnerabilities of the health system and causing major setbacks in most areas of health, from which the country has not fully recovered. At the same time, the pandemic has also given the impetus for the country to strengthen its health system and to move to a new path that leads to faster improvements in health. As summarised by the pioneering work of Jack and Pat Caldwell on health transition in developing nations: 'most effective health services are also the most democratic in that they are easy to access in all parts of the country and to every social group while not imposing high-cost barriers' (1991: 14). With several key infrastructures—including the promise of universal health coverage—in place, Indonesia might be on track to reach the ultimate goal of health for all, but it might be a long and arduous journey after all.

References

Abdurachman, Fira, Richard C. Paddock and Muktita Suhartono. 2021. 'The pandemic has a new epicenter: Indonesia'. *New York Times*, 17 July. www.nytimes.com/2021/07/17/world/asia/indonesia-covid.html

Agustina, Rina, Teguh Dartanto, Ratna Sitompul, Kun A. Susiloretni, Suparmi, et al. 2019. 'Universal health coverage in Indonesia: Concept, progress, and challenges'. *The Lancet* 393(10166): 75–102. doi.org/10.1016/S0140-6736(18)31647-7

Bloom, D.E., S. Chen, M. McGovern, K. Prettner, V. Candelas, et al. 2015. *Economics of Non-communicable Diseases in Indonesia*. World Economic Forum. www.weforum.org/reports/economics-non-communicable-diseases-indonesia

Booth, Anne, Raden Muhamad Purnagunawan and Elan Satriawan. 2019. 'Towards a healthy Indonesia?' *Bulletin of Indonesian Economic Studies* 55(2): 133–55. doi.org/10.1080/00074918.2019.1639509

BPJS-K. 2022. *Laporan Pengelolaan Program Tahun 2021 dan Laporan Keuangan Tahun 2022 (Auditan)* [2021 Program Management Report and Financial Report – Audited]. Jakarta: BPJS-K. www.bpjs-kesehatan.go.id/bpjs/dmdocuments/c988c494fb71090a8d67b6e291a94710.pdf

Britton, Kate, Sayaka Koseki and Arin Dutta. 2018. *Expanding Markets while Improving Health in Indonesia: The Private Health Sector Market in the JKN Era*. Washington, DC: Palladium, Health Policy Plus and Jakarta: TNP2K.

Caldwell, John and Pat Caldwell. 1991. 'What have we learnt about the cultural, social and behavioural determinants of health? From Selected Readings to the first Health Transition Workshop'. *Health Transition Review* 1(1): 3–19. www.jstor.org/stable/40608614

Frenk, Julio, José Luis Bobadilla, Claudio Stern, Tomas Frejka and Rafael Lozano. 1991. 'Elements for a theory of the health transition'. *Health Transition Review* 1(1): 21–38. www.jstor.org/stable/40608615
Jones, Gavin W. and Terence H. Hull. 1997. 'Introduction'. In *Indonesia Assessment: Population and Human Resources*, edited by Gavin W. Jones and Terence H. Hull, 1–15. Singapore: Institute of Southeast Asian Studies.
Kusuma, Dian, Nunik Kusumawardani, Abdillah Ahsan, Susy K. Sebayang, Vilda Amir and Nawi Ng. 2019. 'On the verge of a chronic disease epidemic: Comprehensive policies and actions are needed in Indonesia'. *International Health* 11(6): 422–24. doi.org/10.1093/inthealth/ihz025
Mackenbach, Johan P. 2022. 'Omran's "Epidemiologic Transition" 50 years on'. *International Journal of Epidemiology* 51(4): 1054–57. doi.org/10.1093/ije/dyac020
Mahendradhata, Yodi, Laksono Trisnantoro, Shita Listyadewi, Prastuti Soewondo, Tiara Marthias, et al. 2017. *The Republic of Indonesia Health System Review*. Health Systems in Transition 7(1). World Health Organization. https://apps.who.int/iris/handle/10665/254716
Mboi, Nafsiah, Indra Murty Surbakti, Indang Trihandini, Iqbal Elyazar, Karen Houston Smith, et al. 2018. 'On the road to universal health care in Indonesia, 1990–2016: A systematic analysis for the Global Burden of Disease Study 2016'. *The Lancet* 392(10147): 581–91. doi.org/10.1016/S0140-6736(18)30595-6
Meliala, Andreasta, Krishna Hort and Laksono Trisnantoro. 2013. 'Addressing the unequal geographic distribution of specialist doctors in Indonesia: The role of the private sector and effectiveness of current regulations'. *Social Science & Medicine* 82(April): 30–34. doi.org/10.1016/j.socscimed.2013.01.029
Omran, Abdel R. 1971. 'The epidemiologic transition: A theory of the epidemiology of population change'. *The Milbank Memorial Fund Quarterly* 49(4): 509–38. doi.org/10.2307/3349375
Omran, Abdel R. 1998. 'The epidemiologic transition theory revisited thirty years later'. *World Health Statistics Quarterly* 53(2–4): 99–119. https://apps.who.int/iris/handle/10665/330604
Prabhakaran, Shreeshant, Arin Dutta, Thomas Fagan and Megan Ginivan. 2019. *Financial Sustainability of Indonesia's Jaminan Kesehatan Nasional: Performance, Prospects, and Policy Options*. Washington, DC: Palladium, Health Policy Plus and Jakarta: TNP2K.
Pratiwi, Agnes Bhakti, Hermawati Setiyaningsih, Maarten Olivier Kok, Trynke Hoekstra, Ali Ghufron Mukti and Elizabeth Pisani. 2021. 'Is Indonesia achieving universal health coverage? Secondary analysis of national data on insurance coverage, health spending and service availability'. *BMJ Open* 11(10): e050565. doi.org/10.1136/bmjopen-2021-050565
Santosa, Ailiana, Stig Wall, Edward Fottrell, Ulf Högberg and Peter Byass. 2014. 'The development and experience of epidemiological transition theory over four decades: A systematic review'. *Global Health Action* 7(1): 23574. doi.org/10.3402/gha.v7.23574
Utomo, Budi, Purwa Kurnia Sucahya, Nohan Arum Romadlona, Annette Sachs Robertson, et al. 2021. 'The impact of family planning on maternal mortality in Indonesia: What future contribution can be expected?' *Population Health Metrics* 19(1): 2. doi.org/10.1186/s12963-020-00245-w

Vallin, Jacques and France Meslé. 2004. 'Convergences and divergences in mortality: A new approach of health transition'. *Demographic Research* S2(2): 11–44. dx.doi.org/10.4054/DemRes.2004.S2.2

Witoelar, Firman and Riyana Miranti. 2021. 'COVID-19 and health systems challenges of non-communicable diseases'. In *Economic Dimensions of COVID-19 in Indonesia: Responding to the Crisis*, edited by Blane Lewis and Firman Witoelar, 150–69. Singapore: ISEAS Publishing.

Wulandari, Ratna Dwi, Agung Dwi Laksono, Zainul Khaqiqi Nantabah, Nikmatur Rohmah and Zuardin Zuardin. 2022. 'Hospital utilization in Indonesia in 2018: Do urban–rural disparities exist?' *BMC Health Services Research* 22: 491. doi.org/10.1186/s12913-022-07896-5

PART 1

The Indonesian health system: Challenges and opportunities

2 Post-pandemic trajectory of health-reform financing in Indonesia

Laksono Trisnantoro

The increase in government spending associated with the COVID-19 pandemic between 2020 and 2021 has reduced the Indonesian government's fiscal capacity for financing welfare programs, including financing a much-needed health sector transformation, for at least the next four years. In the past two decades, the health sector in Indonesia has been affected by a number of major reforms. These include multisectoral reforms outside the health sector, such as changes in public service organisation following the 1999 decentralisation, to reforms that focus specifically on the health sector, such as the introduction of universal health care in 2014 (Mahendradhata et al. 2017). Following these health system changes, new and remaining challenges such as the financing of universal health care and the changing landscape of disease have been identified, and the need for further reforms acknowledged. These challenges and the gaps in the health system exposed by the pandemic have prompted the national government to commit to a health sector transformation that involves reorienting and restructuring the health system through a series of reforms (Ministry of Health Regulation No. 13/2022 about the Strategic Plan of the Ministry of Health 2020–2024).[1]

Drawing upon the government's projected fiscal space and data canvassing the health sector conditions before the pandemic, this chapter examines the post-pandemic trajectory of health reforms in the country. I outline lessons learnt during the past two years of the pandemic, and consider pre-existing (i.e. pre-COVID-19) health sector challenges, to

---

1 https://e-renggar.kemkes.go.id/file_performance/1-131313-1tahunan-502.pdf

assess the financing of the health sector transformation. This chapter demonstrates that the costs associated with financing the reforms are huge, and that the pandemic has negatively affected the government's capacity to finance such spending. Although the narrowing fiscal space due to COVID-19 has put pressure on public funding, the government is likely to prioritise the development of the health sector through various policies. One likely policy is the use of private financing. Better-off members of society would pay more for their health services through pre-paid schemes, while the limited public funding would be allocated to preventive and promotive public health services. In the future, a health sector funded by both public and private sources should be examined.

The COVID-19 pandemic impact

The World Health Organization (WHO) declared COVID-19 a pandemic on 11 March 2020 (Cucinotta and Vanelli 2020). Since then, the pandemic has come in a series of waves: new variants have brought new surges in cases. Starting from May 2021, the WHO assigned letters of the Greek alphabet to these variants: Alpha (B.1.1.7), Beta (B.1.351), Gamma (P.1), Delta (B.1.617.2) and Omicron (B.1.1.529). By March 2022, Indonesia had experienced three peaks in the pandemic (January 2021, July 2021, February 2022), as shown in Figure 2.1. Each peak represented the wave of a different variant, which appeared 2–3 months after its first report—the Alpha and Beta cases were correlated with the January 2021 peak, Delta cases correlated with July's 2021 peak, and the Omicron variant surge correlated with February's 2022 peak.

By many accounts, the Delta variant has been the most lethal COVID-19 variant. The number of deaths peaked in July 2021 (Figure 2.2). Indonesia's health system was in crisis and almost collapsed.

Mobility restrictions and social distancing policies have indirectly impacted many health programs. Helmyati et al. (2022) assessed the impact of the pandemic on some key maternal and child health services across districts of Indonesia as of January 2021. Their analysis of nutrition-related programs in 260 districts showed that 23 districts (9%) were severely affected by the pandemic, 101 districts (39%) moderately affected and 61 districts (23%) mildly affected; 75 districts (29%) could not be assessed due to lack of data. Their research also assessed the impact of the COVID-19 pandemic on four of the six nutrition indicators and eight maternal and child health indicators. Growth monitoring and antenatal care coverage (at least four visits) were the most affected (89 and 92 districts affected, respectively), while vitamin A supplementation and family planning services were the least affected (80 and 25 districts, respectively).

Figure 2.1 Number of daily COVID-19 cases in Indonesia, March 2020 to May 2022

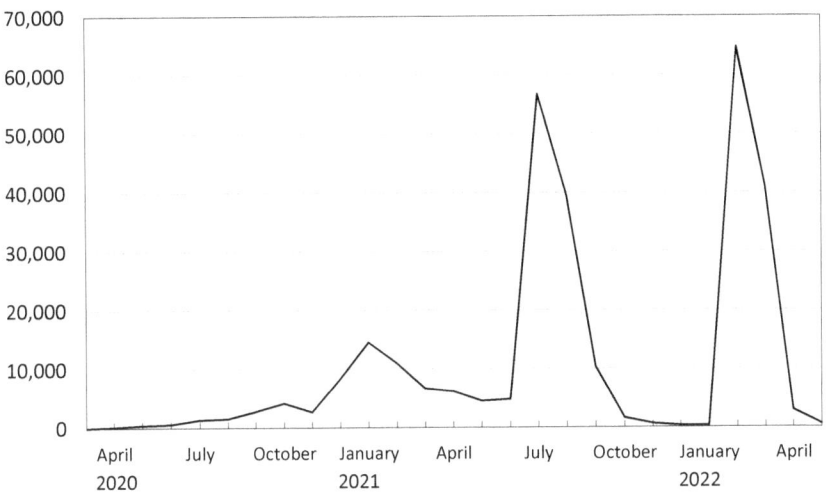

Source: Worldometer, www.worldometers.info/coronavirus/country/indonesia/#graph-cases-daily

Figure 2.2 Number of daily deaths caused by COVID-19 in Indonesia, March 2020 to April 2022

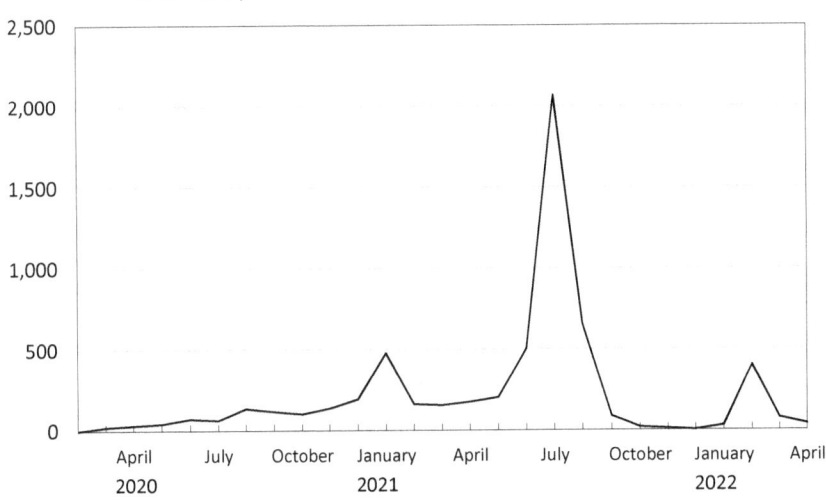

Source: Worldometer, www.worldometers.info/coronavirus/country/indonesia/#graph-cases-daily

The health finance trajectory of COVID-19

Law No. 4/1984 on Infectious Disease Outbreaks stipulates that all health expenses related to infectious disease outbreaks are to be paid by the government. Consequently, the Indonesian government financed most of the country's health expenses related to the COVID-19 pandemic, although local government met some expenses. Central government health expenditure was Rp 83.49 trillion in 2020 and increased to Rp 135.53 trillion in 2021 (January–November 2021) (MoF 2021b). Out-of-pocket expenses for medical services were not calculated. According to Budiarso (2021), health expenditure for COVID-19 in the National Economic Recovery Program was Rp 63.7 trillion. In 2021 the program was allocated Rp 172.8 trillion. The Healthcare and Social Security Agency (Badan Penyelenggara Jaminan Sosial Kesehatan, BPJS-K) did not pay for COVID-19 patients' medical expenses. Limited capacity to mobilise tax revenue means that a significant part of the government budget needs to be financed through government debt (World Bank 2021a). This kind of mechanism has a long-term financial trajectory.

The impact of the pandemic caused Indonesia's gross domestic product (GDP) to contract in 2020 after recording strong growth for two decades. The deepest contraction happened during the second quarter of 2020 (World Bank 2020). The economic contraction happened due to the escalation of virus transmission to which the government responded with various actions to limit economic activity (BKF 2021). During the third quarter of 2020, along with gradually lifted mobility restrictions, GDP showed a partial and slow-paced increase (Figure 2.3). In the third and fourth quarters of 2020, Indonesia experienced its first recession since the Asian financial crisis in the late 1990s.

Prior to the pandemic, Indonesia had experienced low and stagnant tax ratios (the ratio of tax revenue to GDP), with an average of around 10% every year since 2007. The 2020 recession led to a further decrease in government revenue. Fiscal revenue contracted by 15.4% year on year for the first ten months of the year (World Bank 2020). The government responded to this economic recession by issuing several fiscal policies.

Law No. 2/2020 on State Financial Policy and Financial System Stability for Handling the COVID-19 Pandemic gave authority to the government and related institutions to immediately take extraordinary action to conserve the national economy and financial system through relaxation of policies related to the implementation of the State Revenue and Expenditure Budget (Anggaran Pendapatan dan Belanja Negara, APBN), particularly by increasing spending on the health and social safety net (BKF 2021).

Figure 2.3 GDP growth in Indonesia before the pandemic and in 2020 (%)

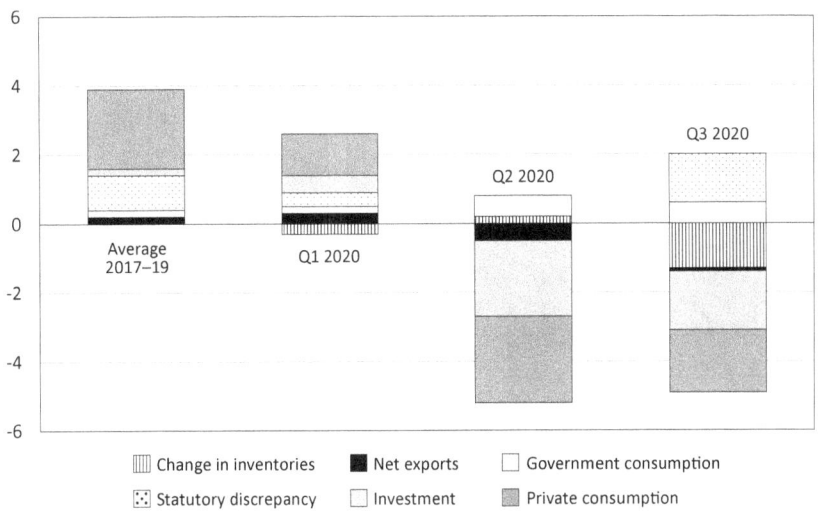

Source: World Bank (2020).

As a policy response, the government released a fiscal package estimated at Rp 695 trillion or 4.3% of GDP, with 12.7% of it given for strengthening health care (World Bank 2020). Figure 2.4 shows how Indonesia's response compares to some of its neighbours. The fiscal package increased Indonesia's net debt to Rp 1,226 trillion or 7.8% of 2020 GDP and interest debt payments to Rp 338.8 trillion or 2% of 2020 GDP. According to the Ministry of Finance, the increased debt will negatively impact the fiscal space for financing welfare programs, including health, for at least the next four years.

The health system situation before the pandemic

Health status

Prior to the onset of the COVID-19 pandemic, Indonesia's performance on a number of health status indicators was relatively poor. The maternal mortality rate, 305 per 100,000 live births in 2015 (BPS 2015), and the prevalence of stunting of children under five, 24.4% in 2021 (MoH 2021a), are still high. Infectious diseases are still problematic. In 2020, Indonesia was ranked third in the world for tuberculosis incidence, or 301 per 100,000 population (WHO 2021c). There are 318 districts/cities in Indonesia with malaria elimination status. Three provinces with high

Figure 2.4 Countries' fiscal response packages, 2020 (% of GDP)

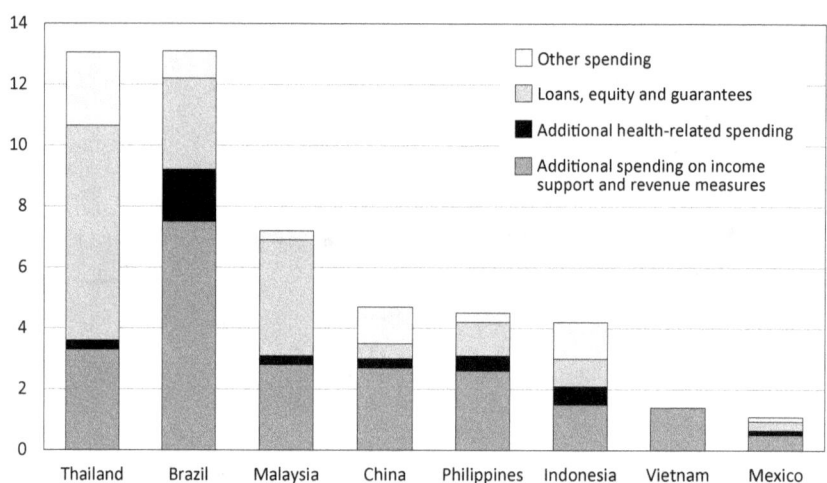

Source: World Bank (2020: 15).

malaria endemicity are Papua, West Papua and East Nusa Tenggara (MoH 2021b). Indonesia has the third-highest number of leprosy cases in the world, after India and Brazil.

Indonesia also has increasing non-communicable disease problems. Cancer, diabetes mellitus, heart and vascular disease have become a heavy burden. The population aged 10–18 years who smoke increased from 7.2% in 2013 to 9.1% in 2018. Hypertension in the population aged over 18 years increased from 25.8% in 2013 to 34.1% in 2018 (MoH 2013, 2018).

Health services

The achievement of complete basic immunisation (*imunisasi dasar lengkap*, IDL) of 57.9% for children aged 12 months (MoH 2018) and 65.8% for children aged 23 months (MoH 2021a) is much lower than the target of 90% to be achieved by 2024, set in the 2020–2024 National Medium Term Development Plan (Rencana Pembangunan Jangka Menengah Nasional, RPJMN). In addition, the percentage of districts/cities that reached 80% of IDL in 2020 was only 37.2% (191 districts/cities), lower than in 2019 (73.5%) and 2018 (72.8%) (MoH 2021d). Enforced lockdowns and reluctance to attend health centres during COVID-19 may have contributed to the low figure in 2020.

The backbone of primary care is the public community health centre—*puskesmas* (around 10,200)—and private clinics (around 14,000). Since the introduction of the national health insurance scheme, Jaminan Kesehatan Nasional (JKN), in 2014, treatment services have tended to be the main activity in public health centres as opposed to preventive services to promote healthy living such as education, surveillance and community empowerment. The Ministry of Health's budget for preventive programs did not increase in the five years leading up to the COVID-19 pandemic (MoF 2020). The involvement of private health services is still low, while the potential for health services provided by the private sector is quite high.

Hospital care has faced problems of numbers, distribution and quality. The current bed ratio for Indonesian hospitals is 1.18 per 1,000 population, which is lower than the Asian average (3.3 per 1,000) and OECD countries (4.8 per 1,000). In addition, there is considerable inequality at the regional level, for example, the ratio of hospital beds in East Nusa Tenggara is only 0.76 per 1,000 while Jakarta has a ratio of 3.03 beds per 1,000 population (Ministry of Health Regulation 13/2022; see also Meliala, this volume). This means that people in rural and regional areas have less access to health facilities. Kharisma (2020) observed a strong correlation between the expansion of health insurance coverage and health care access. However, access to health facilities is still a problem for many because the health insurance scheme does not cover non-medical expenses such as transport and accommodation. Figure 2.5 shows the growth in the number of hospitals across Indonesia between 2012 and 2020.

There was no central government program for financing new medical facilities and human health resources across the country in the five years before the COVID-19 pandemic (MoF 2020), due to central government budget limitations. Most of the Ministry of Health budget is used to finance health social security for the poor. The result is the stagnation of new health facilities development by the central government. Instead, new medical service facilities have been developed by private investors and some local governments. The data show an interesting pattern. New development of hospitals in Indonesia is done mostly by the private sector in partnership with BPJS-K. Most of the development is on Java Island.

Human resources

Human resources consist of medical professionals (e.g. medical doctors and dentists) and other health workers. Although there is no single source of data, the number of medical doctors and dentists is low and suffers from poor distribution across the country. Other health human resources such as nurses and public health professionals in primary health care are

Figure 2.5 The number of hospitals in five regions in Indonesia, 2012–2020

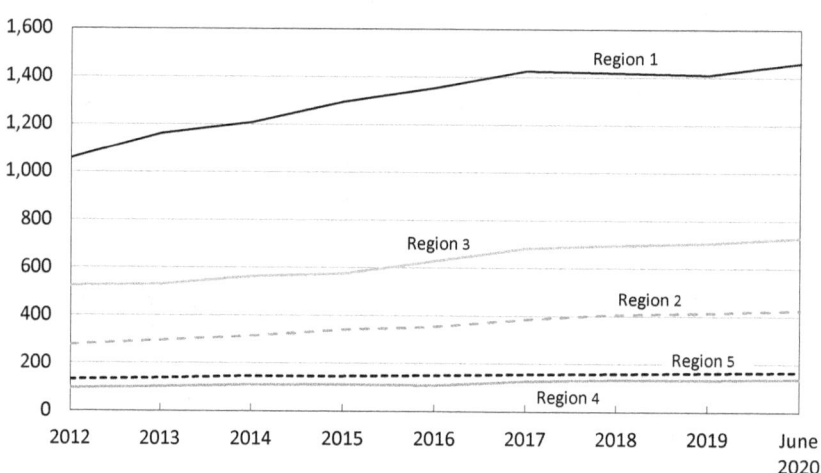

Region 1: Jakarta, West Java, Central Java, Yogyakarta, East Java, Banten
Region 2: West Sumatra, Riau, South Sumatra, Lampung, Bali, West Nusa Tenggara
Region 3: Aceh, North Sumatra, Jambi, Bengkulu, Bangka Belitung, Riau Islands, West Kalimantan, North Sulawesi, Central Sulawesi, South Sulawesi, South East Sulawesi, Gorontalo, West Sulawesi
Region 4: Central Kalimantan, South Kalimantan, East Kalimantan, North Kalimantan
Region 5: East Nusa Tenggara, Maluku, North Maluku, West Papua, Papua

Source: Health System Dashboard (DaSK), https://dask.kebijakankesehatanindonesia.net/data-nasional-pertumbuhan-rumah-sakit-di-indonesia/

also lacking. The distribution of human resources is worse for medical specialists (see Meliala, this volume). The shortage of human resources needs to be addressed with financial investment in education and distribution, but budgets have been affected by COVID-19.

An example of this geographical inequity is in the distribution of cancer surgeons. Figure 2.6 shows the distribution of oncology surgeons in Indonesia based on data from the Ministry of Health's Board for Development and Empowerment of Human Health Resources (BPPSDMK), available on the Health System Dashboard (Dashboard Sistem Kesehatan, DaSK). The highest number of surgical oncology specialists is in Jakarta (81 surgeons), followed by East Java province (55), while West Kalimantan does not have any oncology surgeons at all.

A benefit of the JKN scheme is high-technological and high-cost treatment available for members. However, this kind of medical service is accessible only if medical specialists are available. A strategy for balancing human resources and medical providers is essential for the future of the Indonesian health system.

Chapter 2 Post-pandemic trajectory of health-reform financing in Indonesia 25

Figure 2.6 Distribution of surgical oncology specialists in Indonesia, 2022

Number of oncologists: 1 – 81

Source: Health System Dashboard (DaSK), https://pkmk-ugm.shinyapps.io/sdmkesehatan/

Health system support

The health system relies on survey data instead of routine administrative data (see, for example, Hull, and Contreras Suárez and Cameron, this volume). This situation has arisen because the quality of routine data was very poor and the surveillance system was poorly structured. Bappenas, the National Development Planning Agency, reported that the main obstacle in the health information system is that the application and reporting systems have not been integrated and synchronised. At the central level, the Ministry of Health and BPJS-K have separate information systems. This raises the potential for duplication of entries and increases the administrative burden at the health facility level (Bappenas 2018).

With respect to pharmaceutical supplies, Indonesia is faced with high imports of medicinal raw materials (MoH 2021c). In the medical devices sector, only 3% of the industry had local content production certification in 2021 (Trisnantoro 2021). These conditions made it difficult to respond adequately to the pandemic. (For an analysis of medicine pricing and procurement in Indonesia, see Pisani et al., this volume; for information about availability of assistive devices, see Contreras Suárez and Cameron, this volume.)

Before the pandemic, health spending by the government and private sector in Indonesia remained below average or underfunded for low- and middle-income countries, at only around 3% of GDP in 2019 (WHO 2021b). As a share of GDP, health spending in 2019 ranged from 4.9% on average in lower-middle-income countries to 8.2% in high-income countries (WHO 2021a). Government health spending in Indonesia has been increasing over the years; 49.3% of total health expenditure came from the public sector in 2018. The situation of increased government health spending along with low tax revenue is becoming a challenge for the government, however.

Tax revenue is a fundamental way for the government to finance investments in human capital, infrastructure and social services such as education and health (Akitoby 2018). Unfortunately, Indonesia has always had a narrow tax base and low revenue. From 2007 to 2019, the Indonesian economy experienced steady growth of GDP from less than Rp 4,000 trillion to more than Rp 16,000 trillion (Figure 2.7). Economic growth was not matched by an increase in tax collection, and non-tax income in the same period flattened.

Financial problems in the health system

In 2014, Indonesia introduced a plan to provide universal health coverage to all its citizens by 2019, through JKN, a national health insurance scheme.

Figure 2.7 GDP and tax revenue, 2007–2019 (rupiah trillions)

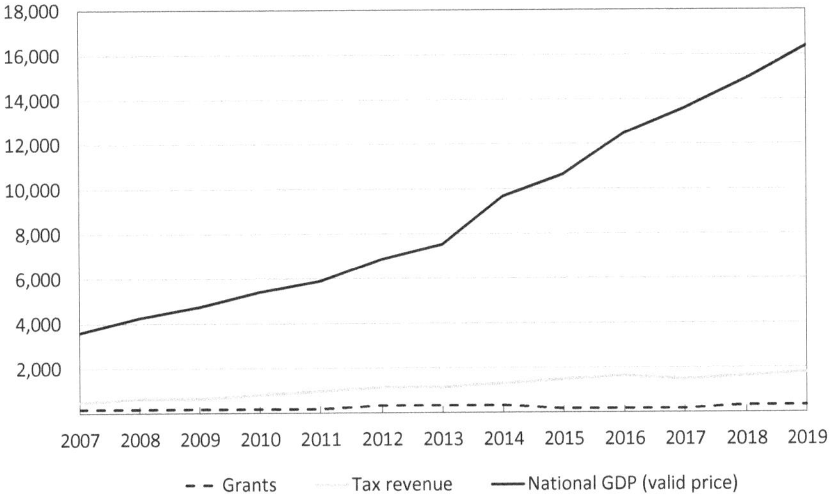

Source: Statistics Indonesia, 2021 and MoF (2021c).

The scheme combines a government subsidy for the poor (*penerima bantuan iuran*, PBI), a voluntary contribution by informal sector workers (*peserta bukan penerima upah*, PBPU) and a compulsory contribution from employees and employers in the formal sector (*pekerja penerima upah*, PPU). The scheme is managed by BPJS-K, using a single-pool mechanism.

The scheme experienced a huge deficit over the years prior to the pandemic in 2020. The informal sector workers, PBPU, contribute the most to the BPJS-K deficit. This occurs because people are more likely to enrol in the health insurance system only when they are likely to use it. Deficits also come from a lack of compliance in paying premiums (only 56% compliance), against a high claim ratio of about 300% (Nugraheni et al. 2020). As BPJS-K pools the surplus from other member segments, these surpluses are used to cover the deficit from informal workers. Each year the Indonesian government has to provide additional finance to cover this deficit, which amounted to around Rp 32 trillion or about US$2.2 billion from 2014 to 2019. A large proportion of payments from the BPJS-K are for treatment services. This is at variance from universal health care as defined by the WHO, where universal health care is a comprehensive concept with the aim that all residents have access to promotive, preventive, curative and rehabilitative services, including access to an appropriate health environment.

As a result, the national budget for health promotion and primary care is under pressure. Even before the COVID-19 pandemic, the directorates general for disease prevention and primary care in the Ministry of Health suffered from budget stagnancy. The infrastructure for public health surveillance was not in place and was underfunded. The Ministry of Finance noted various challenges in health development and the need to escalate health funding in, first, the 'unfinished agenda' such as reducing maternal mortality, overcoming stunting in children under five years, and comprehensive immunisation; and second, the increase in non-communicable diseases that follows the ageing structure of the population.

Health financing relies mostly on the government budget, and little on non-government financial resources. After decentralisation, regional responsibilities for financing health services increased. However, Ministry of Finance Regulation No. 7/2021 on Regional Fiscal Capacity noted that regional fiscal capacity is very limited.[2]

Equity problems in the health system

Fundamental issues in these analyses are the BPJS-K member categories and regional and remote access to services. An equity perspective demonstrates that the deficit actually obscures a much larger problem, namely inequalities in the availability and use of health services by different member groups of the BPJS-K and across different geographic areas of Indonesia.

The WHO reports eleven topics of health inequality in Indonesia, including health facilities and personnel. Inequality in distribution of health care personnel occurs especially at the subnational level. The geographic variation in health services results in urban or wealthier regions getting more benefits from the JKN provider payment scheme. With the prospective provider payment scheme based on services, health care providers with more advanced (or specialised) services will receive a greater benefit in provider payments (Sambodo et al. 2021). Secondary-care providers are paid by claim-based payments using case-based groups (CBGs) of diagnosis-related groups called InaCBGs. The payments are also determined by the class of hospital. Hospitals in a higher class ('type A') have more advanced services, more specialist doctors and are usually located in urban areas or big cities. Therefore, these hospitals will have larger claims using the InaCBG scheme (Agustina et al. 2019).

---

2 https://djpk.kemenkeu.go.id/?p=20896

Future challenges

To project Indonesia's future in health care, the economic situation is an important factor. The economy is predicted to gradually strengthen in 2022 (Table 2.1). This optimistic outlook comes from the gradual improvement in domestic demand and a stronger global economy. The growth of the economy is dependent on the COVID-19 vaccination coverage reaching as many people as possible to ensure improved economic activity in Indonesia (World Bank 2021b). Structural and fiscal reforms that focus on health, education, social protection and infrastructure will be the opportunity to achieve medium-term growth targets (Table 2.2). The government is optimistic that in 2022 it can achieve a better state budget and economic growth higher than before the pandemic (5.2% economic growth). However, this projection is susceptible to effects of any future COVID-19 waves. Further, the uncertainty of global financial conditions combined with a slower-than-expected vaccine rollout could lower Indonesia's growth to 3.1% in 2022 (World Bank 2021b).

Table 2.1 Projection of Indonesia's economy

	2019	2020	2021	2022	2023
Real GDP growth (annual % change)	5.0	−2.1	4.4	5.0	5.1
Inflation (%)	2.8	2.0	2.3	2.8	3.2
Current account balance (% of GDP)	−2.7	−0.4	−1.5	−1.8	−2.0
Fiscal balance (% of GDP)	−2.2	−6.2	−5.4	−4.1	−3.0
Public debt (% of GDP)	30.2	39.4	41.2	42.6	43.0

Source: World Bank (2021b).

Table 2.2 State budgets, 2019–2022

	2019	2020	2021 (Outlook)	2022 (RAPBN)
Deficit to GDP (%)	−2.2	−6.14	−5.82	−4.85
Economic growth (%)	5.0	−2.1	3.7	5.2
Deficit (rupiah trillions)	−384.7	−947.7	−961.5	−868.0

Note: RAPBN = Rancangan Anggaran Pendapatan dan Belanja Negara (Draft State Revenue and Expenditure Budget)

Source: MoF (2021a).

Uncertainties around the progress of the COVID-19 pandemic mean that economic projections should be done with caution and monitored continuously. The pandemic has compelled the Indonesian government to allocate resources to COVID-19 programs while sustaining welfare programs and infrastructure. To do this, the government has taken on more debt, resulting in a projected deficit of the central government's 2022 budget of 4.85% of GDP and narrowing the fiscal gap for welfare programs. Tax revenue is predicted to grow to 9.5% in 2022; however, the tax ratio is still low. The picture of tax revenue before and after the pandemic is relatively unchanged and the government will still be faced with weak fiscal capacity. However, private financing is promising.

To achieve the proposed state budget in 2022, the government plans structural and fiscal reform. The reforms will focus on the health sector and strengthening community protection while remaining flexible to the uncertainties of the pandemic. Structural reform will focus on human capital such as quality education, integrated and reliable health systems, lifelong and adaptive social protections, and the economic transition.

Tax reform, spending reform, and innovative, prudent and sustainable financing are part of the fiscal reforms that need to occur. The government allocated Rp 255.4 trillion, or 9.4% of state expenditure, to the health sector in the 2022 state budget bill. This is aimed at continuing to respond to the pandemic, reforming the health care system, reducing childhood stunting and continuing the JKN program (MoF 2021a). The health budget comprises Rp 139.4 trillion of the regular budget and Rp 115.9 trillion of the National Economic Recovery Program budget (Dana PEN). Figure 2.8 shows the increase of public spending in health, but still under low tax revenues and an increasing debt burden to the government.

Transforming the health sector

During the years of the pandemic, the Minister of Health developed three main objectives: (1) prioritise the acceleration of vaccination, (2) end the pandemic as soon as possible and (3) reform the health system to restore economic conditions. The first objective was gradually achieved during 2021. In response to the third objective, the government of Indonesia decided to use the pandemic momentum to plan reforms to the Indonesian health system. Plans for the health system transformation include accommodating the increased community needs attributed to the COVID-19 pandemic, keeping universal health coverage and sustaining essential health programs, while improving the pre-pandemic health system weaknesses (Ministry of Health Regulation No. 13/2022).

Figure 2.8 National health budget, 2017–2022 (rupiah trillions)

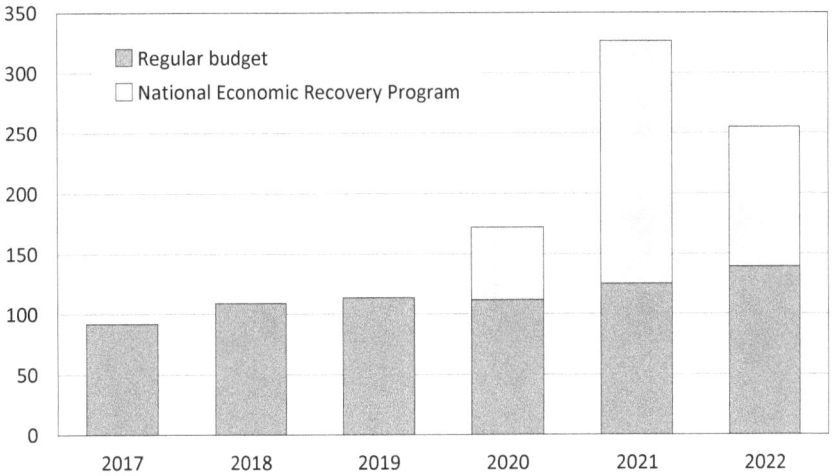

Source: MoF (2021a).

The health system transformation is described in the National Health Strategy 2021–2024 and based on six main pillars (Figure 2.9). The first pillar is primary health care, and aims to strengthen basic health services through strengthening promotive and preventive functions, increasing the capacity and capability of *puskesmas* and other private care services, and strengthening disease control. The second pillar aims to improve curative health care by increasing the ratio of hospital beds and other infrastructure, improving service quality and hospital accreditation, and improving health services in remote and underdeveloped regions through mobile health services. The third pillar focuses on health system resilience, to create resilience through increasing the independence of pharmacy and medical equipment and strengthening emergency responses.

The fourth pillar is about strengthening the foundation of health financing. Some of its strategies are the integration of health financing (universal health coverage) between the government and the private sector; strengthening and developing schemes for better equity, and efficient and effective health financing; and strengthening health financing for promotive and preventive activities. The fifth pillar is to implement human resource transformation. Its strategies include quality improvement through strengthening education, competence and training; and redistribution of health human resources to remote, isolated and underdeveloped areas. The sixth pillar aims to transform

Figure 2.9 Indonesia's national health transformation, 2021–2024

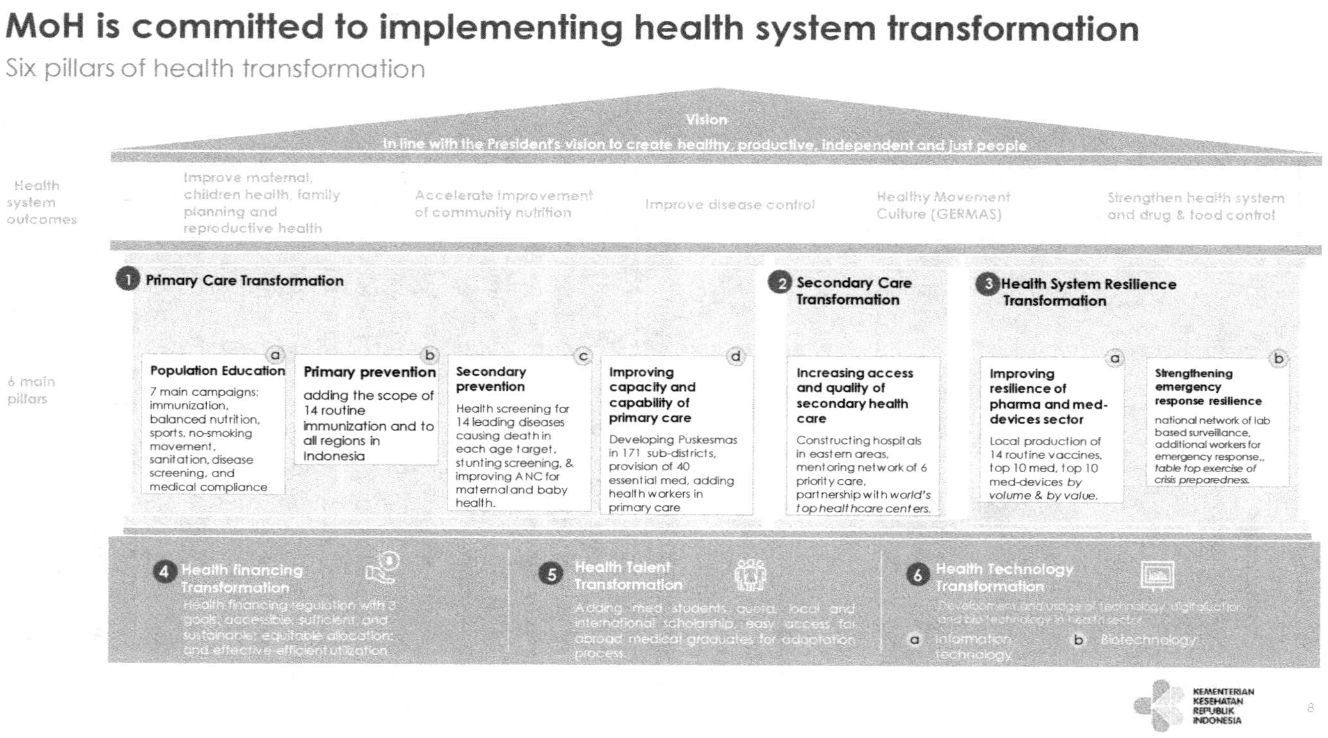

Source: MoH presentation, 2022.

digital health and biotechnology development. It will include health data system integration and development; telemedicine development and digitisation of *posyandu*, *puskesmas* and hospital services; and health technology ecosystem development. This is to support better health policy decision-making.

The health transformation depicted in Figure 2.9 uses the health system outcomes set by Bappenas before the pandemic, indicating that the pre-pandemic objectives of the health system still apply.

Financing and maintaining the health sector transformation will be a challenge. The financial trajectory of the COVID-19 pandemic shows that due to increased public debt, the government's fiscal capacity to finance welfare programs has been reduced. Development of health services infrastructure will have increased operating costs. For example, if equity in access to health services across the country is achieved, the costs for medical treatment will be higher. There is uncertainty whether government fiscal capacity is able to finance the construction and operating costs of the new facilities. At present, the central government has a World Bank loan to finance the construction of three large hospitals in remote provinces: Maluku, East Nusa Tenggara and Papua. Moreover, the capacity of BPJS-K to pay the InaCBG claims may be in doubt.

Another example is the screening program for non-communicable diseases. If the screening program is successful, persons identified in the program as needing treatment should proceed to the next level of care. Higher numbers of people requiring treatment will lead to higher demands on the health care system; these costs are to be financed by the government and BPJS-K.

Should the health sector rely on public spending, or include more private spending? For example, it is difficult to finance the deficit of the BPJS-K after the pandemic without increasing member premiums for the informal sector workers (*peserta bukan penerima upah*). If the health sector relies on public spending, tax revenue is likely to be insufficient to pay for medical expenses. Increasing the income tax rate is not politically palatable. As mentioned earlier, the fiscal gap for financing welfare programs is narrowing due to the long-term impacts of the COVID-19 pandemic combined with pre-pandemic health status indicators.

Therefore, the government's plans to transform the health sector are severely fiscally constrained. Realistic health finance policies are necessary. In this transformation, increasing financing from the private sector needs to be explored to see whether private investment can be mobilised to reduce the burden on government spending. The main strategy in financing the health sector post COVID-19 is to ensure the health budget in the national and local government budgeting process and to persuade better-off society members to pay more for their health needs (vaccinations and non-basic curative care). The economic structure of Indonesia with its low tax ratio (under 10%) should be emphasised. In this situation, it is not prudent to increase health care financing mostly from government resources. Individuals who are able to pay should pay more through pre-paid health insurance.

Careful use of the limited government resources is warranted. The Ministry of Finance has a plan for increasing the central government budget fiscal capacity for health through 'earmarked' cigarette taxes on the grounds that cigarette consumption causes health problems. However, these additional funds should be used for preventive and promotive programs related to cigarette smoking. It is not appropriate if the 'earmarked' cigarette tax or other sin taxes are used to finance expensive medical technologies without clear effectiveness. The limited government funds should be allocated to investment in innovative technology for reducing the burden of widespread diseases such as tuberculosis, malaria and neglected tropical diseases (for approaches to dengue control, see Utarini, this volume). Immunisation and other preventive programs should be financed by the government. Government funds should also be used for constructing health care facilities across the archipelago. A policy for 'pro-public good' should be enacted.

For individual needs (including high-technology medical interventions) there should be an increase in private sector involvement. The development of high technology for a limited number of beneficiaries should be managed as a private good. This will have an impact on the tier system of health care delivery. Not all needs and demands can be fulfilled by the JKN. The BPJS-K should be promoted as a health social security agency whose main task is becoming a safety net organisation. The main task is to ensure that all citizens have access to basic and standard health care. In the future, a two-tier system will become clearer in the Indonesian health services landscape. To support the funding of BPJS-K, a philanthropic scheme should be promoted. Innovative health financing should be encouraged, such as public–private partnerships, as well as corporate social responsibility.

References

Agustina, Rina, Teguh Dartanto, Ratna Sitompul, Kun A. Susiloretni, Suparmi, et al. 2019. 'Universal health coverage in Indonesia: Concept, progress, and challenges'. *The Lancet* 393(10166): 75–102. doi.org/10.1016/S0140-6736(18)31647-7

Akitoby, Bernardin. 2018. 'Raising revenue: Five country cases illustrate how best to improve tax collection'. *Finance & Development*, March. www.imf.org/en/Publications/fandd/issues/2018/03/akitoby

Bappenas (Badan Perencanaan Pembangunan Nasional, National Development Planning Agency). 2018. *Modul Sinkronisasi RPJMD-RPJMN Bidang Kesehatan dan Gizi Masyarakat* [RPJMD-RPJMN Synchronisation Module for Community Health and Nutrition]. Jakarta: Bappenas.

BKF (Badan Kebijakan Fiskal, Fiscal Policy Agency). 2021. 'Kajian dampak COVID-19 terhadap pasar tenaga kerja dan respons kebijakan di kawasan Asia dan Pasifik' [Assessment of the impact of COVID-19 on the labour market and policy responses in the Asia Pacific region]. Ministry of Finance. https://fiskal.kemenkeu.go.id/kajian/2021/08/18/2433-kajian-dampak-covid-19-terhadap-pasar-tenaga-kerja-dan-respons-kebijakan-di-kawasan-asia-dan-pasifik

BPS (Badan Pusat Statistik, Statistics Indonesia). 2015. *Profil Penduduk Indonesia Hasil Supas 2015* [Indonesian Population Profile 2015—Supas Results]. Jakarta: BPS.

Budiarso, Adi. 2021. 'COVID-19 socioeconomic impact in Indonesia: Policy responses and strategies'. Presentation to the 5th Annual Islamic Finance Conference, Jakarta. Fiscal Policy Agency, Ministry of Finance.

Cucinotta, Domenico and Maurizio Vanelli. 2020. 'WHO declares COVID-19 a pandemic'. *Acta Biomedica* 91(1): 157–60.

Helmyati, Siti, Dhian P. Dipo, Insan Rekso Adiwibowo, Maria Wigati, Erri Larene Safika, et al. 2022. 'Monitoring continuity of maternal and child health services, Indonesia'. *Bulletin of the World Health Organization* 100(2): 144–54. doi.org/10.2471/BLT.21.286636

Kharisma, Dinar Dana. 2020. 'Indonesian health system performance assessment: The association between health insurance expansion with health status and health care access'. *Jurnal Perencanaan Pembangunan: The Indonesian Journal of Development Planning* 4(3): 312–26. doi.org/10.36574/jpp.v4i3.134

Mahendradhata, Yodi, Laksono Trisnantoro, Shita Listyadewi, Prastuti Soewondo, Tiara Marthias, et al. 2017. *The Republic of Indonesia Health System Review. Health Systems in Transition* 7(1). World Health Organization. https://apps.who.int/iris/handle/10665/254716

MoF (Ministry of Finance). 2020. 'Data analysis from LKPP and financial note 2015–2019'. Jakarta: MoF.

MoF (Ministry of Finance). 2021a. 'Advertorial. Proposed 2022 budget economic recovery and structural reformation'. https://anggaran.kemenkeu.go.id/api/Medias/3a2c2884-b467-4598-9123-e814419f4076

MoF (Ministry of Finance). 2021b. *APBN Kita: Kinerja dan Fakta* [Our Budget: Performance and Facts]. December. https://djpk.kemenkeu.go.id/?portfolio=apbn-kita-edisi-desember-2021

MoF (Ministry of Finance). 2021c. 'Informasi APBN 2021'. https://anggaran.kemenkeu.go.id/api/Medias/45aa9080-850d-4356-9601-1dd7daecc4c7

MoH (Ministry of Health). 2013. *Hasil Riset Kesehatan Dasar (Riskesdas)* [Basic Health Research Results (Riskesdas)]. Jakarta: Badan Penelitian dan Pengembangan Kesehatan.

MoH (Ministry of Health). 2018. *Hasil Riset Kesehatan Dasar (Riskesdas)* [Basic Health Research Results (Riskesdas)]. Jakarta: Badan Penelitian dan Pengembangan Kesehatan.

MoH (Ministry of Health). 2021a. *Buku Saku Hasil Studi Status Gizi Indonesia (SSGI) Tahun 2021* [Pocket Book of Indonesian Nutrition Status Study Results 2021]. Jakarta: MoH.

MoH (Ministry of Health). 2021b. 'Data malaria di Indonesia'. www.malaria.id/laporan

MoH (Ministry of Health). 2021c. *Ketahanan Industri Farmasi* [Pharmaceutical Industry Resilience]. https://industri-obat-alkes.net/forum-nasional-kemandirian-dan-ketahanan-industri-sediaan-farmasi-pameran-virtual-sediaan-farmasi-dalam-negeri-dan-business-matching/

MoH (Ministry of Health). 2021d. *Profil Kesehatan Indonesia 2020* [Indonesia Health Profile 2020]. MoH: Jakarta. https://pusdatin.kemkes.go.id/resources/download/pusdatin/profil-kesehatan-indonesia/Profil-Kesehatan-Indonesia-Tahun-2020.pdf

Nugraheni, Wahyu P., Asri Hikmatuz Zahroh, Risky Kusuma Hartono, Ryan Rachmad Nugraha and Chang Bae Chun. 2020. 'National health insurance deficit in Indonesia: Identification of causes and solutions for resolution'. *Global Journal of Health Science* 12(13): 58. doi.org/10.5539/gjhs.v12n13p58

Sambodo, Novat Pugo, Eddy Van Doorslaer, Menno Pradhan and Robert Sparrow. 2021. 'Does geographic spending variation exacerbate healthcare benefit inequality? A benefit incidence analysis for Indonesia'. *Health Policy and Planning* 36(7): 1129–39. doi.org/10.1093/heapol/czab015

Trisnantoro, Laksono. 2021. 'Pengantar diskusi: Dinamika regulasi di alat kesehatan dan kebutuhan akan community of practice' [Discussion: The dynamics of regulation in medical devices and the need for community of practice]. PowerPoint presentation. Ministry of Health.

WHO (World Health Organization). 2021a. *Global Expenditure in Health: Public Spending on the Rise?* Geneva: WHO.

WHO (World Health Organization). 2021b. Global Health Expenditure Database. Accessed 27 November 2021. https://apps.who.int/nha/database/country_profile/Index/en

WHO (World Health Organization). 2021c. *Global Tuberculosis Report 2021*. Geneva: WHO.

World Bank. 2020. *Indonesia Economic Prospects, December 2020: Towards a Secure and Fast Recovery*. Washington, DC: World Bank. http://hdl.handle.net/10986/34930

World Bank. 2021a. 'Indonesia Emergency Response to COVID-19 Additional Financing'. https://documents1.worldbank.org/curated/en/817781624240832504/pdf/Indonesia-Emergency-Response-to-COVID-19-Program-Additional-Financing.pdf

World Bank. 2021b. *Indonesia Economic Prospects, June 2021: Boosting the Recovery*. World Bank. www.worldbank.org/en/country/indonesia/publication/indonesia-economic-prospects-iep-june-2021-boosting-the-recovery

3 The right to health and the politics of health policy reform in post–New Order Indonesia

Andrew Rosser and Luky Djani

Since the fall of Suharto's New Order in 1998, Indonesia's political elite has made significant changes to Indonesian law affording greater recognition to the right to health (R2H).[1] Between 1999 and 2002, the People's Consultative Assembly amended the 1945 constitution to introduce new rights to 'obtain health services', 'have a good and healthy living environment', have access to social security and 'develop oneself through the fulfilment of basic needs'. In accordance with these new rights, it also imposed a new obligation on the state to provide 'health service facilities' and declared that the state would develop a social security system for all people. In the midst of and following these amendments, the national parliament (DPR) enacted a number of laws that reaffirmed—and in some cases expanded upon—these rights and obligations (Rosser 2017: 6–7). These included Law No. 36/2009 on Health which stipulates, among other things, that the government has obligations to provide health services, ensure resources for the health sector, and try to realise the highest possible standard of health (Pūras 2018: 5).

These legal commitments have been accompanied by health policies and programs that have sought to promote R2H in various ways. As the

---

1 R2H entails 'a right to the enjoyment of a variety of facilities, goods, services and conditions necessary for the realization of the highest attainable standard of health' (UNCESCR 2000: Article 9). It incorporates not merely a right to quality health services but also to the underlying preconditions for health (OHCHR and WHO 2008: 4).

United Nations' (UN) special rapporteur on R2H, Dainius Pūras, noted in a 2018 report, the Indonesian government has 'made considerable progress with regard to the realization of the right to health, particularly by expanding universal health coverage'. It has also promoted R2H by increasing health expenditure as a share of the government budget. However, many commentators have suggested that the government has stymied progress vis-à-vis R2H by failing to address discrimination and inequality in access to health services, improve the quality of health services, address the growing burden of non-communicable diseases, enhance access to clean water and sanitation, control addictive and harmful substances, ensure healthy environmental conditions, and—particularly since the onset of the COVID-19 pandemic in 2020—ensure the country is protected from emerging infectious diseases.

The purpose of this chapter is to shed light on the reasons for this outcome and the likely future trajectory of health policy in Indonesia by examining the political dynamics that have shaped health policy in post–New Order Indonesia. We argue that the greater overall priority given to R2H in Indonesian law and policy has reflected the broad realignment of power relations that accompanied the fall of the New Order. This realignment—which entailed a shift in power away from predatory elites nurtured under the New Order towards technocratic, progressive, populist and popular elements—created a political context more conducive to rights-based health policy. At the same time, however, the fact that predatory elites were able to maintain, and have recently reasserted, their political dominance has imposed significant constraints on the extent of such change. The result has been an uneven process of rights-oriented reform in which the fate of rights-oriented initiatives has depended on whether they have threatened the interests of predatory elites and attracted support from popular and populist elements. Broadly, we suggest, reform has proceeded furthest where reform initiatives have sought to enhance access to health services and least where they have sought to address the underlying preconditions of health, reflecting the fact that the former has created new stakeholders, altering electoral and mobilisational politics, while the latter has not (cf. Nelson 2004). This uneven trajectory of change, we suggest, is likely to continue into the foreseeable future in the absence of any fundamental realignment in underlying power relations. It remains to be seen whether COVID-19 will produce such realignment.

We begin our analysis by providing an overview of the main actors who have been involved in health policymaking in post–New Order Indonesia and the interests and agendas they have pursued. We then examine how political dynamics have shaped health policy in broad terms and specific issue areas. We conclude by examining the likely future trajectory of health policy in Indonesia.

Actors, interests and agendas

Broadly speaking, five main sets of actors have shaped health policy in post–New Order Indonesia, each of which has had distinct interests and a distinct agenda with regard to R2H. The first of these has been liberal economic technocrats in government and their supporters within the donor community and other bodies controlling mobile capital. This coalition has often expressed a commitment to human rights (including R2H) but it has tended to privilege economic growth and free markets over human rights (O'Connell 2007). With respect to health policy, it has supported state investment in public health services and measures to improve the preconditions for health as a way of building the country's human resources and, in so doing, contributing to economic growth (Boediono 2009: 13, 31, 44). It has also supported social safety net schemes and increased government health expenditure to provide basic social protection for the poor (ADB 2000). At the same time, however, it has argued that public health programs need to be affordable, cost-effective and based on evidence about what works and why; supported high levels of private health care provision; and been concerned about the potential for environmental health regulations to impact negatively on economic growth (Rokx et al. 2009; Wanner 2015). The influence of this agenda has reflected powerful structural pressures on the Indonesian government emanating from budget constraints, the power of mobile capital due to its ability to relocate to alternative jurisdictions (Winters 1996), and the technocrats' access to policymaking processes due to their positions within the state apparatus.

The second main set of actors has been predatory political, military and bureaucratic officials who have occupied the state apparatus and the domestic and foreign business groups to which they have been connected (in many cases through family and other personal relationships). Members of this coalition have sought to exploit their positions and connections to generate rents for personal enrichment and lubricate personal and political networks (Robison and Hadiz 2004). In general, they have had little commitment to human rights. With regard to health policy, they have recognised that state investment in public health services and measures to promote the underlying preconditions of health are conducive to promoting economic growth through their contribution to human resource development. But they have had a stronger interest in limiting government spending on health to free up resources for other areas (for instance, infrastructure, industrial projects, subsidised credit programs) more central to their business activities or promoting their political bases. To the extent that the government has spent money on health, they have had a further interest in ensuring that such expenditure privileges military and bureaucratic officials—for instance, by providing them with insurance benefits or opportunities to enrich themselves, lubricate patronage networks and buy votes (van Diermen 2017: 58–59).[2] Members of this coalition have exercised influence over health policy by virtue of their direct access to the policymaking process and role in implementing health policy.

The third main set of actors has been progressive elements in the non-government organisation movement, academia, health professional organisations such as the Indonesian Medical Association (IDI) and the Indonesian Public Health Association (IAKMI), and various UN organisations. This set of actors has sought to promote improved access to health services as well as measures to provide for the underlying preconditions for health in accordance with R2H (KUIS 2005; Pūras 2018). As the World Health Organization (WHO) has noted, in terms of policy, R2H requires states to: (i) refrain from 'interfer[ing] directly or indirectly with the enjoyment of the right to health' by, for instance, 'limiting access to health-care services or marketing unsafe drugs'; (ii) 'prevent third parties from interfering with the right to health' by, for instance, 'ensur[ing] that private companies provide safe environmental conditions for their employees and surrounding communities'; and (iii) 'adopt appropriate legislative, administrative, budgetary, judicial, promotional and other measures to fully realize the right to health' (WHO n.d.). In pursuing this agenda, members of this coalition have not had much direct access to the health policymaking process because they have largely been situated outside the state apparatus. But they have nevertheless exercised influence due to their ability to access the media, conduct strategic litigation, leverage the support of popular elements (on occasion), and in the case of UN organisations and IDI/IAKMI figures, secure some access to policymakers, especially in the Ministry of Health.

The fourth set of actors has been Indonesian politicians—especially those running for or occupying national or local executive offices such as president, provincial governor and district head—who have sought to mobilise support from the poor by promoting or at least claiming credit

---

2 Such opportunities include illegal fees by public health service providers, corrupt deals over supply of medical equipment and other materials to these providers, and delivery of cash transfers (with health-related objectives) in the lead-up to elections.

for populist/redistributive policies. Politicians have employed strategies that comprise, in varying ways and to varying extents (i) the cultivation of mafia networks through patronage distribution; (ii) the consolidation of party machines through measures to enhance their institutional capacity; and (iii) the mobilisation of the poor through populist/redistributive policies (Tans 2011). To the extent that they have sought to mobilise the poor through populist/redistributive policies, they have widened the scope for rights-oriented health policies, although, as Mietzner (2020) has noted, populist strategies can also lead to rights-unfriendly anti-scientism.

The fifth and final set of actors has been popular forces such as organised labour and farmers. This set of actors has had contradictory interests with regard to R2H. On one hand, these actors have stood to benefit in health terms from improved access to health services as well as measures to provide for the underlying preconditions for health. On the other hand, some elements have stood to lose from measures such as stricter tobacco-control policies to the extent that such measures negatively affect their employment and income. Their agenda with regard to health policy has thus varied significantly by policy issue and the popular element concerned.

The politics of health policy reform

During the New Order, predatory elements were the dominant set of political actors. At the same time, liberal economic technocrats and their supporters also exercised significant influence, reflecting the New Order's need to attract mobile investment to drive economic growth, particularly during economic crises (Winters 1996). Progressive, popular and populist elements were largely excluded from the policymaking process due to authoritarian controls on civil society, professional organisations and political opposition, and in particular their ability to raise human rights concerns (Robison and Hadiz 2004). In the realm of health policy, the result was ambivalent government commitment to R2H. On one hand, the New Order endorsed the 'Alma Ata declaration' in 1978. This asserted that health is a fundamental human right and outlined a range of other principles and actions consistent with a rights-based approach to health. The New Order also dramatically expanded the public health system during the oil boom era when it was awash in petrodollars, significantly improving access to health services.

However, it invested little in the public health system thereafter, reflecting technocratic concerns to rein in government spending following the collapse of oil prices and the interests of predatory elites in maintaining other areas of spending and rent seizure. Instead, it encouraged private provision of health services and tolerated legal and illegal fees at public health facilities, constructing health services as a private good rather than a right-based entitlement and transforming public health facilities into mechanisms for the generation and distribution of rents by predatory officials (Rosser 2012). At the same time, underfunding of the public health system meant that public health services were 'substandard, reflecting a combination of low-quality health personnel and poor equipment' (Suwandono et al. 2003: 133). Finally, the New Order failed to adopt adequate measures to ensure the underlying preconditions for health—for instance, many Indonesians lacked access to clean water and sanitation, controls on addictive and harmful substances were weak, and many people lacked healthy working and environmental conditions (Moodie et al. 2000). As one indication of the New Order's ambivalence towards R2H, its main piece of health legislation, Law No. 23/1992 on Health, did not explicitly provide for a right to health services or the underlying preconditions to health.[3]

The onset of the Asian financial crisis in 1997 and subsequent collapse of the New Order in 1998 shifted power away from predatory elites and towards technocratic, progressive, populist and popular elements. The former dramatically strengthened the position of government technocrats and their donor allies by forcing the government to negotiate a rescue package with the International Monetary Fund and accept increased aid. The latter witnessed the removal of key obstacles to organisation by civil society groups, improvements in freedom of expression, greater autonomy for professional organisations, and the creation of new policy spaces (such as the Constitutional Court) that popular elements and their allies could access (Rosser 2012). It also created an incentive for politicians to promote redistributive policies because of their electoral popularity, with local political figures, newly empowered by decentralisation implemented in 2001, often taking the lead in this respect (Djani et al. 2018). At the same time, however, this reconfiguration of the balance of power between competing political and social elements was limited by predatory elites' ability to maintain their control over the state apparatus by establishing new parties and forging new alliances (Robison and Hadiz 2004). Over coming years, they even clawed back some lost ground through attacks on the anti-corruption commission and moves to recentralise authority and undermine democratic reforms (Power and Warburton 2020).

---

3 Article 4 vaguely stated that: 'All people have the *same* right to obtain an optimal standard of health' (italics added).

The overall effect of these changes, as noted earlier, was an uneven process of rights-oriented reform: while the government adopted a range of legal and policy changes giving greater recognition to R2H and seeking to promote its fulfilment in practice, the fate of specific rights-oriented initiatives varied from case to case. Below we examine the reasons for this in greater detail by analysing the politics of health policy in three areas: health insurance, tobacco control and health security. We argue that the fate of rights-oriented reforms in these areas depended on the extent to which they disrupted predatory interests and attracted support from popular and populist elements: where reforms avoided seriously disrupting predatory interests, they proceeded relatively smoothly; where they disrupted these interests, reform outcomes depended on whether these initiatives attracted support from popular and/or populist elements. We further note that among our case studies, reforms that enhanced access to health services fared better than reforms addressing the underlying preconditions of health, suggesting the possibility of a wider pattern along these lines. Our analysis with respect to each case is summarised in Table 3.1.

Table 3.1 Health policy case studies: Outcomes and politics

	Case	Type of reform	Reform outcome
Disrupted predatory interests and attracted support from popular/populist elements	1. Health insurance	Access-enhancing	Extensive
Disrupted predatory interests and did not attract support from popular/populist elements	2. Tobacco control	Addressing underlying preconditions for health	Limited
Did not disrupt predatory interests	3. Health security	Addressing underlying preconditions for health	Significant

Health insurance

During the New Order, the Indonesian government pursued an approach to health insurance consistent with the 'productivist' model of social welfare (van Diermen 2017). In this model, economic policy is prioritised over social policy and benefits are concentrated on 'productive' elements in society (Holliday 2000). More specifically, the government provided subsidised health insurance to civil servants, military officials and veterans through the Askes health insurance scheme and made available health care benefits to formal-sector workers who contributed to the Workers' Social Insurance (Jamsostek) scheme. But it provided little if any coverage to other Indonesians, leaving them exposed to potentially catastrophic out-of-pocket health costs when faced with illness or disease. The Asian financial crisis in 1997–1998 saw the Indonesian government move away from this approach towards one more consistent with the rights to health and social security. It did so through the introduction of new national and local health insurance schemes covering variously the poor, the near-poor and eventually all Indonesians.

Initially, it introduced the Social Safety Net – Health scheme (Jaringan Pengaman Sosial – Bidang Kesehatan, JPS-BK) with donor financial support to provide protection to the poor during the Asian financial crisis. Intended only to be a temporary measure, this scheme was gradually wound down and ceased to exist by 2003. Subsequently, the government established the Health Safety Net for Poor Families (Jaringan Pengaman Sosial – Keluarga Miskin, JPS-Gakin) (2003–2004) and Health Insurance for Poor Communities (Asuransi Kesehatan Masyarakat Miskin, Askeskin) (2004–2008). Both of these schemes provided state-funded health coverage to the poor, in the former case according to a managed care model styled on a United States health maintenance organisation and in the latter case according to a social health insurance model. In 2008, the government replaced the latter with National Health Insurance for the Poor and Near Poor (Jaminan Kesehatan Masyarakat, Jamkesmas) (Rokx et al. 2009: 36; Rosser 2012: 258–59). In the midst of these changes, it granted local governments the authority to establish local health insurance programs to cover people not included in national schemes (Djani et al. 2018). Finally, in 2014, it introduced a national health insurance program, Jaminan Kesehatan Nasional (JKN), a mandatory social insurance scheme that provides universal health coverage. Administered by the Social Health Insurance Agency (Badan Penyelenggara Jaminan Sosial Kesehatan, BPJS-K), the scheme requires the government to pay health insurance premiums for the poor and near-poor while others pay their own premiums based on the quality of insurance cover chosen.

This change in direction posed a significant threat to predatory elements. To free up the funds to establish the new health insurance schemes (and the wider set of social assistance programs of which they were part), the government had to cut fuel subsidies that primarily benefited business and the middle class (van Diermen 2017). The creation of the JKN and accompanying social security reforms related to labour protection also entailed increased costs for business due to mandatory social security charges (Pisani et al. 2017). They also entailed the transfer of control over social security funds from the traditional social security state-owned enterprises—PT Askes, PT Jamsostek, PT Taspen and PT Asabri—to two new agencies, BPJS-K and BP Jamsostek (BPJS Labour). This was important because these funds were a source of funding for strategic government initiatives and rents for government officials, well-connected business groups and senior officials in these state-owned enterprises. The result was a series of protests from the business community—or instigated by it—against cuts to fuel subsidies and the implementing legislation for the JKN (van Diermen 2017). But, in the end, such protests proved ineffective, reflecting the broad nature of coalition that formed in support of the new health insurance programs and, specifically, the fact that it included populist and popular elements.

Initially, this change in policy direction reflected concern among technocratic and progressive elements about the social impact of the Asian financial crisis and a view that the government needed to provide better and more equitable health coverage than the New Order (KMUK 1999; van Diermen 2017). Technocratic elements expressed concern about the fiscal sustainability of the new health insurance schemes, especially the JKN, reflecting the fact that BPJS-K has incurred large deficits since its inception (World Bank 2020), but they nevertheless supported the country's moves towards greater health coverage. For their part, progressive elements pushed for expanded health coverage through advocacy, research and engagement work as well as participation in lobbying and strategic litigation (Rosser 2017). Some key figures became involved in related intra-governmental policymaking processes. For instance, Hasbullah Thabrany, a prominent public health expert, joined the team that drafted Law No. 40/2004 on a National Social Security System, the legal foundation for the JKN (van Diermen 2017: 154).

Over time, however, this change in direction became increasingly driven by support from local and national politicians, especially ones running for or occupying executive offices, and popular forces. The new insurance schemes proved popular with the public, making them a potential vote-winner in Indonesian elections (Pisani et al. 2017). As a result, several politicians included health insurance reforms as part of their campaign strategies. At the local level, these included I Gede Winasa in Jembrana and Joko Widodo when he ran for the governorship of Jakarta in 2012. At the national level, Susilo Bambang Yudhoyono incorporated health insurance–related promises into his successful presidential campaigns in 2004 and 2009 (van Diermen 2017: 172, 185). Widodo also did so when he ran for president in 2014. In his campaign for the Jakarta governorship, Widodo introduced the Jakarta Health Card (Kartu Jakarta Sehat, KJS) as a means of ensuring that all Jakartans would receive free hospital treatment regardless of their economic status. In his presidential campaign, he scaled up KJS to the national level, announcing that he would introduce a Kartu Indonesia Sehat (Pisani et al. 2017: 273). At the same time, the JKN also drew crucial support from sections of the trade union movement. When the government delayed passage of crucial implementing legislation due by October 2009, thousands of labour activists held demonstrations across the country, calling for the quick endorsement and subsequent enactment of the bill. Combined with a series of strategic court cases, these demonstrations put enormous pressure on the government to pass the legislation (Rosser 2017).

Tobacco control

Indonesia has experienced a severe tobacco epidemic for many decades, impairing the country's ability to promote R2H. According to de Beyer and Yurekli (2000: 2), annual cigarette consumption in Indonesia rose by 159 per cent during the 1970s, 67 per cent during the 1980s and 47 per cent during the 1990s. It has continued to rise further to the point that the country has become the world's third-largest cigarette market. This increase in cigarette consumption has been driven largely by growing smoking rates among Indonesian men. According to the most recent statistics, 62.9 per cent of men and 4.8 per cent of women smoke. The country also has a severe child smoking problem and 60 per cent of Indonesians are exposed to passive smoke at home (IAKMI-SEATCA 2020: 29–30, 39). Such widespread consumption of and exposure to tobacco has had devasting health consequences, with more than 225,700 Indonesians dying each year from tobacco-related diseases (ibid.: 174). Since the onset of COVID-19, experts have warned that this situation will worsen the pandemic's impact by causing more severe illness (Widiadana 2020).

During the New Order, the Indonesian government did almost nothing to combat—and virtually everything to encourage—the tobacco epidemic. There were few restrictions on the sale, marketing and use of tobacco products; taxes on tobacco products were very low, making cigarettes affordable even for many poor people; and the government actively promoted the production of tobacco products. Following the fall of the New Order, however, the government moved fitfully and inconsistently towards tougher tobacco-control policies. It included a provision in the 2009 Health Law identifying tobacco as an addictive substance, introduced requirements for cigarette packets to include pictorial warnings and harsher written warnings, set maximum nicotine and tar levels, imposed restrictions on tobacco advertising in electronic media, and introduced provisions for local governments to establish smoke-free zones. But it backtracked, partly or fully, on some tobacco-control measures (most notably those on tobacco advertising in electronic media, and nicotine and tar levels); kept tobacco excise rates low;[4] continued to promote increased domestic tobacco production; and refused to sign the WHO's Framework Convention on Tobacco Control, the key international standard on tobacco control (Rosser 2015). At the same time, studies suggest that local government implementation of smoke-free zones has been uneven (Septiono et al. 2019). Overall, the result has been a tobacco-control policy regime that, while stronger than the New Order's, still has major weaknesses.

Like health insurance reforms, tobacco-control measures posed a serious threat to predatory elements, specifically those associated with the country's tobacco industry. Tobacco companies in Indonesia are extremely powerful, reflecting their economic size and political connections. Two cigarette companies are among the ten largest companies on Indonesia's stock exchange and the owners of Indonesian tobacco companies regularly feature in lists of the country's wealthiest people (Astuti et al. 2020: 10). Tobacco companies are also major employers, fund a range of education, cultural, musical and sporting events through their philanthropic/corporate social responsibility arms, and provide substantial state revenues in the form of tobacco excise payments. They are also widely believed to be a key source of election campaign finance for politicians and political parties. Finally, they have had the capacity to mobilise popular forces—most notably tobacco farmers and workers—in support of their agenda (Rosser 2015).

Unsurprisingly, they have pushed back against tobacco-control measures. For instance, figures associated with the tobacco industry campaigned strongly against recognition of tobacco as an addictive substance in the 2009 Health Law. There was even a scandalous attempt to engineer the removal of the relevant provision from the law after it was passed by the DPR (*Tempo* 2010). Similarly, the two peak industry associations representing cigarette companies' collective interests, the Indonesian Cigarette Manufacturers Association (GAPPRI) and the White Cigarette Producers Association (GAPRINDO), have been active in campaigns against the government endorsing the Framework Convention on Tobacco Control (Rosser 2015).

---

4   There were, however, marked rises in tobacco excise rates in 2020 and 2021 (IAKMI-SEATCA 2020: 92).

Importantly for our purposes, this resistance from predatory forces has not been offset by support from populist or popular elements, as in the case of health insurance reform. The campaign for tobacco control has been led by progressive figures based in non-government organisations, universities, IDI, IAKMI (many of which have been supported by the Bloomberg Foundation) and technocratic figures in the WHO and the World Bank. In general, executive political figures at the local and national level have baulked at championing tobacco-control measures (although there have been some notable exceptions such as Bima Arya, the mayor of Bogor) (Kartika and Thaariq 2019). This reflects the political clout of the tobacco companies and a sense that there are few votes in limiting a popular pastime and doing harm to an industry that is a major employer and source of government revenue and funding for social and cultural activities. Nor have tobacco-control advocates been able to mobilise support from popular elements. In 2010, Muhammadiyah, one of Indonesia's main Islamic social organisations, and the Council of Indonesian Ulama (MUI), the country's peak clerical body, both declared smoking *haram* (forbidden). But in the latter's case this was only for children and pregnant women and in public spaces. At the same time, Nahdlatul Ulama (NU), the country's other main Islamic organisation, determined that smoking was merely *makruh* (something to be avoided but not necessarily sinful). Underlying the responses of the MUI and NU was the fact that tobacco farmers are a key part of NU's support base, which is geographically situated in East Java and Central Java, both major tobacco-growing areas. Not surprisingly, to the extent that NU has mobilised in relation to tobacco-control measures, it has been to defeat them: in 2012, for instance, NU's Agricultural Development Institute launched a Constitutional Court challenge to the provision in Law No. 36/2009 identifying tobacco as an addictive substance (Rosser 2015).

In this context, tobacco-control advocates have found it difficult to advance their agenda beyond piecemeal reforms. These reforms have made some inroads into tobacco consumption—the most recent Ministry of Health data suggest that tobacco consumption rates among both men and women fell slightly between 2013 and 2018.[5] But the limited nature of reforms makes it likely that the tobacco epidemic in Indonesia will continue for decades, with obvious implications in terms of R2H.

---

5   The falls were from 66.0 to 62.9 per cent in the case of men and 6.7 to 4.8 per cent in the case of women (IAKMI-SEATCA 2020: 29).

Health security

Under the New Order, the Indonesian government invested significant resources in combating established infectious diseases such as tuberculosis, polio, diphtheria, pertussis, tetanus and measles, all of which posed a major threat to the health of Indonesian citizens. However, it did little to combat emerging infectious diseases, despite the fact that its rule saw HIV/AIDS become one of history's worst pandemics and globalisation and the proliferation of biological weapons raise concern about the emergence of new diseases. For instance, while it took some initial steps to combat HIV/AIDS, these were limited in nature and poorly funded in accordance with the low prevalence recorded in early sentinel surveillance among high-risk groups (Elmendorf et al. 2005: 4).

The onset of the SARS and avian influenza outbreaks in the early to mid-2000s, as well as the country's new commitment to promoting R2H following the fall of the New Order, prompted the government to change tack in this respect. In 2003, through ASEAN, it called on the WHO to revise the International Health Regulations (IHR)—an international legal instrument which 'defines countries' rights and obligations in handling public health events and emergencies that have the potential to cross borders' (WHO 2016)—to take into account the lessons of the SARS experience (WHO 2003: 61). Subsequently, it moved to implement the revised IHR, holding a series of self- and joint-assessment exercises and establishing an IHR national committee to accelerate this process (Government of Indonesia 2020). Implementation entailed the development of a set of 'core capacities' that are 'required to detect, assess, notify and report events, and respond to public health risks and emergencies of national and international concern'.[6] These capacities relate to matters to do with legislation, points of entry, surveillance and response, laboratory capacity, human resource development, food safety, chemical radionuclear safety and multisectoral collaboration.

The government's self-assessments suggest that these moves led to a dramatic improvement in the country's IHR capacities[7] over subsequent years—indeed it claims that it fully implemented the IHR in 2014 (Government of Indonesia 2020). A 2017 joint external evaluation (JEE) by the government and international partners also presented a positive

---

6 www.emro.who.int/international-health-regulations/about/ihr-core-capacities.html
7 See Indonesia's Electronic State Party Self-Assessment Annual Reporting Tool (e-SPAR) scores, https://extranet.who.int/e-spar/#capacity-progress

picture of Indonesia's progress in implementing the IHR, although it identified room for improvement in all assessed areas (WHO 2018).

But the government's ineffective management of COVID-19 in 2020–2021—by mid-2021, Indonesia had become the global epicentre of the pandemic with new cases peaking at more than 50,000 per day—revealed that many of these presumed capacities were markedly weaker than claimed. An August 2020 evaluation of Indonesia's COVID-19 response carried out by the WHO, other UN agencies, and the Indonesian government rated a subset of the country's IHR capacities substantially lower than the government's self-assessments and the JEE. Overall, the evaluation results suggest that the country had at best achieved a significant improvement rather than a dramatic improvement in this area of policy (WHO 2021: 25). This is a matter of concern to the extent that there is an association between strong IHR capacities and reduced rate of incidence and mortality from emerging infectious diseases and COVID-19 particularly (Wong et al. 2021).

In contrast to rights-oriented reform in both the health insurance and tobacco-control cases, the development of IHR core capacities did not significantly disrupt entrenched predatory interests. Building these capacities was largely a matter of developing new processes, facilities and coordination mechanisms rather than withdrawing benefits from or imposing costs on powerful political and corporate interests. The exercise of specific capacities within the context of particular disease outbreaks was, of course, a different matter. For instance, as Hameiri (2014: 348) has noted, there was significant pushback from predatory elements in the poultry industry to culling as a strategy for addressing the spread of avian influenza in the late 2000s despite the fact that this was the preferred approach of the WHO, the Food and Agriculture Organization, and the World Organisation for Animal Health. Likewise, during COVID-19, there has been pushback from the business sector against proposals for the government to implement hard lockdowns to combat the spread of COVID-19 because of concerns they would harm investment and employment (Aditya and Heijmans 2021). But, in general, the prior development of the required capacities was uncontroversial and encountered little resistance from predatory elements, facilitating reform.

Conclusion

The post–New Order period has seen the Indonesian government introduce changes to Indonesian law that have afforded greater legal recognition to R2H and a series of health policies and programs that have sought to promote R2H in various ways. However, the extent to which it has adopted such policies and programs has varied across issue areas. Drawing on an analysis of the political dynamics of health policymaking in three areas, this chapter has suggested that this pattern of reform has reflected (i) the broad realignment of power relations that accompanied the fall of the New Order—by which there was a shift in power away from predatory elites, who at best had only a modest interest in R2H, towards technocratic, progressive, popular and populist elements who have a more significant interest in this right; and (ii) the extent to which specific rights-oriented reforms have threatened predatory interests and attracted support from popular and populist elements. In short, we suggest that, within an overall political context more conducive to rights-oriented health policy reform, the extent of such reform has depended on the nature of the coalitions that have formed vis-a-vis specific policy issues and the balance of power between them. In some cases, resistance from predatory forces has been limited or offset by contestation from diverse rights coalitions, facilitating reform, while in other cases it has not, impairing reform. The greatest gains for R2H have been made where reforms enhanced citizens' access to health services while fewer gains were made where reforms addressed the underlying preconditions of health, reflecting the fact that the former created new stakeholders, altering electoral and mobilisational politics.

What does this analysis suggest about the likely future trajectory of health policy in Indonesia? Broadly, it suggests that if Indonesia continues to move towards more rights-oriented policy settings, it will do so in an asymmetrical manner, with reform progressing further in some areas than others. It also suggests that reform will reach a point, if it has not already, where it is unable to progress further because politically feasible health policy reforms have been exhausted. This is because there is little prospect of fundamental change in underlying power relations in the foreseeable future. In fact, as noted earlier, if anything the trajectory in recent years has been towards a reassertion of predatory dominance over Indonesian politics and increasing exclusion of technocratic, progressive, populist and popular elements, constraining potential for rights-oriented change. COVID-19—and the government's mishandling of it—may prove to be a game-changer in this respect but so far there is little sign that it has produced a fundamental realignment of power relations in favour of elements more supportive of R2H. Indeed, the Indonesian government's response to COVID-19 has been accompanied by moves to sideline progressive and technocratic elements by seeking to silence criticism of the president and, in particular, his government's handling of the pandemic (Mietzner 2020: 244).

Even if COVID-19 does not shift the overall alignment of power relations in Indonesia, it is possible that it will alter the political dynamics surrounding specific areas of health policy. Clearly, the most likely area for this to happen is health security. We are yet to see evidence that COVID-19 has generated new forms of large-scale popular mobilisation seeking to promote rights-oriented health security policy reform: indeed, as in many other parts of the world, popular mobilisations that have occurred vis-a-vis government handling of the pandemic have typically involved opposition to measures such as lockdowns and 'mandatory' vaccination. However, recent efforts by senior political figures to promote greater self-sufficiency in the production of medical instruments (such as ventilators and testing instruments), medicine, vaccine and oxygen suggest the potential for populist impulses to drive rights-oriented health security policy reform forward (Pribadi 2020; Saputri 2021). In the other areas of health policy covered in this chapter, we are yet to see evidence of either populist-driven reform or new popular mobilisations—indeed, in the case of health insurance, the government has increased insurance premiums to stem the growing costs of the JKN despite the fact that 2020 saw a fall in BPJS-K participation (Pratama 2021). The future may, however, see a change in this respect as elections approach, given the potential appeal of further health insurance reform.

Acknowledgements

We would like to thank the Indonesia Democracy Hallmark Research Initiative at the University of Melbourne for providing a grant to support the preparation of this chapter; Fahmy Badoh and Wahyudi Tohar for their research assistance; and Firman Witoelar Kartaadipoetra, Ariane Utomo and Sophie Rosser for their feedback on earlier drafts. The usual caveat applies.

References

ADB (Asian Development Bank). 2000. *Asian Development Outlook 2000*. Manila: ADB.

Aditya, Arys and Philip Heijmans. 2021. 'How anti-lockdown elites swayed Jokowi, fueling Indonesia crisis'. Bloomberg, 21 July. www.bloomberg.com/news/features/2021-07-21/how-anti-lockdown-business-elites-swayed-jokowi-fueling-indonesia-crisis

Astuti, Putu, Mary Assunta and Becky Freeman. 2020. 'Why is tobacco control progress in Indonesia stalled? A qualitative analysis of interviews with tobacco control experts'. *BMC Public Health* 20: 527. doi.org/10.1186/s12889-020-08640-6

Boediono. 2009. *Ekonomi Indonesia Mau Ke Mana? Kumpulan Esai Ekonomi* [Where Is Indonesia's Economy Going? A Collection of Economic Essays]. Jakarta: Gramedia and Freedom Institute.

de Beyer, Joy and Ayda Yurekli. 2000. 'Curbing the tobacco epidemic in Indonesia'. East Asia and the Pacific Region Watching Brief, 6.

Djani, Luky, M. Didit Saleh and Putut Aryo Saputro. 2018. 'Claiming a welfare state: Universal health insurance and the labour movement. Case study of Jamkes Watch in Bekasi, West Java, Indonesia'. In *The Politics of Welfare: Contested Welfare Regimes in Indonesia*, edited by Wawan Mas'udi and Cornelius Lay, 49–78. Jakarta: Pustaka Obor Foundation, PolGov Fisipol UGM and University of Oslo.

Elmendorf, A. Edward, Eric Jensen and Elizabeth Pisani. 2005. *Evaluation of the World Bank's Assistance in Responding to the AIDS Epidemic: Indonesia Case Study*. Washington, DC: World Bank.

Government of Indonesia. 2020. National Action Plan for Health Security Indonesia. Jakarta: Government of Indonesia.

Hameiri, Shahar. 2014. 'Avian influenza, "viral sovereignty", and the politics of health security in Indonesia'. *Pacific Review* 27(3): 333–56. doi.org/10.1080/09512748.2014.909523

Holliday, Ian. 2000. 'Productivist welfare capitalism: Social policy in East Asia'. *Political Studies* 48(4): 706–23. doi.org/10.1111/1467-9248.00279

IAKMI (Ikatan Ahli Kesehatan Masyarakat)-SEATCA (Southeast Asia Tobacco Control Alliance). 2020. *Fakta Tembakau Indonesia 2020* [Indonesian Tobacco Facts 2020]. Jakarta: IAKMI.

Kartika, Widya and Rahmanda Thaariq. 2019. 'Strengthen govt support to help smokers quit'. *Jakarta Post* 12 October.

KMUK (Koalisi Masyarakat Untuk Kesehatan). 1999. 'Usulan untuk amendemen UUD 45 dan GBHN hak terhadap pelayanan kesehatan' [Recommendation for amendments to the 1945 constitution and the Broad Outlines of State Policy on the right to health services]. Mimeo.

KUIS (Koalisi Untuk Indonesia Sehat). 2005. *Sehat Itu Hak: Panduan Advokasi Masalah Kesehatan Masyarakat* [Health Is a Right: Guidelines for Public Health Advocacy]. Jakarta and Yogyakarta: KUIS and INSIST.

Mietzner, Marcus. 2020. 'Populist anti-scientism, religious polarisation, and institutionalised corruption: How Indonesia's democratic decline shaped its COVID-19 response'. *Journal of Current Southeast Asian Affairs* 39(2): 227–49. doi.org/10.1177/1868103420935561

Moodie, Rob, Chris Borthwick, Seri Phongphit, Rhonda Galbally and Bridget H.-H. Hsu-Hage. 2000. 'Health promotion in South-East Asia: Indonesia, DPR Korea, Thailand, the Maldives and Myanmar'. *Health Promotion International* 15(3): 249–57. doi.org/10.1093/heapro/15.3.249

Nelson, Joan. 2004. 'The politics of health sector reform: Cross-national comparisons'. In *Crucial Needs, Weak Incentives: Social Sector Reform, Democratization and Globalization in Latin America*, edited by Robert Kaufman and Joan Nelson, 23–64. Washington, DC: Woodrow Wilson Center and Johns Hopkins University Press.

O'Connell, Paul. 2007. 'On reconciling irreconcilables: Neo-liberal globalisation and human rights'. *Human Rights Law Review* 7(3): 483–509. doi.org/10.1093/hrlr/ngm015

OHCHR (Office of the High Commissioner for Human Rights) and WHO (World Health Organization). 2008. 'The Right to Health'. Fact Sheet No. 31. www.ohchr.org/documents/publications/factsheet31.pdf

Pisani, Elizabeth, Maarten O. Kok and Kharisma Nugroho. 2017. 'Indonesia's road to universal health coverage: A political journey'. *Health Policy and Planning* 32(2): 267–76. doi.org/10.1093/heapol/czw120

Power, Thomas and Eve Warburton, eds. 2020. *Democracy in Indonesia: From Stagnation to Regression?* Singapore: ISEAS – Yusof Ishak Institute. doi.org/10.1355/9789814881524

Pratama, Wibi P. 2021. 'Jumlah peserta BPJS Kesehatan merosot 1,64 juta orang, kenapa ya?' [The number of BPJS Kesehatan participants has decreased by 1.64 million people. Why?]. *Bisnis Indonesia* 13 January. https://finansial.bisnis.com/read/20210113/215/1342316/jumlah-peserta-bpjs-kesehatan-merosot-164-juta-orang-kenapa-ya#:~:text=Moneter-,Jumlah%20Peserta%20BPJS%20Kesehatan%20Merosot%201%2C64%20Juta%20Orang%2C%20Kenapa,sebanyak%20222%2C46%20juta%20orang

Pribadi, Indra A. 2020. 'Industri dalam negeri siap produksi ribuan ventilator atasi COVID-19' [Domestic industry is ready to produce thousands of ventilators to fight COVID-19]. Antara, 15 April. www.antaranews.com/berita/1423281/industri-dalam-negeri-siap-produksi-ribuan-ventilator-atasi-covid-19

Pūras, Dainius. 2018. Report of the Special Rapporteur on the Right of Everyone to the Enjoyment of the Highest Possible Standard of Physical and Mental Health on His Mission to Indonesia. Document No. A/HRC/38/36/Add.1. Geneva: UN Human Rights Council.

Robison, Richard and Vedi R. Hadiz. 2004. *Reorganising Power in Indonesia: The Politics of Oligarchy in an Age of Markets.* London and New York: RoutledgeCurzon.

Rokx, Claudia, George Schieber, Pandu Harimurti, Ajay Tandon and Aparnaa Somanathan. 2009. *Health Financing in Indonesia: A Reform Road Map.* Washington, DC: World Bank. doi.org/10.1596/978-0-8213-8006-2

Rosser, Andrew. 2012. 'Realising free health care for the poor in Indonesia: The politics of illegal fees'. *Journal of Contemporary Asia* 42(2): 255–75. doi.org/10.1080/00472336.2012.668351

Rosser, Andrew. 2015. 'Contesting tobacco-control policy in Indonesia'. *Critical Asian Studies* 47(1): 69–93. doi.org/10.1080/14672715.2015.997083

Rosser, Andrew. 2017. *Litigating the Right to Health: Courts, Politics and Justice in Indonesia.* Honolulu: East West Center.

Saputri, Dessy. 2021. 'Moeldoko disuntik vaksin Nusantara oleh Terawan' [Moeldoko inoculated with Nusantara vaccine by Terawan]. *Republika* 30 July. www.republika.co.id/berita/qx1x3h328/moeldoko-disuntik-vaksin-nusantara-oleh-terawan

Septiono, Wahyu, Mirte A.G. Kuipers, Nawi Ng and Anton E. Kunst. 2019. 'Progress of smoke-free policy adoption at district level in Indonesia: A policy diffusion study'. *International Journal of Drug Policy* 71: 93–102. doi.org/10.1016/j.drugpo.2019.06.015

Suwandono, Agus, Qomariah, Suhardi and Ingerani. 2003. 'Case study—Indonesia'. In *Long-Term Care in Developing Countries: Ten Case Studies*, edited by Jenny Brodsky, Jack Habib and Miriam Hirschfeld, 119–70. Geneva: World Health Organization.

Tans, Ryan. 2011. 'Mafias, machines and mobilization: The sources of local power in three districts in North Sumatra, Indonesia'. MA thesis. National University of Singapore.

Tempo. 2010. 'Dua coret ayat dua' [Two delete paragraph two]. *Tempo* 28 March: 88–89.

UNCESCR (United Nations Committee on Economic, Social and Cultural Rights). 2000. General Comment No. 14: The Right to the Highest Attainable Standard of Health (Art. 12).

van Diermen, Maryke. 2017. 'Welfare in transition: The political economy of social protection reform in Indonesia'. PhD thesis. University of Adelaide.

Wanner, Thomas. 2015. 'The new "passive revolution" of the green economy and growth discourse: Maintaining the "sustainable development" of neoliberal capitalism'. *New Political Economy* 20(1): 21–41. doi.org/10.1080/13563467.2013.866081

WHO (World Health Organization). n.d. 'A human rights-based approach to health'. www.who.int/hhr/news/hrba_to_health2.pdf

WHO (World Health Organization). 2003. Fifty-Sixth World Health Assembly: Resolutions and Decisions, Annexes. Geneva: WHO. https://apps.who.int/iris/handle/10665/259836

WHO (World Health Organization). 2016. *International Health Regulations 2005*, 3rd edition. Geneva: WHO. www.who.int/health-topics/international-health-regulations#tab=tab_1

WHO (World Health Organization). 2018. Joint External Evaluation of the IHR Core Capacities of the Republic of Indonesia: Mission Report: 20–24 November 2017. Geneva: WHO.

WHO (World Health Organization). 2021. *Intra-action Review of Indonesia's Response to COVID-19: Summary Report for Partners*. Jakarta: WHO.

Widiadana, Rita. 2020. 'Indonesia fails in tobacco control measures'. *Jakarta Post* 13 May. www.thejakartapost.com/life/2020/05/12/indonesia-fails-in-tobacco-control-measures.html

Winters, Jeffrey A. 1996. *Power in Motion: Capital Mobility and the Indonesian State*. Ithaca, NY: Cornell University Press. doi.org/10.7591/9781501711541

Wong, Martin C.S., Junjie Huang, Sunny H. Wong and Jeremy Y.-C. Teoh. 2021. 'The potential effectiveness of the WHO International Health Regulations capacity requirements on control of the COVID-19 pandemic: A cross-sectional study of 114 countries'. *Journal of the Royal Society of Medicine* 114(3): 121–31. doi.org/10.1177/0141076821992453

World Bank. 2020. *Indonesia Public Expenditure Review: Spending for Better Results*. Washington, DC: World Bank.

4 The importance of the 2020 Population Census for health data

Terence H. Hull

It is a matter of great pride and frequent comment that Indonesia is the fourth most populous nation and the third most populous democracy in the world. This factoid, much beloved by journalists and schoolchildren, opens the door to bickering among other nations' politicians, but it lays out two vital issues: Indonesia as a nation and Indonesia as a democracy. Both point to the importance of reliable population estimates for the workings of health, education and electoral systems. Demography provides tools to measure population dynamics. The *demos* in both demography and democracy refers to people—the citizens of a nation. For Indonesia, the demographic story goes back to the early nineteenth century when Sir Thomas Stamford Raffles' short-lived British administration of Java included a census count. In the subsequent hundred years a restored Dutch administration, riding the trends of modernisation, industrialisation and enlightenment, adopted many innovations to improve the counts of the rapidly growing population, initially in Java but inexorably spreading through the archipelago.

In the historical effort to understand disease and death, doctors and governments used these census results to measure and analyse human experiences of health challenges. At the core of recording disease and death is the importance of understanding population size, characteristics and trends. Public health was growing as a discipline in European medical schools, and administrators were learning to use rates and ratios to evaluate the impact of their actions. Numerators were counts of the blows to the individuals suffering from infectious diseases, nutritional insults or violent attacks. But they gained rational explication when denominators turned them from simple reports into forms of logical analysis. More often than not these denominators were measures of the population including age and sex structure. In the face of pandemics and hunger, the government fostered ever more demographically informed health data throughout the late nineteenth and twentieth centuries.

In this chapter, the history of censuses and health statistics is followed through to the innovations of the reform-era political leaders of the twenty-first century. Two themes stand out. First, following five decades of progress in building statistical strengths in government, bureaucrats have recently backtracked in important ways. Whether in terms of budget cuts or regulatory barriers, data are less available to researchers than was the promise two decades ago. Second, the COVID-19 pandemic has shaken, and in some ways destroyed, the complex structure of data collections built up by Statistics Indonesia (Badan Pusat Statistik, BPS), the Health Department and the Ministry of Home Affairs. Health and population data systems were crippled by 'long COVID' between 2020 and 2022. Can they recover quickly? Even if there is a strong recovery of data collection quality, there remains the challenge of improving public access to public data.

Historical censuses

Widjojo Nitisastro's (1970) magisterial overview of Indonesia's population history describes the wide variety of ways governments have counted and characterised their populations over the centuries. In line with Enlightenment economics, the wealth of nations was measured in terms of land, labour and capital, with labour being counted as heads of households under the control of rulers. Dutch overlords relied on a select number of local leaders to report population sizes to facilitate extraction of workers, tribute and retainers.

The first ambitious comprehensive census of Java was carried out during the short administration of Raffles, who sent lieutenants across the island to enumerate the whole population for purposes of administration and tax. It was overwhelmingly a listing of men, as heads of families (*chácha*). Children were not central to the count. Given the high rates of infant mortality at the time, young children were often left out of official counts until they were old enough to play a part in the family economy. Uncounted children are a feature of censuses even today. Javanese officials also distinguished between insiders and aliens in their regions and largely ignored the aliens. Raffles (1817) was aware of the shortcomings of his census, but it was only in the mid-twentieth century that social science researchers came to an agreement that his methods of determining a population of under 5 million were likely to have overlooked an equal number. Java's true population in 1815 was most probably close to 10 million in contrast to his published figures of less than 5 million (Peper 1970).

Across the nineteenth century, the restored Dutch administration improved methods for assessing labour–power to mobilise workers for plantations, transport infrastructure and colonisation. Over time, increasing recognition of social welfare needs among the colonised peoples of the archipelago sharpened the methods of enumeration. The British imperial censuses of the 1880s took the innovations of household enumeration in the colonial centre and spread them through the peripheral units held under their dominion. The Dutch and other colonial powers followed suit. By 1900 standardisation of census methodologies included attempts to define households according to the interests of colonial administrations, including sex and age groups, work categories and marital status. The Netherlands Indies administration was also concerned with literacy, religion and ethnicity as it attempted to pull together the strands of multiculturalism to unify the putative nation. The counts became more elaborate and by 1930 most of the archipelago was included in a comprehensive enumeration, though without detailed age data due to the belief that the populace was ignorant of a common chronology of life. In other countries, governments tried to overcome such problems through the use of registers and guesstimates of age using physical characteristics or memories of historical events. Parallel with the census, health services attempted to improve household counts as part of their efforts to control infectious diseases, provide services to assist childbirth and improve the sanitation of communities.

Despite the weakness of age data in 1930, plans were made for better counts in 1940, but these were interrupted by the Japanese invasion in 1941 and a decade of war and revolution. Over the three-decade gap between the censuses of 1930 and 1961, Indonesia's attention to population numbers focused on two major collection procedures: the civil registration procedures run by local officials, and community health surveys carried out by the growing network of clinics administered by doctors or paramedics (*mantri kesehatan*). In both of these activities, the government attempted to monitor vital statistics—calculating birth and death rates by comparing reports of events experienced in the community with estimates of total populations. The reliability of these rates varied greatly across the country, but over time the administrators pressed families to contribute data as a matter of civic duty. Gradually these habits grew, though it would take decades to reach reasonable levels of reliability. The problem identified with a routine registration system is that it is only as strong as its weakest links, in contrast to the standardisation and concentration of census procedures focusing on counting the full population using well-trained and supervised teams of interviewers. Unfortunately, the colonial half of the twentieth century was unkind to the Netherlands Indies' census attempts.

Censuses of independent Indonesia

Indonesia entered the second half of the twentieth century freed from the colonial yoke but burdened by the task of rebuilding an economy and a government ravaged by years of privation. The Japanese occupation had changed the nature of local government organisation with a new set of expectations for village and hamlet management of population data. There were still large gaps between the central islands of Java and Bali and the mosaic of ethnic groups in the rest of the sprawling archipelago but, from the outset, the national government set high priority to unifying the administrative, educational, cultural and political institutions of the nation. This included the creation and management of a professional statistical institution in BPS (Statistics Indonesia). In common with most nations, Indonesia has held a census every decade (since 1961). In the first four counts—1961, 1971, 1980, 1990—every residence was visited for a full headcount, but only a sample of houses participated in the detailed questions related to education, marital status, occupation and fertility. In 2000 and 2010, the government decided to carry out a detailed questionnaire in every household to gain reliable data producing reliable estimates down to the village level. This innovation was in furtherance of the purposes of the year 2000 implementation of political and economic decentralisation that shifted the locus of decision-making from the central agencies to districts and democratising village governments.

Major innovations in the 2020 Population Census

On the instructions (Perpres No. 39/2019) of President Joko Widodo (Jokowi), the 2020 Sensus Penduduk (Population Census) was designed to produce a single unified estimate of population numbers, called 'Satu Data' (or One Data). This was meant to put an end to perennial tensions between BPS and the Ministry of Home Affairs over the question of what constitutes an 'official' estimate of population numbers. From 2020 on, it was declared, BPS and the ministry would collaborate in the collection and announcement of demographic data used for government administration and planning.

The plan was for BPS to carry out two distinct enumerations just over one year apart and to combine these with the continuous registration system administered by the ministry. The first BPS enumeration would be a multistaged, full count of every household in the nation between February and July 2020. The forms administered both online and in paper form would be 'short', but in fact the demands of government departments meant that they would include many detailed questions, including ethnicity, education, religion and migration. BPS would use the registration data from the population administration division of the ministry (the Administrasi Kependudukan, Adminduk) as a baseline for these online and household collections, in this way validating the data.

In mid-2021 BPS planned a second enumeration using a longer, more detailed form administered by highly trained interviewers visiting a small sample of households. This would be in line with many other nations where a full count is followed by a more detailed sample count, and was much like the Indonesian censuses before 2000, except that those did not have such a long time gap between the full and sample activities. Again, the planners spoke of comparing the BPS and the Adminduk data for purposes of verification and completion. Unfortunately, as I will discuss below, these plans collapsed in the face of the pandemic.

The two phases of BPS census data collection offered analytical bonuses in the form of checking and rechecking the reliability of data, calculating changes in sample households between their first information in 2020 and the planned second visit in 2021. It would be an understatement to say that the demographers at BPS were excited by the promises of their planned innovations. In particular, they looked forward to a greatly expanded use of digital questionnaires to be filled in directly by families with access to the internet.

The full count kicked off on 15 February 2020 with the launch of a digital data collection website. Citizens were issued with passwords and encouraged to open the questionnaire online and fill in information for every household member. The operation centre in the BPS central office tracked submissions in real time and produced maps and tables of key variables for evaluation. Some families shared the responsibility of recording information online among the members capable of the task, while in other households all information was entered by one 'head' of the family. The initial reports of this digital collection were promising. People who had difficulties with logging in could contact a helpline, and the returns were flowing smoothly through the end of February.

By then, though, dark clouds gathered as reports of a novel coronavirus originating in Wuhan, China, raised concerns that a global pandemic could strike Indonesia. The first infections were reported in Jakarta on 2 March 2020 and within a month the virus had spread throughout the archipelago. Jakarta declared a health emergency on 20 March. Even though the census forms could be filled in online without risking the danger of the direct spread of infection inherent in face-to-face interviewing, the census procedures were still severely disrupted as BPS staff were forced to work from home and respondents were swept up in the panic of waves of regulations, warnings and by the end of March hundreds of daily deaths. The reports of deaths and hospitalisations climbed into the thousands by May. Though the online census was originally planned to end on 31 March, it soon became clear time extensions would be needed. More than that, it was clear that the entire plan for the face-to-face collection of census data required an overhaul.

On 3 April 2020, Jokowi issued Perpres No. 54, completely overhauling the government budgets to respond to the growing resource demands of the pandemic. BPS learned that the budget for the census would be cut by 74 per cent. In terms of US dollars, the per capita cost of the enumeration dropped from $1.03 to $0.26. This was a stunning blow to the country's largest-ever demographic data collection. By this point, there was no turning back, just a turning down of the speed and intensity of the enumeration.

The digital collections stretched out to 29 May 2020. The field data activities originally planned for July were delayed to September and the entire concept of the operation was revised to respond to the dangers of the pandemic. As early as the first week of May 2020, Suharyanto, then head of BPS, was briefing parliamentarians that in-person training of the 390,000 field staff to be recruited for the census would need to be replaced by online designs. In addition, the questionnaires would be distributed by 1.2 million hamlet heads (*ketua rukun tetangga*) and the interviewers were limited to direct collection if no household member could complete and return the form.

The ambitions for an innovative direct population count in 2020 were transformed into a search for innovative ways to manage data collection under pandemic conditions. The online census pressed ahead, but field verification could no longer be as direct and socially nuanced as planned. Face masks, visors and rubber gloves were issued to staff dispatched to household visits. Despite the precautions, census workers were still caught up among the precipitous rise of case numbers sweeping across the country.

The hope for a sample collection in 2021 flickered and, eventually, BPS had to admit that this was a bridge too far. By the middle of 2021, it was announced that the sample enumeration would be delayed till 2022, or perhaps 2023. For the 2020 Population Census, what BPS had collected before the end of the year would be what it had for analysis and planning for the foreseeable future. There could be no more attempts to complete a full household enumeration. This was a bitter pill, but in a land of *jamu* (herbal medicines) people are used to bitter pills.

Population numbers

Over 2020, as the tidal wave of COVID-19 infections reached into the millions and deaths passed the hundreds of thousands, the Indonesian government was pressed to release timely data on population numbers. Journalists speculated that birth rates would plummet, and as international borders closed it was clear that migration flows would be strangled, so the demand for updated population estimates was palpable.

On 21 January 2021 BPS and Dukcapil[1] jointly released a series of preliminary census publications, the most important of which was deemed a 'portrait' of the 2020 census (BPS 2021a). This included a preliminary report of a total census population of 270.2 million broken down by five-year age groups based on links to the population administration registration data. As the first example of Satu Data, this exercise was confusing since it did not follow the decades-long methodology of BPS. Usually, BPS would give a census quick-count with responses recorded from the house-to-house collection. The preliminary population numbers in this announcement were neither fully census nor exclusively registration counts and thus did not allow comparisons of the distinct methodologies to validate the data.

Instead, the presentation was heavier on explaining the problems of the pandemic enumeration than the explanation of contrasting results drawn from the online count, the face-to-face count, the forms filled in by respondents and submitted via hamlet heads, and the reports based on the administrative holdings of family and individual ID cards. Instead, irrespective of the way the information was collected, the tables were simple compilations. The first two tables gave the populations of each province by sex and the provincial numbers showed residence either matching or differing from the Kartu Keluarga (Family Card), which forms the base of the civil registration system. Nearly 10 per cent of individuals lived away from the address of their family card registration place.

Over the next six months, BPS worked on the editing and tabulation of the full census results to reach a final count. Two major changes were made to the age structure. First, the ages reported on the census form were used to correct the ages from the registration system used in the preliminary results. Second, the more than 2 million 'missing' and 'don't

---

1 Direktorat Jendral Kependudukan dan Catatan Sipil—the Population and Civil Registry, Ministry of Home Affairs.

know' age responses were imputed into the full age distribution to ensure that individuals' records had information on age and sex. Remarkably these so-called 'final' census numbers did not vary much from January's preliminary total even though the numbers in each age group changed substantially. According to the Satu Data approach, the population of Indonesia in September 2020 was 270,203,917 (Table 4.1a). By mid-2021 the published adjusted estimates gave a total population of 270,273,152, an increase of slightly under 70,000 people (Table 4.1b). This was a minor adjustment at best and showed no application of the factors coming out of post-enumeration surveys used in most countries to adjust the counts of an enumeration.

Over the decade between the censuses of 2010 and 2020, Indonesia's population growth rate averaged 1.25 per cent per year. At that rate, the population would double in 55 years. The fact that it was a declining rate of growth compared to the years before 2010 meant there was no expectation that Indonesia would ever reach the half-billion level implied in that concept of doubling. Nonetheless, growth was still high and worthy of policy concern.

Beyond the issue of growth, the 2020 census age distribution contained some puzzling characteristics. Figure 4.1 is a standard population pyramid, with the light-coloured outline of 2020 overlaying the darker bars of the 2010 census. Even with the BPS adjustments, it is intriguing that the population numbers from birth to age 15 in 2020 were smaller in absolute terms than those a decade earlier. Above age 15 the pyramid bars for 2020 were larger than those for 2010 in every age group, and for both males and females. These are symbolically typical of an ageing population, and may reflect net inmigration at some point. Being a comparison of two cross-sectional counts, it is premature to talk of immigration or even of changing death rates to explain the puffing out of the pyramid, but it is important to consider the reliability of the two census experiences.

The stories embedded in the pyramid point to some real conundrums for the government efforts to develop policies based on the census. Eyeballing the differences of successive cohorts sparks questions about what we can make of recent trends in fertility and mortality. Luckily there are some methods available to address these questions.

Total fertility estimates

The engine room of demographic growth in most countries is fertility. In nations with well-functioning civil registration systems, the measurement of the levels and trends of fertility are published regularly with analysis by geographic regions and social characteristics. For many low- and middle-income countries, including Indonesia, the registration data are of insufficient coverage to be reliable, and other approaches to calculate fertility rates must be developed. Demographers have developed an array of methods to estimate fertility rates from census or survey data on the age and sex structure of the population, essentially comparing the numbers of recent births (children aged 0 to 4) and the current age of women of child-bearing age (15 to 49 years old). The population census of 2010 produced a total fertility estimate of 2.4. The data for 2020 in Table 4.1a are sufficient for a comparable calculation.

Imagine the surprise when analysts applied the technique to the preliminary results issued on 21 January 2021. The small cohort of 15 million children aged 0–4 produced an estimated total fertility rate (TFR) of 1.4 births per woman, a huge decline compared with the demographic and

Table 4.1a 2020 census age structure, preliminary release 2021

Age group	Preliminary 2020 census release, issued 21 January 2021			
	Male	Female	Sex ratio	Total
0–4	7,996,762	7,456,932	107	15,453,694
5–9	12,054,557	11,293,112	107	23,347,669
10–14	12,248,242	11,501,707	106	23,749,949
15–19	11,890,104	11,232,889	106	23,122,993
20–24	11,799,983	11,151,534	106	22,951,517
25–29	10,983,136	10,594,469	104	21,577,605
30–34	10,678,855	10,444,990	102	21,123,845
35–39	11,127,884	11,030,421	101	22,158,305
40–44	10,363,207	10,340,154	100	20,703,361
45–49	9,259,566	9,271,800	100	18,531,366
50–54	8,066,156	8,083,777	100	16,149,933
55–59	6,445,652	6,617,735	97	13,063,387
60–64	5,104,332	5,169,843	99	10,274,175
65–69	3,445,786	3,340,480	103	6,786,266
70–74	1,943,260	2,205,321	88	4,148,581
75+	2,221,406	2,805,338	79	5,026,744
Total numbers	135,628,888	132,540,502	102	268,169,390
Don't know	1,033,011	1,001,516	103	2,034,527
Total population	136,661,899	133,542,018	102	270,203,917

Source: BPS (2021a, 2021b).

Chapter 4 The importance of the 2020 Population Census for health data   65

health surveys' string of TFR estimates of 2.6 over more than a decade and 2.4 from the 2010 census. This calculation put Indonesian fertility below every other Southeast Asian nation, bar Singapore, and level pegged with Thailand. Looking at the Population Reference Bureau's 2021 Data Sheet, China's and Japan's TFRs of 1.3 made the 1.4 figure for Indonesia look plausible, but the well-known histories of those two East Asian fertility transitions cast a shadow on the Indonesian number. Neither China nor Japan had a fertility drop of one full child in such a short time. The idea of such a large fertility decline between 2010 and 2020 was all the more unlikely when it was observed that the 2015 estimates were well over 2.0.

Before too long the BPS demographers made adjustments to the age distributions, overturning the early estimate to produce the columns titled Final 2020 census release in Table 4.1b. The calculation of TFR of 1.4 was

Table 4.1b   2020 census age structure, final release 2021

Age group	Final 2020 census release, developed through July 2021			
	Male	Female	Sex ratio	Total
0–4	11,293,711	10,778,786	105	22,072,497
5–9	11,295,307	10,799,048	105	22,094,355
10–14	11,449,769	10,746,111	107	22,195,880
15–19	11,495,696	10,816,894	106	22,312,590
20–24	11,632,238	11,050,132	105	22,682,370
25–29	11,410,784	10,945,191	104	22,355,975
30–34	11,109,053	10,795,496	103	21,904,549
35–39	10,556,654	10,354,273	102	20,910,927
40–44	10,014,632	9,928,479	101	19,943,111
45–49	9,025,557	8,996,940	100	18,022,497
50–54	7,872,400	7,873,992	100	15,746,392
55–59	6,546,325	6,574,527	100	13,120,852
60–64	5,091,717	5,117,776	99	10,209,493
65–69	3,681,457	3,772,554	98	7,454,011
70–74	2,179,067	2,374,851	92	4,553,918
75+	2,007,532	2,686,203	75	4,693,735
Total numbers	136,661,899	133,611,253	102	270,273,152
Don't know	–	–	–	–
Total population	136,661,899	133,611,253	102	270,273,152

Source: BPS (2021a, 2021b).

Figure 4.1 Population pyramid (millions)

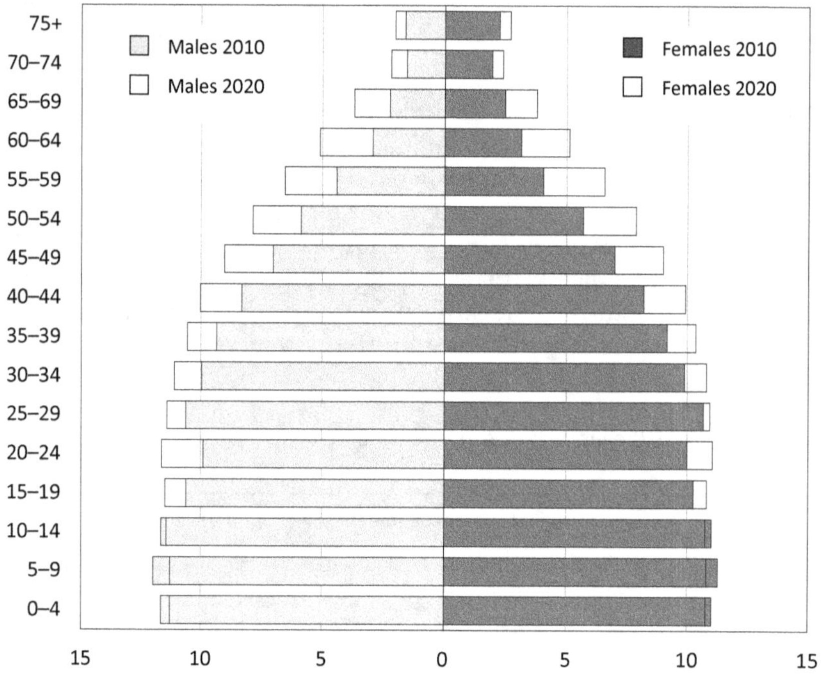

[Population pyramid showing Males 2010, Males 2020, Females 2010, Females 2020 across age groups from 0–4 to 75+]

Source: BPS (2013, 2021a, 2021b).

displaced by the more believable rate of 2.1. This implied that in the years before the enumeration the pace of child-bearing declined slowly to the notional replacement level where couples child-bearing would, over a long term, tend to a stationary population. At the national level replacement fertility made sense and, in comparison with the rest of Asia, it was to be expected. Across the huge archipelago, the history of the national family planning program demanded a more fine-grained discussion of fertility. For this, an examination of the 2015 assumptions of provincial fertility levels used by government planners for their official projections can be stood against the final 2020 census estimates, in Table 4.2.

Projection assumptions are obviously not definitive measures of fertility since they are subject to many political pressures and speculations about an unknowable future, but the numbers chosen by Bappenas (the National Development Planning Agency) in 2013 for the foundation of its calculations were widely regarded as reasonable. They are for the period 2010–2015, or on average 2012. Since the 2020 census estimates use data

Table 4.2 Provincial total fertility rates (TFRs) from the 2013 official population projection assumptions compared to the 2020 census indirect estimates of fertility

Province	2013 TFR assumption 2012	2020 TFR estimate 2017	Decline or increase (%)
Indonesia	2.44	2.12	13.1
Aceh	2.79	2.38	14.6
North Sumatra	3.01	2.43	19.3
West Sumatra	2.94	2.19	25.4
Riau	2.86	2.43	15.2
Jambi	2.41	2.25	6.8
South Sumatra	2.53	2.39	5.7
Bengkulu	2.40	2.24	6.5
Lampung	2.60	2.25	13.3
Bangka Belitung Islands	2.43	2.10	13.7
Riau Islands	2.31	2.25	2.7
DKI Jakarta	1.88	1.91	−1.7
West Java	2.42	2.07	14.4
Central Java	2.26	1.96	13.3
DI Yogyakarta	1.90	1.83	3.9
East Java	2.01	1.84	8.6
Banten	2.47	2.19	11.3
Bali	2.08	1.83	12.1
West Nusa Tenggara	2.65	2.42	8.6
East Nusa Tenggara	3.61	2.77	23.3
West Kalimantan	2.66	2.24	15.8
Central Kalimantan	2.58	2.08	19.5
South Kalimantan	2.67	2.35	11.9
East Kalimantan	2.64	2.13	19.3
North Kalimantan		2.13	
North Sulawesi	2.39	2.08	13.1
Central Sulawesi	2.78	2.42	12.9
South Sulawesi	2.54	2.05	19.3
South East Sulawesi	3.14	2.49	20.8
Gorontalo	2.48	2.09	15.7
West Sulawesi	3.03	2.53	16.4
Maluku	3.34	2.17	34.9
North Maluku	3.14	2.39	23.8
West Papua	2.90	2.20	24.3
Papua	2.66	2.46	7.5

Source: BPS (2013, 2021a, 2021b).

for the five years before the census date to calculate the TFRs, they have an average reference year of 2017 or about five years after the baseline of the projections.

The differences between 2012 and 2017 are instructive. In the earlier period, six provinces had TFR values in excess of three children per woman and only two provinces had TFRs below two children (shading in Table 4.2). In 2017, according to the 2020 census, only two provinces were above 2.5 TFR, and five provinces appear to have TFRs below two children per woman. This result confirms the success of the national family planning program in meeting fertility reduction targets set decades ago, but you would search in vain for any celebration of this event. Instead, politicians decried population ageing. Demographers have long pointed to ageing as a welcome sign of demographic transition away from rapid population growth. Preventing unwanted births and delaying inevitable deaths are the cardinal goals of any competent health system. Indonesia seems to be on the right track by bringing fertility below the putative replacement level.

Survivorship

The age structures of successive censuses shown in Table 4.1 allow us to follow age cohorts over the decade to calculate the proportions of a group who survive, or die, in the time period. Table 4.3 compares numbers in cohorts from 2010 who survived to become the cohort ten years older in 2020. For the cohort aged 0–4, 98 per cent of both males and females accomplished this feat.

Oddly, over 100 per cent of the age cohorts 10–14, 15–19, 20–24 and 30–34 were reported to have survived to ten years later. While it is clear that population figures are not simply a matter of births and deaths, and most countries have small but meaningful numbers of net migrants adding or subtracting from the cohorts, Indonesia is so large that we would not expect international migration to be a major influence, especially among teenagers and young adults in 2010. If anything, we would expect them to follow work opportunities overseas. Instead, the numbers increase slightly and it is unlikely there were people in these age groups coming into the country in large numbers prior to 2020. One speculation is that many in the cohort were missed in the 2010 census, but what explains the situation in the pandemically crippled 2020 enumeration? Most demographers are more sceptical about the pandemic census than the count a decade earlier.

Table 4.3 Ratio of age cohort surviving for 10 years from the 2010 census to the 2020 census

Age group in 2010 = x	(x + 10)/(x)		
	Male	Female	Total
0–4	0.98	0.98	0.98
5–9	0.96	0.96	0.96
10–14	1.00	1.00	1.00
15–19	1.08	1.07	1.07
20–24	1.12	1.08	1.10
25–29	0.99	0.97	0.98
30–34	1.01	1.00	1.01
35–39	0.97	0.98	0.97
40–44	0.95	0.96	0.95
45–49	0.93	0.94	0.93
50–54	0.87	0.90	0.88
55–59	0.84	0.93	0.88
60–64	0.74	0.76	0.75

Source: Calculated by the author from census data (BPS 2013, 2021a, 2021b).

Conclusions

COVID-19 disrupted the 2020 Population Census in ways that will be difficult if not impossible to overcome. Striking precisely at the start of the innovative digital online collection of information, and rapidly spreading through times of quarantine and isolation, it was inevitable that the traditional house-to-house visits by trained interviewers would be constrained. It was not recognised at the time that the census operations would be thrown back to the Raffles era when censuses depended on reports from village heads and registers of families, as interviewers were prevented from field visits by isolation rules. As in the Raffles census, this undoubtedly led to underenumerations, misenumerations and delays. It also meant that the vital check on data reliability, the Post Enumeration Survey (PES), would also be inhibited. To date, no reports are available on the PES, and it is not clear if any insights from the PES have guided the adjustments made to the preliminary census data that appeared in January 2021.

Can we believe the preliminary count announced in January 2021 as the One Data innovation melding the BPS census and the Home Affairs Adminduk registration returns? I cannot. Until the PES is published and the anonymised micro (individual) records released for independent analysis, it will not be possible to validate the returns. Similarly, the national registration numbers are not routinely published, so it is impossible to validate those returns. In the meantime, the fertility and survivorship data discussed above are warnings to all discussions of Indonesian population trends. Fertility does seem to be declining, mortality does seem to be falling, and for the time being the Indonesian diaspora seems to be shrinking as expatriates seek to return to the comfort of family and home during the pandemic. The fact that over 270 million Indonesians were counted in the 2020 Population Census stands as a remarkable triumph over adversity by BPS and Home Affairs staff. If the true population was actually 280, or even 285 million, the difference will not bother most policymakers. It is something researchers should set as a priority question for the next four years when hopefully the pandemic is brought under control and an intercensal enumeration can produce a corrective assessment of population, fertility and mortality. Until then, people interested in population numbers will need to lobby BPS, the Ministry of Home Affairs and the Ministry of Health for more accessible and transparent data.

References

BPS (Badan Pusat Statistik, Statistics Indonesia). 2013. *Proyeksi Penduduk Indonesia* [Indonesia Population Projection]. Jakarta: Bappenas, BPS and United Nations Population Fund.

BPS (Badan Pusat Statistik, Statistics Indonesia). 2021a. *Potret Sensus Penduduk 2020: Menuju Satu Data Kependudukan Indonesia* [Portrait of the 2020 Population Census: Towards One Indonesia Population Data]. Jakarta: BPS. https://www.bps.go.id/publication/2021/01/21/213995c881428fef20a18226/potret-sensus-penduduk-2020-menuju-satu-data-kependudukan-indonesia.html

BPS (Badan Pusat Statistik, Statistics Indonesia). 2021b. 'Hasil sensus penduduk 2020' [Population census results 2020]. Jakarta: BPS. PowerPoint presentation from the 21 January 2021 launch of the census results.

Nitisastro, Widjojo. 1970. *Population Trends in Indonesia*. Ithaca, NY: Cornell University Press. Reprinted by PT Equinox Publishing Indonesia, 2006.

Peper, Bram. 1970. 'Population growth in Java in the 19th century'. *Population Studies* 24(1): 71–84. doi.org/10.1080/00324728.1970.10406113

Population Reference Bureau. 2021. World Population Data Sheet. Washington, DC: PRB. https://www.prb.org/news/2021-world-population-data-sheet-released/

Raffles, T. 1817. *The History of Java*. London: Black, Parbury, and Allen, Booksellers to the Hon. East India Company. Reprinted by Oxford University Press, Oxford in Asia Historical Reprints, 1978.

5 Addressing regional disparities in access to medical specialists in Indonesia

Andreasta Meliala and Srimurni Rarasati

The unequal distribution of health care workers between urban and rural areas—and across subnational regions—has been a persistent policy challenge in many low- to middle-income countries, including Indonesia. Previous studies in other country settings have suggested that although the types of diseases and severity of illness experienced by rural residents are becoming increasingly similar to those found in urban populations, the access to and patterns of use of medical specialist services are very different. That is, amid increasing prevalence of non-communicable diseases and chronic illness, a significant share of the rural and regional population in the Global South continues to have limited access to medical specialist care (DeBenedectis et al. 2022; Duke et al. 2021; Lorch et al. 2021; Nguyen-Pham et al. 2014). Studies have shown that patients with chronic diseases such as diabetes, congestive heart failure, cancers and obstructive pulmonary disease who live in rural areas with fewer doctors per capita have fewer consultations and diagnostic tests (Corallo et al. 2014). Further, the lack of access to medical specialist services has a compounding impact on the quality of care for rural patients. For example, prehospital time for rural patients is prolonged compared to that for urban patients (Ashburn et al. 2022). Patients who live in regions with fewer beds will experience fewer hospitalisations and a lower likelihood of being treated in intensive care units (Wennberg 2002).

This chapter addresses the issue of regional disparities in access to and use of medical specialist services in Indonesia. While the unequal distribution of specialist physicians has been a longstanding problem in Indonesia, we argue that the required policy response to address this issue has become more complex because of decentralisation. In the context of increasing complexity in the planning and management of human resources for health following decentralisation, we present our assessment of the two broad strategies that have so far been employed by the government: the attempts to produce more doctors, and strategies to invite the private sector and foreign investment to meet the demand for private hospitals with specialist doctors.

Regional disparities in health care facilities and access to medical specialist services

Indonesia is the world's fourth most populous country with 270 million people; a little over half the population (56.7%) lives in urban areas (BPS 2021). With a geographical expanse spanning six major islands—Java, Bali, Sumatra, Kalimantan, Sulawesi and Papua—and more than 17,000 small islands, Indonesia has faced a rural–urban disparity in health services for years. To date, the dynamic of health care services has followed market rules, in which highly populated areas have had favourable access to a wide range of clinical services, while less-populated areas have had reduced access to health services. With respect to medical specialist services in particular, which are usually attached to a high level of hospital care, the disparity is greater (Meliala et al. 2013).

Following the fall of the New Order government in 1998, Indonesia shifted to a decentralised system to govern what is now a national territory with 34 provinces, 514 districts and more than 7,000 subdistricts. Nationally, the Ministry of Health performs the role of policy formulation and guidance about health matters to provincial and district-level governments. Services for districts and municipalities are coordinated by the provincial governments.

The health system in Indonesia has both public and private components. The Ministry of Health leads the central government's arm, providing strategic direction and standards setting, regulating the health sector, creating policy for human resources management, and regulating hospitals. Provincial governments provide technical oversight of provincial hospitals and district health services, and also manage cross-district health issues. The system applies to both public and private sectors.

The health care system in Indonesia uses a referral system that starts from primary care, moving up through levels to tertiary care (Figure 5.1). The primary health care level plays a gatekeeper role and will admit patients when they need to be treated at a higher level of service. At the

Figure 5.1 The decentralised health service in Indonesia

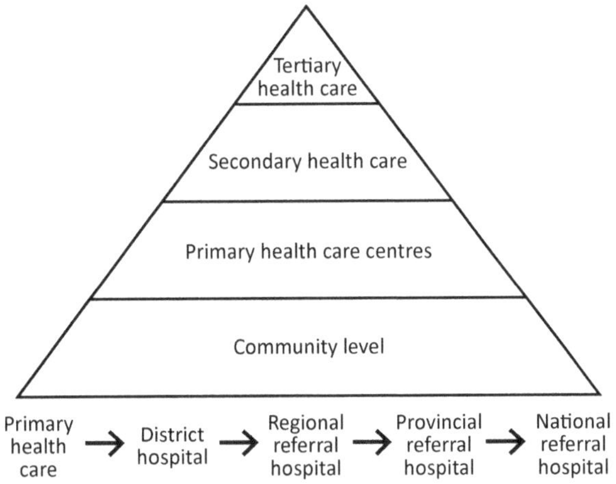

```
                    Tertiary
                   health care

                Secondary health care

              Primary health care centres

                  Community level
```

Primary health care → District hospital → Regional referral hospital → Provincial referral hospital → National referral hospital

Source: MoH (2020a).

community level are health posts run by health cadres and supervised by doctors within the primary health care system. District and municipal governments are responsible for managing both local hospitals and the primary health centres called *puskesmas*. *Puskesmas* are important in the context of universal health coverage, acting as the first point of call for public health efforts through their focus on prevention and health promotion at the primary level.

In 2014 the Indonesian government implemented a national health insurance scheme, Jaminan Kesehatan Nasional (JKN), towards achieving universal health coverage. To support the national scheme, the government established BPJS-K (Badan Penyelenggara Jaminan Sosial Kesehatan, Healthcare and Social Security Agency) to administer the payments system. The government encourages the even distribution of health care services nationwide, and for all citizens to join the JKN.

However, the growth of medical services has not kept pace with population growth or demographic changes. One of the intentions for the JKN is to increase access to health care services for rural citizens. The universal health coverage plan in the 2019 National Mid-Term Development Plan (Rencana Pembangunan Jangka Menengah Nasional) aimed to bring the whole population under coverage by the end of that year. However, there have been challenges for both participants and service providers in adapting to the new system. Obstacles have included a lack of health care providers. Most health care facilities are located on

Java Island and in the main cities of the other big islands (Figure 5.2), and the number of health care facilities remains low in rural areas (Bappenas 2019a). Uneven distribution of health care facilities across Indonesia creates more challenges to the implementation of the JKN, which constitutes the world's largest public health insurance program.

Figure 5.2 Number of private and public hospitals by province, 2020

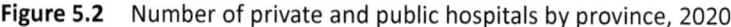

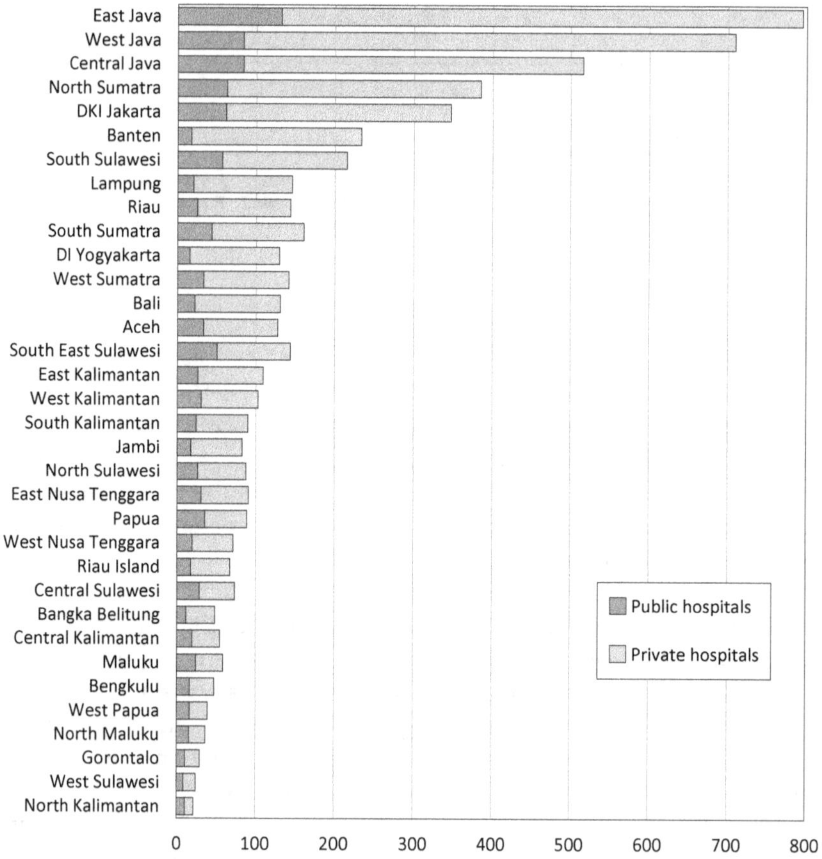

Source: Hospital Information System (SIRS), https://sirs.kemkes.go.id/fo/#

Availability of medical specialists

As human resources are critical to the provision of health care services, there has been growth in the number of medical graduates in efforts to meet the growing demand for, and to fill the gap in regional disparities of, access to medical specialists. Currently, Indonesia has hundreds of health professional schools and produces thousands of health professionals each year. In 2019, for example, 25,636 general practitioners graduated and in 2020 there were 18,928 graduates (MoH 2020c, 2021a). However, a Ministry of Health presentation about health services transformation in 2021 stated that 513 (about 5%) of the 10,326 *puskesmas* across Indonesia were reported to have no medical doctor (MoH 2021c).

The problem extends to the unequal distribution of medical specialists across the archipelago. The government defines seven basic medical specialists that should be available in hospitals: interns, general surgeons, paediatric specialists, obstetricians-gynaecologists, anaesthesiologists, radiologists and clinical pathologists (Ministry of Health Regulation No. 30/2019 on Hospital Classification and Licensing). But some provinces still lack these medical specialist services. Even though a hospital is available in a particular area, it does not mean it has medical specialists. Current regulations specify four different types of hospital in Indonesia. Type A hospitals, as top referral hospitals, offer many subspecialty services. Teaching hospitals owned by the Ministry of Health are also in this category. Type B hospitals provide some subspecialist and many specialist services. As a referral point from a district hospital, type B hospitals are located in each provincial capital. Type C hospitals offer limited specialist services that include at least four services: internal medicine, surgery, paediatric medicine and obstetric services. Type D hospitals provide general medicine and dental health services and are intended to be developed into type C hospitals. Type C and type D hospitals receive referrals from public health centres or *puskesmas* (Mahendradhata et al. 2017).

However, data from a 2019 Bappenas report suggest that only 54.2% of type C hospitals have a complete configuration of medical specialists. The situation is even worse for medical subspecialists—neurosurgeons, oncologists and neonatologists—who are available only in the major city of the main provinces, especially in Java (Bappenas 2019b). This phenomenon is related to the limited production of medical specialists and subspecialists. In Indonesia, medical specialists and subspecialists are trained only by government medical schools and the capacity of production is inadequate to fulfil the growing demand for their services.

The stakeholders: Decentralisation and provision of human resources for health

Since decentralisation, the planning and management of human resources for health (HRH) has become the responsibility of regional governments. The central government still has the authority to deploy health workers, including medical specialists, to the area where they are most needed under a special assignment policy. HRH challenges become more complex in settings involving multi-tiered networks of actors. We list the institutions and actors regulating the planning and management of HRH—and medical specialists in particular—in Indonesia in Table 5.1.

Table 5.1 Institutions and human resources for health planning in Indonesia

Stakeholders	Role and responsibility in HRH planning
General Directorate of Health Workforce, Ministry of Health	Main task is to formulate policies that will ensure production of health workers (including medical specialists) according to the required number, equitable distribution and performance quality improvement. Its duties are planning, utilisation, distribution and assessment of HRH.
Ministry of Administrative and Bureaucratic Reform	Responsible for planning, recruitment and placement of medical specialists as civil servants.
Ministry of Internal Affairs	Guides medical specialists as civil servants.
Ministry of Finance	Responsible for medical specialists' salaries.
Ministry of Education, Culture, Research and Technology	Responsible for production of medical specialists via universities that offer medical specialist education. Universities are responsible for medical residents recruitment. Teaching hospital—place for training during medical specialist education.
National Civil Service Agency	Registers all medical specialists who work as civil servants.
Professional Associations	
Indonesian Medical Association	Is the only professional medical association in Indonesia.
Medical Specialist Association	Is part of the Professional Service Development Council, which consists of Indonesian Medical Association members who have the same profession in certain medical specialties. It has duties to ensure the quality, safety and effectiveness of services provided by its members to the community.

Medical specialist colleges	There were 38 medical specialist and subspecialist colleges in Indonesia in 2016. Colleges have the task of maintaining the quality of medical professional education, including managing the education of medical specialists and subspecialists. Colleges have the following duties: • prepare and develop National Medical Education Standards which will then be ratified by the Indonesian Medical Council (KKI) • implement national competency exam • issue national professional competency certificates (certification) • issue additional qualification certificates • facilitate the accreditation of medical professional education by the Indonesian Accreditation Agency for Higher Education (LAMPTKES), prepared by the Medical Specialist Education Institute (IPDS) • foster and monitor the implementation of education in educational institutions • prepare competency standards and education standards, which will then be approved by KKI • recommend and evaluate the opening of new educational institutions • assess the feasibility of the new study program (based on KKI Regulation No. 15/2013).
Indonesian Medical Council (Konsil Kedokteran Indonesia, KKI)	Medical specialists need to register with the council as a licensing requirement. The council performs professional regulation as its function of regulating, ratifying, determining and fostering doctors who carry out medical practice, in order to improve the quality of medical services. Medical Practice Law No. 29/2004 states that the Indonesian Medical Council has three tasks: (1) to register doctors and dentists (including medical specialists), (2) to establish medical education standards for health professionals and (3) to supervise and improve the quality of medical practice. For the education function stated in point (2), the council determines the standard of medical education and delegates the management of professional education to a medical college.
Local government	Prepares local regulations together with the Regional Employment Agency, which recruits medical specialists for government hospitals.
Provincial health office	Issues practice licences for medical specialists.
District health office	Provides recommendations and regulations for the practice licences of medical specialists.
Local public hospital	Medical specialists' workplace.

From the list of stakeholders involved, the complexity of policy and management of medical specialists is evident.

Addressing the medical specialist supply gap

The national government has two broad strategies to reduce the gap between rural and urban health care facilities. The first strategy is to produce more health workers and deploy them to rural areas. The second strategy is to bring in the private sector—through both domestic and foreign investment—to build and develop health care facilities. We discuss these two broad strategies below.

The production of medical specialists

In 2016, there were only 17 centres with authorisation to educate medical specialists out of 91 medical schools in Indonesia (KKI 2017). All 17 institutions are public medical schools. The capacity of each centre varies. The other restriction to educating medical specialists is the ratio of lecturers to medical specialist trainees (also known as residents) and the availability of type A teaching hospitals. In Indonesia, none of the private hospitals belong to the type A hospital group.

The health care system and medical education are two separate systems. The two systems are one of the factors that determine the number and distribution of specialist doctors in Indonesia. Medical specialist education in Indonesia that adheres to the university-based system is one example of the non-integration of the two systems. Admission of residents is carried out by the Faculty of Medicine, not based on the needs of the health care system.

The number of medical specialist university graduates in 2020 was 2,625 people spread across 12 provinces. Most medical specialist graduates were surgeons (387 graduates), followed by interns (354). The smallest category of medical specialist who graduated in 2020 was 62 medical rehabilitation specialists and anatomical pathologists.[1]

The Indonesia Health Profile 2020 (MoH 2021b) reported that there are 38,400 medical specialists nationwide. The highest number of medical specialists was found in the capital, DKI Jakarta (7,175 specialists), followed by West Java (6,310). Meanwhile, the provinces with the least number of medical specialists were West Sulawesi (118) and North Maluku (124). There were 265 medical specialists who practised in rural and remote areas in 2020. That figure is only about 0.7% of all HRH.

---

1 Data from Hospital Information System (SIRS), https://sirs.kemkes.go.id/fo/#

Table 5.2 The numbers and ratios of registered health workers per 1,000 population in 2018 and the targeted ratio by 2025

Category of health worker	Number of registered health workers	Health worker ratio per 1,000 population	
		2018	2025 target
Medical specialist	38,782	0.15	0.12
Medical doctor	134,459	0.52	0.50
Dentist	29,194	0.11	0.14
Nurse	639,356	2.46	2.00
Midwife	590,920	2.27	1.30
Public health officer	54,138	0.21	0.18
Nutritionist	41,021	0.16	0.18
Environmental health officer	2,826	0.01	0.20
Total	1,530,696	5.89	

Source: MoH (2020a, 2021b).

Despite the many stakeholders that oversee HRH (Table 5.1), the data on HRH varies considerably. For example, the differences in numbers of medical specialists can be seen in the Indonesia Health Profile 2020 and HRH Country Profile reports, summarised in Table 5.2.

As of 2018, the ratio of medical specialists per 1,000 population was 0.15. This ratio is low compared to other categories of health workers. In 2020, the ratio of medical specialists per 1,000 population was 0.14 (Figure 5.3). Population growth has been faster than the growth of specialist doctors. Looking at each province, we can see that the distribution gap between the provinces with the most and the fewest medical specialists is striking.

The growth of private hospitals

The availability of private hospitals is another reason medical specialists are reluctant to work in rural areas. Medical Practice Law No. 29/2004 states that medical professionals in Indonesia may practise in three places: in government-owned health care facilities, in the private sector or in individual private practice.

In a 2008 study, 15 specialist doctors identified their practice locations in non-government hospitals and private clinics, in addition to government hospitals. Three is the maximum number of sites for which doctors' licences are granted, but 11 of the specialists visited more than 3 sites. The non-compliance was known but overlooked due to the shortage of

Figure 5.3 Medical specialists ratio per 1,000 population, 2020

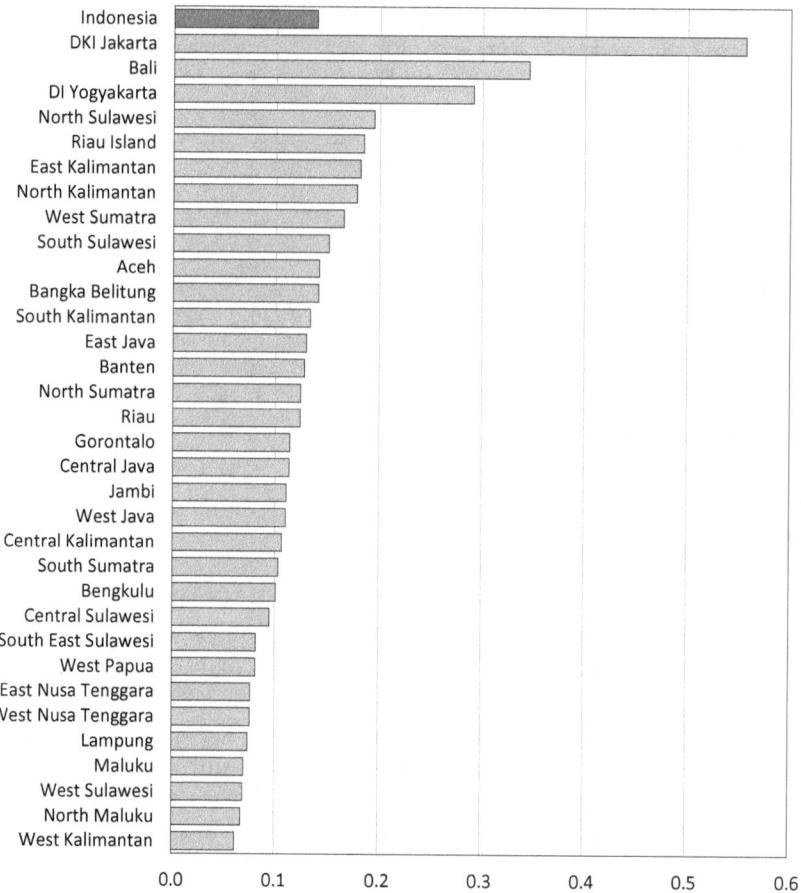

Source: Data processed from the Development and Empowerment of Human Resources for Health Agency and Statistics Indonesia, 2020.

medical specialists (Meliala et al. 2013). Now, in big cities, the policy trend is mono-loyalty, whereby medical specialists focus on one hospital.

Moonlighting has been a practice for years, known since the Dutch colonial era. Dual practice provides more opportunities for doctors to earn more income. According to research by Anderson et al. (2014) and WHO (2020), the number of medical specialists is proportional to the number of private hospitals. This means the preference of medical specialists to work in a particular location is related to the availability of private hospitals. In reality, the difference between public and private hospitals in Indonesia is not clear. The majority of health care professionals are civil servants but are also registered to conduct private professional practice. In terms of entity, some public facilities have been used to deliver private services. Therefore, it is difficult to clearly define private medical specialists and public medical specialists. All type A and B hospitals already have internal medical specialists, but there are still some type C and D hospitals that do not (Table 5.3). Overall, the availability of internal medical specialists is higher in private hospitals.

Table 5.3 The share of public and private hospitals with internal medical specialists, by category

Hospital ownership	Hospital type (%)				
	Type A	Type B	Type C	Type D	Total
Public	100	100	95.3	66.0	89.5
Private	100	100	97.5	90.5	94.9

Source: Risnakes, 2017.

Data from the Hospital Information System (Sistem Informasi Rumah Sakit, SIRS) in 2019 indicated the number of private hospitals in Indonesia is increasing faster (7% annual growth rate) than public hospitals (around 3% growth per year) (Figure 5.4). Private hospitals now make up 63% of hospitals that support BPJS-K services. The introduction of BPJS-K has enabled the number of private hospitals to grow steadily, as they cater to a larger volume of patients who are now able to access health care services.

Domestic investment for hospital services has been more progressive in the past ten years. Public hospitals are outnumbered by private ones — more than 60% of hospitals in Indonesia belong to the private sector (Bappenas 2019a). For-profit companies are now starting to develop their hospital businesses in other major cities, for example Jayapura (Papua), Ambon (Maluku) and in several cities in Sulawesi. This activity is related to the implementation of the JKN system in Indonesia in 2014. Before then, the growth of private hospitals was driven by market mechanisms. Since 2014, it has been driven by the JKN, which enables hospitals to be accessible for the people who join the national health insurance scheme. As of March 2022, more than 230 million people had joined the JKN (DJSN 2022).

The Indonesian health care market has investment promise. Indonesia's total health expenditure in 2018 was around Rp 435 trillion. Out-of-pocket spending was also quite high, around 35% of total health expenditure,

Figure 5.4 The growth of private hospitals in Indonesia, 2012–2018

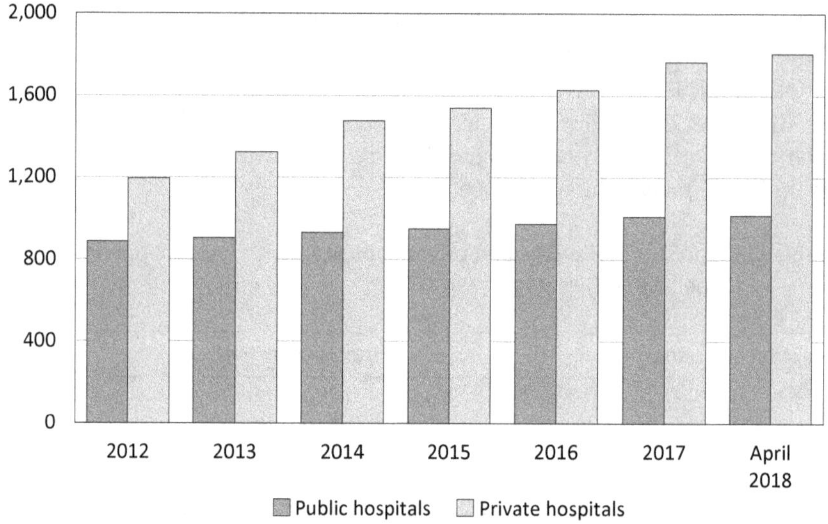

Source: Hospital Information System (SIRS), https://sirs.kemkes.go.id/fo/#

compared to the government's spending on health insurance of about 17%. This means that more money was spent by the people to access health care services, rather than government money (MoH 2020b). Normally, out-of-pocket money is spent in the private sector, which provides more specialist services and shorter waiting times. These figures show that both markets are promising for investors. Private hospitals and clinics continue to attract higher-income patients and are likely to see benefits from the country's expanding health expenditure. Public facilities are challenged by long queues and insufficient human resources; more patients are electing to seek care from private providers.

Foreign investment in the Indonesian health sector

Another policy response to address unmet needs in health care is to open the domestic health care market to foreign investment. Presidential Regulation No. 44/2016 on Lists of Business Fields That Are Closed to and Business Fields That Are Open with Conditions to Investment allows foreign investment in hospital businesses up to 67% for non-ASEAN investors and up to 70% for ASEAN investors. Singapore, Australia and China were the largest foreign investors in health care facilities in 2019 (Figure 5.5). The objective of this policy is to provide better hospital services for Indonesian citizens. Indonesia appears to be an open market

Figure 5.5 Foreign direct investment in Indonesian health care, by country (US$ millions)

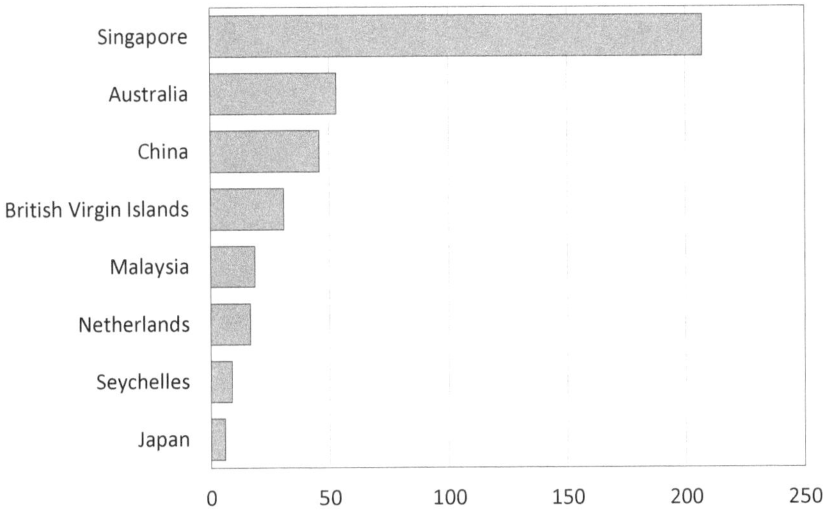

Country	US$ millions (approx.)
Singapore	~205
Australia	~50
China	~45
British Virgin Islands	~30
Malaysia	~18
Netherlands	~18
Seychelles	~8
Japan	~5

Source: Asia Taskforce (2020).

in this sector. However, Presidential Regulation No. 44/2016 states that foreign-owned private hospitals can operate in all capital cities in eastern Indonesia, with the exceptions of Makassar and Manado.

The Indonesian government Law No. 11/2020 on Job Creation, known as the omnibus law (Cipta Kerja), has liberalised several sectors, including certain subsectors of the health care industry. Following passage of the omnibus law, several follow-up regulations were created. One is Presidential Regulation No. 10/2021 on Investment Sectors (known as the New Investment List). Under this regulation, hospitals are now open to 100% foreign investment. Clinics that offer specialised health care, *klinik utama*, are also open to 100% foreign investment, whereas *klinik pratama* (clinics that offer primary health care services) are closed to foreign investors and are reserved for local small and medium-sized businesses. Even though the private sector has been given access to become a player in the national health system, the regulations haven't pushed it to rural areas.

A Ministry of Health regulation further provides that hospitals owned by a foreign investment limited liability company (Perseroan Terbatas Penanaman Modal Asing, PT PMA) must have at least 200 beds and be established based on international cooperation. The number of beds is in accordance with the minimum number of beds in type B general hospitals.

This regulation is in line with Presidential Regulation No. 47/2021 on Administration of the Hospital Sector.

In terms of human resources, subject to Indonesian laws and regulations on foreign manpower, a foreign-invested hospital may employ foreign nationals as medical and non-medical workers according to the hospital's service needs. In practice, this policy conflicts with other regulations that allow foreign health workers to work in Indonesia as consultants or medical practitioners only when they are not available within the country.

Discussion

Health indicators show that the Indonesian health system is generally improving—living conditions are better and access to health services has increased. However, this achievement has been partly offset by the growth of non-communicable diseases such as diabetes, high cholesterol, high blood pressure, obesity and smoking. These diseases are growing evenly across Indonesia, implying a growing demand for access to medical specialist services in hospitals nationwide.

Health financing through BPJS-K had covered 237,923,846 people by March 2022 (DJSN 2022). This is a huge membership. The system provides access for citizens to all levels of health care and to a wide benefit package. Combined with strong growth in health care spending and the positive economic outlook in 2022, Indonesia is a promising option for private investment within the health system, particularly in health care services. In addition, passage of the omnibus law in 2020 opened more opportunities for foreign investors to invest directly in the country's health care sector.

Disparity in health care services still exists and can be a challenge in an archipelago comprising thousands of islands, with 270 million inhabitants spread across rural and urban areas.

The government strategy to produce more medical doctors is not matched by the capacity of medical schools to train more medical specialists. The limitations of medical specialist institutions to produce more medical specialists need to be addressed by the government.

The demand side of the health care market has been growing since 2014 but the supply side, particularly availability of medical specialists, remains relatively low. The cause of this issue should be further explored to find solutions. For example, increasing the capacity of medical specialist production without compromising quality standards is a strategy that can be employed now to improve medical specialist availability.

The association between the number of medical specialists and number of hospitals is clear. To improve the number of medical specialists in rural areas, the government should also increase the number of private hospitals. However, dual-practice policy and market-based distribution of medical specialists should also be reviewed since these are a barrier to entry. A redeployment strategy could be applied if private hospitals are already available in rural areas.

The strategy to invite the private sector to invest in the health care system needs to be examined. The effectiveness of this policy can be observed only in Indonesia's major cities and is ineffective in remote and rural areas. Foreign investment in remote and rural areas is still insignificant, except for the service provided by foreign companies exclusively for their own staff. Currently, all levels of government have a responsibility to build hospitals in rural areas; the private sector has several reasons to be absent from this area due to logistics challenges and a lack of qualified professionals.

Facing a shortage of hospitals in underserved areas, the government could encourage private providers to collaborate in providing universal health coverage to Indonesians. The Ministry of Health together with other ministries should welcome a greater role for the private sector in health care provision, and offer incentives to private investors willing to establish more hospitals in rural areas. In the context of decentralised governance, governments at all levels should consider closer partnerships between the private sector and the government in care provision, particularly to provide health care workers and a supportive investment climate. The government should also create an opportunity for private hospitals to serve more BPJS-K members to relieve pressure on the public health care system.

The open market strategy is not the solution for patients who live in remote and rural areas. The bottleneck of medical specialists production might be one of the causes. While the national government encourages foreign and domestic investment to contribute to health care services, production of medical specialists, the most important medical professional in hospitals, is limited. As a result, private hospitals and medical specialists are both available mostly in the major cities. Training more health workers and encouraging private sector investment—the government's two main policies to reduce the disparity in access to health services between rural and urban residents—have not been effective. Further research to find ways to overcome this disparity is needed.

References

Anderson, Ian, Andreasta Meliala, Puti Marzoeki and Eko Pambudi. 2014. *The Production, Distribution, and Performance of Physicians, Nurses, and Midwives in Indonesia: An Update*. Discussion Paper No. 91324. Washington, DC: World Bank.

Ashburn, Nicklaus P., Anna C. Snavely, Ryan M. Angi, James F. Scheidler, Remle P. Crowe, et al. 2022. 'Prehospital time for patients with acute cardiac complaints: A rural health disparity'. *American Journal of Emergency Medicine* 52: 64–68. doi.org/10.1016/j.ajem.2021.11.038

Asia Taskforce. 2020. *Investing In Indonesian Healthcare: Opportunities for Australian Businesses*. Asia Taskforce Discussion Paper No. 5. https://asiasociety.org/australia/investing-indonesian-healthcare-asia-taskforce-discussion-paper

Bappenas. 2019a. *Penguatan Sistem Pelayanan Kesehatan* [Strengthening the Health Services System]. Jakarta: Badan Perencanaan Pembangunan Nasional.

Bappenas. 2019b. *Sumber Daya Manusia Kesehatan* [Human Health Resources]. Jakarta: Badan Perencanaan Pembangunan Nasional.

BPS (Badan Pusat Statistik, Statistics Indonesia). 2021. 'Hasil sensus penduduk 2020' [Population census results 2020]. Jakarta: BPS. PowerPoint presentation from the 21 January 2021 launch of the census results.

Corallo, Ashley N., Ruth Croxford, David C. Goodman, Elisabeth L. Bryan, Divya Srivastava and Therese A. Stukel. 2014. 'A systematic review of medical practice variation in OECD countries'. *Health Policy* 114(1): 5–14. doi.org/10.1016/j.healthpol.2013.08.002

DeBenedectis, Carolynn M., Lucy B. Spalluto, Lisa Americo, Casey Bishop, Asim Mian, et al. 2022. 'Health care disparities in radiology—A review of the current literature'. *Journal of the American College of Radiology* 19(1, Part B): 101–11. doi.org/10.1016/j.jacr.2021.08.024

DJSN (Dewan Jaminan Sosial Nasional). 2022. 'Sistem Monitoring Terpadu: Aspek Kepesertaan' [Integrated monitoring system: participation]. Accessed 23 May 2022. http://sismonev.djsn.go.id/kepesertaan/

Duke, Sean M., Karina A. González Otárula, Thomas Canales, Elaine Lu, Amber Stout, et al. 2021. 'A systematic literature review of health disparities among rural people with epilepsy (RPWE) in the United States and Canada'. *Epilepsy & Behavior* 122: 108181. doi.org/10.1016/j.yebeh.2021.108181

KKI (Konsil Kedokteran Indonesia). 2017. *Laporan Tahunan KKI 2016* [Annual Report of the Indonesian Medical Council 2016]. Jakarta: KKI.

Lorch, Scott A., Jeanette Rogowski, Jochen Profit and Ciaran S. Phibbs. 2021. 'Access to risk-appropriate hospital care and disparities in neonatal outcomes in racial/ethnic groups and rural–urban populations'. *Seminars in Perinatology* 45(4): 151409. doi.org/10.1016/j.semperi.2021.151409

Mahendradhata, Yodi, Laksono Trisnantoro, Shita Listyadewi, Prastuti Soewondo, Tiara Marthias, et al. 2017. *The Republic of Indonesia Health System Review*. Health Systems in Transition 7(1). World Health Organization.

Meliala, Andreasta, Krishna Hort and Laksono Trisnantoro. 2013. 'Addressing the unequal geographic distribution of specialist doctors in Indonesia: The role of the private sector and effectiveness of current regulations'. *Social Science & Medicine* 82(April): 30–34. doi.org/10.1016/j.socscimed.2013.01.029

MoH (Ministry of Health). 2020a. *Human Resources for Health: Indonesia Country Profile*. Jakarta: MoH.

MoH (Ministry of Health). 2020b. 'National Health Accounts Indonesia 2018'. Sekretariat Jenderal Pusat Pembiayaan dan Jaminan Kesehatan. Jakarta: MoH.

MoH (Ministry of Health). 2020c. *Profil Kesehatan Indonesia Tahun 2019* [Indonesia Health Profile 2019]. Jakarta: MoH. https://pusdatin.kemkes.go.id/resources/download/pusdatin/profil-kesehatan-indonesia/Profil-Kesehatan-indonesia-2019.pdf

MoH (Ministry of Health). 2021a. 'Peta/Data PEMDA yang memiliki anggaran untuk kontrak tenaga kesehatan di puskesmas dan rumah sakit' [Map/data of local governments that have budgets for contracting health workers at *puskesmas* and hospitals]. PowerPoint presentation. Jakarta: MoH.

MoH (Ministry of Health). 2021b. *Profil Kesehatan Indonesia Tahun 2020* [Indonesia Health Profile 2020]. Jakarta: MoH.

MoH (Ministry of Health). 2021c. 'Transformasi SDM Kesehatan'. PowerPoint presentation. Jakarta: MoH.

Nguyen-Pham, Sallyanne, Janni Leung and Deirdre McLaughlin. 2014. 'Disparities in breast cancer stage at diagnosis in urban and rural adult women: A systematic review and meta-analysis'. *Annals of Epidemiology* 24(3): 228–35. doi.org/10.1016/j.annepidem.2013.12.002

Wennberg, John E., 2002. 'Unwarranted variations in healthcare delivery: Implications for academic medical centres'. *BMJ* 325(7370): 961–64. doi.org/10.1136/bmj.325.7370.961

WHO (World Health Organization). 2020. *Improving Retention of Health Workers in Rural and Remote Areas: Case Studies from the WHO South-East Asia Region*. New Delhi: WHO.

6 Pill pushers: Politics, money and the quality of medicine in Indonesia

Elizabeth Pisani, Relmbuss Biljers Fanda, Amalia Hasnida, Mawaddati Rahmi, Yunita Nugrahani, Bachtiar Rifai Pratita Ihsan, Ayuk Lawuningtyas Hariadini, Diana Lyrawati and Aksari Dewi

Law No. 9/1960 on Basic Health declared that all Indonesians had the right to be physically, mentally and spiritually healthy, while Article 8 declared the government responsible for ensuring that all Indonesians had access to health services. Four decades then passed before President Megawati Sukarnoputri, in her last act as head of state, signed legislation supporting universal health insurance. Although her successor did little to advance the health care agenda nationally, initiatives at the district level established that the provision of 'free' health care played very well at the ballot box (Rosser et al. 2011). One of the beneficiaries was Joko Widodo. As governor of Jakarta, he enthusiastically rebranded a city health insurance scheme inherited from his predecessor, taking credit for the popular Jakarta Health Card (Kartu Jakarta Sehat, KJS). When Widodo ran for president in 2012 under the banner of Sukarnoputri's Indonesian Democratic Party of Struggle (Partai Demokrasi Indonesia-Perjuangan, PDI-P), he promised to extend the scheme nationwide should he win, thus cementing universal health coverage as a PDI-P legacy (Pisani et al. 2017).

When Indonesia's mandatory, universal, single-payer insurance system (Jaminan Kesehatan Nasional, JKN) was formally launched in 2014, it was thus freighted with political importance. Many vested interests were involved in preparing for that launch, including those of the powerful state insurance firms which preceded JKN's implementer,

Badan Penyelenggara Jaminan Sosial Kesehatan (BPJS-K). The details of the scheme's implementation were thus hammered out largely on the anvil of political expedience rather than through careful technical calculus (Aspinall 2014). The result was a generous insurance program that could not cover its costs. For Rp 25,500 a month (covered by the government for the poor and near-poor), all Indonesians had a right to full coverage for a wide range of care, including sophisticated procedures such as hip replacements. Many hospitals provided private rooms for patients paying 'first class' premiums of Rp 80,000 per month. The price of diagnostic tests and all 300-odd medicines on the national essential medicines list was included at all levels, with no co-payments required (Mboi 2015).

Unsurprisingly, the scheme ran at a deficit from its inception until premiums rose in 2020. The total deficit increased more than fivefold in the first five full years of operation, from Rp 9.1 trillion in 2015 to 51 trillion in 2019, according to the National Audit Agency (Badan Pemeriksa Keuangan, BPK). In part because it is politically important to the Widodo government that the JKN should succeed, in addition to paying premiums for the poor, near-poor and state employees—currently some 70% of registered participants—the government provided cash infusions totalling Rp 22.2 trillion in the five years to 2019 (BPK 2021).

A planned increase in premiums was cancelled by the Supreme Court in February 2020, but reinstated by presidential decree three months later. This contributed to a 25% rise in premium income, while spending on care fell by 13%, in part due to restricted access to non-COVID-19 services during the pandemic. Income was further boosted by additional revenue from a hypothecated tax on cigarettes, so that BPJS-K reported an operational surplus for the first time in 2020 (BPJS-K 2021).

The historic deficits would likely have been far greater if more Indonesians had access to the health services that the insurance is meant to pay for. Analysis of National Socioeconomic Survey (Survei Sosio-Ekonomi Nasional, Susenas) and Village Potential (Potensi Desa) data for 2018 showed a 40% gap in hospital use between the best- and worst-served fifth of districts, even though the worst-served districts were generally those with the highest JKN insurance coverage. Meanwhile, BPJS-K spending on services per registered participant was 49% higher in the best-served regions (Java and Bali) than in the rest of the country (Pratiwi et al. 2021). It's thus likely that if all Indonesians could access services at the same rate as those in Java and Bali, operational surpluses would again be threatened. In its most recent report on the JKN, BPK continues to warn that the deficit problem remains unresolved.

While the deficit is clearly structural, public and policy rhetoric has until very recently continued to focus on the high price of medicines as a prime contributor to the expense of JKN. In his speech on National Health Day, 12 November 2019, for example, the minister of health said tackling the high price of medicines was a national health priority (Putranto 2019).

In fact, BPJS-K has worked from its inception to bring costs down to levels closer to its income in two principal ways. The first tackled spending on services, financing through capitation fees and diagnostic groups rather than fee-for-service. The second reformed procurement to squeeze down the price of medicines and other consumables. Falling medicine prices led some international companies to withdraw from the market; elicited complaints from domestic producers that their very viability was threatened; and awakened public anxiety, reflected in press reports, that medicines provided in the public system are of poor quality (Hasnida et al. 2021).

The remainder of this chapter focuses on efforts to use procurement policies to contain medicine costs, describing how those polices shape incentives in the medicine supply chain, and in turn affect the availability and quality of medicines in Indonesia.

Methods

This chapter draws on a review of published and grey literature, press reports and regulations relating to medicine pricing and procurement in Indonesia, and on data collected in three separate but linked studies focusing on the procurement, distribution and dispensing of medicines in Indonesia. Secondary data were collected from national institutions in Jakarta, while primary data were collected in Kabupaten Malang (East Java), and in two districts in Nusa Tenggara Timur (NTT): Kupang and Timor Tengah Selatan (TTS). We conducted in-depth interviews, collected data on stocks and prices of medicines from pharmacies and public health facilities, and conducted mystery shopper surveys to establish actual prices charged by pharmacies, private health care providers and informal sellers.

We selected respondents for in-depth interviews for their familiarity with medicine procurement, sale or dispensing. They included employees of distributors, pharmacies, hospitals and the district health office, as well as other health workers. We also approached medicine producers, but none consented to be interviewed, though some participated in our informal study advisory group. We obtained written consent from all participants, and recorded and transcribed interviews. We conducted a total of 39 formal interviews, 20 in Malang and 19 in NTT.

Stock, pricing and dispensing data were requested from the head pharmacist of public medical warehouses, hospitals and *puskesmas*;

and private distributors, hospitals, clinics and pharmacies. In total, we collected information from six public and three private outlets in Malang, and two public and four private outlets in TTS.

We conducted field surveys in which study staff posing as patients bought samples of six commonly prescribed medicines (amlodipine, amoxicillin, captopril, furosemide, glibenclamide and simvastatin), recording the sale price and details of the product (brand, expiry date, etc.). We collected a total of 238 samples of 6 medicines in Malang, and 22 samples of 2 medicines (amoxicillin and amlodipine) in NTT. Data were analysed using the software package Stata 17.

Ethical approval for data collection in NTT was obtained from the Faculty of Medicine at the University of Gajah Mada, Yogyakarta. Ethics approval for data collection in Malang, East Java, was obtained from the Faculty of Medicine at the University of Brawijaya, Malang, and the University of New South Wales, Sydney. Data collected at the national level received ethical approval from the University of Indonesia.

Results

JKN represents a significant change in the way health care in Indonesia is structured. Many recent investigations of medicine pricing and accessibility have thus understandably focused on the changes in the public sector. However, we found that the interaction between public and private markets is likely to be a critical influence on the quality of medicines taken by Indonesian patients in both sectors.

History of price controls in the Indonesian medicine market

Our literature review found that policies aiming to bring down the price of medicines in Indonesia were implemented long before the start of JKN. In 2004, when most spending on medicines was out of pocket even in public facilities, a Ministry of Health report found that innovator brands were on average 22 times more expensive in Indonesia than the international reference price, while the Indonesian market leader (usually a branded generic version of the medicine) was between five and seven times more, with slightly higher prices in private facilities than in the public sector (MoH 2005: 62).

In the private sector, cost-containment efforts were limited to setting a ceiling retail price for medicines. The *harga eceran tertinggi*, maximum retail price or HET, is set in consultation between the Ministry of Health and manufacturers, and is printed on medicine packaging. Public sector physicians have been required to prescribe generic medicines since 1989; this may have fuelled the market for 'branded generics' produced by many domestic manufacturers. Price caps on essential generic medicines were set in 2004; this appears to have brought down costs for non-branded generics (known in the pharmaceutical industry as international non-proprietary name or INN generics) but it did little to control prices for branded versions. A 2009 study comparing the price of ciprofloxacin internationally found that domestic-branded generics sold in Indonesia's private sector were among the most expensive globally. Indonesia's INN generics, however, were among the cheapest (HAI 2009).

From 2010, the public sector has been obliged to procure and prescribe INN generics. This significantly reduced public sector spending on medicines long before the procurement reforms that came with JKN (Anggriani et al. 2014). However, it was unevenly enforced across the highly fragmented procurement landscape; public sector hospitals, in particular, continued to buy branded generics and the narrative of high medicine prices continued.

One of the core policies introduced with JKN was a single-winner (per province) auction system for essential medicines, designed to consolidate procurement, facilitate the oversight of INN-only policies and push down prices. Ceiling prices (based on *harga perkiraan sendiri*, HPS) were set by the Ministry of Health, according to an undisclosed formula. Bidders had to pitch their prices below that level and promise to fulfil orders up to the demand forecasts provided by the Ministry of Health, and the medicine had to have a valid market authorisation. Beyond that, tenders were awarded in auctions administered by the Public Procurement Policy Board (Lembaga Kebijakan Pengadaan Barang dan Jasa Pemerintah, LKPP) based solely on lowest price.[1] Winning bidders sell products through an electronic platform known as e-catalogue, where buyers place orders with manufacturers directly, for fulfilment by their designated distributor.

Despite low ceiling prices, the promise of exclusive access to the potentially vast public market proved attractive to many companies, some of them with limited experience of large-scale production or distribution. As manufacturers undercut one another, the price for many products dropped precipitously, often to levels well below the international reference price (Anggriani et al. 2020; Kristina et al. 2020). For example, LKPP data show that the public sector price of amlodipine 5 mg, a blood pressure lowering medicine among the most commonly prescribed in Indonesia, dropped from Rp 240 per tablet in 2013 to Rp 53 in 2020—a fall of 78% before considering inflation.

---

1 According to LKPP, this system is expected to change in 2022, when any prequalified company will be allowed to offer products at any price up to the public procurement ceiling price (HPS).

Industry's response to low public sector prices

Companies can protect profit margins by cutting costs, protecting against losses and/or increasing revenues. We found that the first line of defence against low public sector prices for both manufacturers and distributors was to reduce exposure to potential losses. For example, at least one international manufacturer of higher-end generics withdrew from the Indonesian market entirely (Hasnida et al. 2021).

Domestic manufacturers participated actively in early e-catalogue auctions. However, their enthusiasm waned as the ceiling price, set in response to earlier low bids, fell ever lower. Some domestic manufacturers have avoided or progressively reduced exposure to e-catalogue, and/or focused greater attention on over-the-counter products whose prices continued to be constrained only by the negotiated maximum retail price. As a result, auctions for many products fail, leaving public facilities without a central source for some essential medicines. Table 6.1 shows the medicines for which there was no bidder in the initial round of bidding for the 2018 e-catalogue (which remained in force until late 2020), together with the estimated unmet demand.

Companies that win auctions are sometimes exposed to losses because they underestimated the cost of production, or because costs rise following increases in the price of active ingredients (which are mostly imported, thus also affected by exchange rates).

In an open letter to health authorities, the head of GP Farmasi, the Indonesian pharmaceutical manufacturers association, complained that the price per kilogram of imported paracetamol rose by 93% between late 2017 (when 2018 e-catalogue price bidding took place) and March 2020, when the winning prices were still in force (Tirtokoesnadi 2020). Some producers react by simply halting production of e-catalogue products.

> [E-catalogue] auction winners are supposed to ensure that they can meet demand from government hospitals … But once they've won the tender, then suddenly they say 'oh, we can't get raw materials any more'. They all want to win the tender, but then they shouldn't be allowed to say they've run out of raw materials … There should be sanctions for e-catalogue winners [who don't produce enough to fulfil orders] so that they think twice before bidding.
>
> Pharmacist, public sector 2, TTS

Indeed, even where products are available, distributors sometimes selectively refuse to fulfil orders. There are two reasons for this. The first is that the maximum price variation between districts, which amounts to a potential distribution margin, is regulated. LKPP divides Indonesia

Table 6.1 Estimated demand for products in areas where no company bid successfully to supply e-catalogue products, 2018

Molecule	Dose	Form	Estimated unmet demand (counting units)
Amoxicillin	500 mg	tablet	598,394,368
Ampicillin	1,000 ml	vial	2,813,816
Cefixime	100 mg	tablet	64,202,608
Clindamycin	300 mg	tablet	21,529,398
Domperidone	5 ml	liquid	129,676
Ethambutol	500 mg	tablet	25,374,616
Loperamide	2 mg	tablet	21,728,884
Loratadine	10 mg	tablet	33,377,290
Mefenamic acid	250 mg	tablet	17,303,408
Metformin	500 mg	tablet	310,519,456
Nifedipine	10 mg	tablet	33,740,776
Propylthiouracil	100 mg	tablet	22,740,012
Ranitidine	150 mg	tablet	126,151,152
Sodium bicarbonate	500 mg	tablet	18,649,908
Sucralfate	500 mg	tablet	9,440,184

Source: Public Procurement Policy Board (Lembaga Kebijakan Pengadaan Barang dan Jasa Pemerintah, LKPP).

into five zones for the purposes of pricing. The e-catalogue price in each zone is for delivery to the district level.[2] Yet the ceiling price of products in the most remote (and sparsely populated) provinces is limited to 20% more than the ceiling price in populous Java. For low-value products, this may represent a very small amount in real terms, and will in many cases not cover the fee paid to distributors for delivery to remote areas, let alone the real costs of transport.

> In reality, a product that costs 100 there [in Java] can cost 700 here [in TTS], with container shipment that takes two weeks, maybe a month if the weather is bad.
>
> Panel pharmacy, Kupang

---

2 An exception is the easternmost province of Papua, where the price includes delivery only to the provincial warehouse.

It is thus in the interests of both producers and distributors to prioritise sales to lower-cost, higher-volume destinations, as well as to focus on higher-value products.

> It's business logic. [INN] generics are cheap, and the distribution fee we get from the producer is based on the value. Seven per cent. And imagine, out of that I also have to cover customers that don't pay.
>
> Distributor, national

Though public procurement agency LKPP can impose sanctions for non-delivery of medicines through e-catalogue, there is no record of it doing so. This may be in part because distributors sometimes have good reason for refusing to supply: because clients had not paid for previous shipments.

> We serve many BPJS-K clients, and [public] hospitals, well, you know, there's no way they're going to pay cash. Usually the payment gets put off ... If we've given them 90 days to pay and they still don't pay, we won't serve them again.
>
> Distributor, national

Hospitals in turn complain that they cannot pay distributors because the public insurer delays payments and reimbursement for JKN patients, leaving hospitals with no cash on hand. In 2018 GP Farmasi reported that this had caused a backlog of Rp 3.5 trillion in unpaid bills to distributors and manufacturers (GP Farmasi 2018).

State-owned distributors report being particularly hard hit, because public sector clients assume they will write off debts, even though the companies are run for profit and are required to pay dividends to the government.

> It's as though because we're state-owned, [public hospitals] think it's fine for us to operate at a loss, but that's just not true.
>
> Distributor, national

On the revenue-boosting side of the equation, manufacturers and distributors react mostly by seeking to increase profits in the private sector, as discussed below.

Health care providers' response to low public reimbursement

Primary health services (*puskesmas*) are expected to provide medicines to JKN patients for free. They can order medicines from e-catalogue through the district medicine warehouse, or sometimes directly. If e-catalogue medicines are not available, *puskesmas* must procure them using the

Table 6.2 Ratio of median maximum retail price (HET) to average public procurement price, 2020

Medicine	Dose (tablet, mg)	E-catalogue price (rupiah)	Median HET (rupiah)	Ratio
Amlodipine	10	70	2,530	36.1
Amlodipine	5	53	1,311	24.7
Amoxicillin	250	194	2,200	11.3
Amoxicillin	500	201	1,267	6.3
Captopril	12.5	65	154	2.4
Captopril	25	75	241	3.2
Furosemide [a]	40	77	318	4.1
Glibenclamide	5	82	385	4.7
Simvastatin	10	68	693	10.2
Simvastatin	20	97	1,375	14.2

a = There was no winner for the auction covering 2020. This price was valid in 2019. HET = *harga eceran tertinggi* (maximum retail price).

Source: E-catalogue data, LKPP, 2021. HET data: market survey, Malang and Nusa Tenggara Timur, 2021.

capitation funds they receive from BPJS-K. Hospitals may order medicines for public patients through e-catalogue, or may source other brands in the 'regular' market; in both cases, medicines are supposed to be provided for free to JKN patients, and are paid for out of the flat fee reimbursed to the hospital according to the patient's diagnosis.

In all of these cases, the revenue is fixed (and usually very constrained), while the cost of acquiring the medicines varies. Compensation is generally calculated on the basis of e-catalogue prices; these are commonly far below the market median for the same products. As Table 6.2 shows, we found, for example, that across ten dosages of six common essential medicines, the median HET (maximum retail price) for the products collected in our survey was more than double the public procurement price for all products. For half of the products, the median price was over ten times the e-catalogue price.

If they cannot access e-catalogue products, service providers may have to pay more for medicines than the capitation/reimbursement is designed to cover. They are thus incentivised not to serve those patients, or to find the very cheapest alternative supplier.

We had proposals from lots of distributors to supply the health centre. Usually the procurement team compares their price proposals, and it turns out [Distributor A] was the cheapest, so we appointed [Distributor A].

Puskesmas pharmacist, Malang

This raises the question: how does 'Distributor A' undercut the opposition? A common practice we identified was itself designed to avoid losses on the part of manufacturer or distributor: deep discounting of products nearing expiry.

Industry norms, and in some cases regulations, allow or oblige expired medicines to be returned to distributors and/or manufacturers for disposal. Medicines close to their expiry date thus represent two types of potential losses: sales forgone, and the cost of return and disposal. Because of this, manufacturers and distributors are both keen to shift stock as it approaches its expiry date. National and local distributors and pharmacists all described the widespread practice of deep discounting of overstocked medicines close to expiry, in order to avoid the cost of sales forgone.

> If we've got a lot of stock, we suggest a [promotional] program so that there's not too much expiry ... If there's only a year left [on the expiry date] we will discount 50%, as long as there is some profit, or even just a small loss ... It's better to sell at a small loss than to let it die in the warehouse and suffer a great big loss.

Panel pharmacy, Kupang

In some cases, distributors simultaneously protected themselves against the potential cost of processing returns by stipulating that these discounted products are not eligible for returns.

> If we've already given a big discount, and also for BPJS-K [e-catalogue] medicines, we don't accept returns. We've already paid out a lot [for distribution] and they still want to send it back?!

Distributor, national

Some respondents warned that these products also easily find their way into the informal end of the private supply chain:

> There are people selling amoxicillin in village [market stalls] ... What worries me is that these are expired medicines that haven't been properly disposed of, and just repackaged ... It's so easy with the technology now.

Pharmacist, public sector, TTS

If health services providing care for JKN patients are unable to procure e-catalogue medicines and are unwilling to provide free medicines sourced elsewhere, they have two further options. The first is to send the patient away to pay for medicines out of their own pocket. This reduces spending

Figure 6.1 Proportion of different brands of furosemide dispensed by Malang district hospital by volume and revenue, January–October 2021

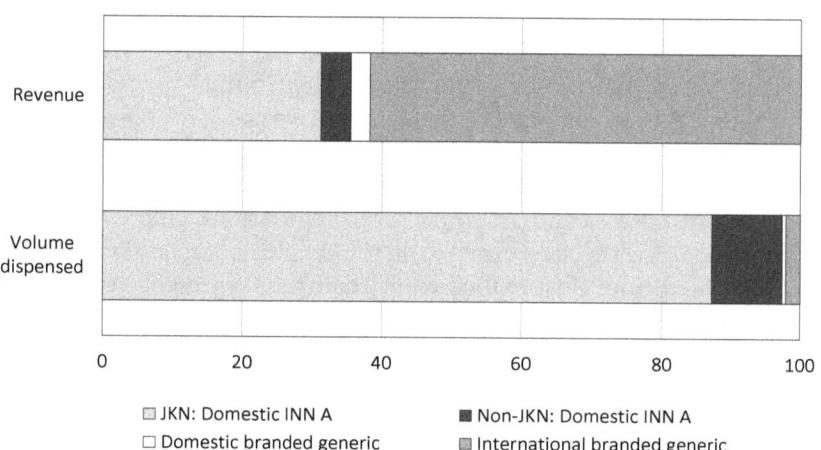

☐ JKN: Domestic INN A ■ Non-JKN: Domestic INN A
☐ Domestic branded generic ▨ International branded generic

and thus costs. The second strategy increases revenues: 'upsell' the JKN patient to an alternative medicine provided by the hospital pharmacy, again at the patient's own expense. Some respondents suggested that this strategy has become more necessary as JKN eats away at hospital income, and slow reimbursement obstructs cash flow.

An NTT hospital explained that they charged public patients 25% more than the wholesale list price, so higher-priced medicines yield higher margins. The importance of this to a hospital's bottom line was clear from an analysis, shown in Figure 6.1, of revenue from dispensing of different brands of furosemide in the district hospital in Malang. While the most expensive brand accounted for just 2.1% of furosemide dispensed, it accounted for 61.7% of earnings from the medicine.

Less ethical health care providers line their own pockets while reducing outlay for the hospital. They turn patients away from the public sector when there is a stock-out of an e-catalogue medicine (and sometimes even when there is not), instead issuing prescriptions on which they designate a pharmacy in which they have a financial interest.

> When I was at the public hospital, there was one specialist doctor who would write prescriptions ... for branded medicines, even though we had a generic version in the hospital pharmacy. That was a [source of] conflict between me and the doctor. The patient was [insured by] JKN, they had a right to free medicine, so why go and buy medicine at 300,000 [rupiah]?

… [This doctor] writes pharmacy A, B or C right on the prescription. As I understand it, he has a collaboration [with the pharmacy].

Pharmacist, public sector, TTS

The bureaucrats' view

The cataclysmic changes wrought by JKN came not very long after an energetic burst of *'pemekaran'*: the subdivision of districts in remoter parts of Indonesia, and the simultaneous indigenisation of the civil service. Local autonomy increased the need for experience and skills in local government; it also reduced the supply of those skills (Kimura 2010). As procurement functions using unfamiliar technologies fell to less-experienced staff, oversight mechanisms also increased. This has changed the incentive structure for some civil servants; we found several instances of pronounced risk avoidance, ultimately affecting service provision.

Many public sector health workers now fear being audited or otherwise held responsible for any deviation from prescribed procedures, even when those procedures don't match local conditions or needs across Indonesia's hugely diverse settings. This discourages flexibility and proactive problem-solving, such as the use of capitation funds to restock medicines before existing stocks are exhausted. 'I wouldn't dare' is commonly given by public sector health providers as a reason for not acting more proactively.

> The biggest problem is when [the national procurement agency] LKPP can't find a winner, because the profit is too small or whatever … Like, in 2019, there was no paracetamol, ibuprofen, asemefenamat, really essential medicines [offered through e-catalogue].
>
> Interviewer: So did you procure those directly?
>
> No, we wouldn't dare, because according to the system, we were supposed to use e-catalogue … Eventually we met with [the National Audit Agency] BPK to come to an agreement … and from this year we are doing direct purchasing.
>
> Interviewer: So in those two years, if [an essential medicine] wasn't available on e-catalogue, where did you get it from?
>
> We just didn't buy it.
>
> District health office staff, Malang

This risk aversion, and the stock-outs it leads to, have the same effect as turning patients away: patients are driven into the for-profit medicine market, discussed in the next section.

'Regular' market medicines: Exploitation or subsidy?

Faced with a specialist doctor's unethical prescribing practices, the public sector pharmacist quoted above volunteered this opinion:

> If it's a private patient, fine, they can afford it. But don't do it to a [public insurance] patient who will have to borrow money to buy those medicines.
>
> Pharmacist, public sector, TTS

Almost all manufacturers, distributors and pharmacists are in business to make a profit, and many health care providers are, too. It's to be expected that they behave like most other business people, trying to maximise profit where possible; below, we discuss many of the strategies they share with traders of other commodities. However, the pharmacist's comments highlight two important ways in which medicines differ from most other commodities. First, they are usually not discretionary or interchangeable purchases. Each medicine is specific to a condition, and patients have to take them to stay alive and healthy. Second, doctors get to dictate what medicine and sometimes also what brand a patient takes, by issuing a prescription. Where doctors or their employers have a financial interest in dispensing, this creates the opportunity for exploitative prescribing.

While the Indonesian pharmaceutical industry's code of conduct on marketing forbids producers and distributors from paying or otherwise incentivising doctors to prescribe a specific brand (GP Farmasi 2016), several respondents reported direct and indirect encouragement to favour specific brands.

> If a doctor prescribes a branded product, the manufacturer will give them an incentive against the prescription.
>
> Distributor, multinational

Deals with hospitals are also common.

> The business model to get medicines into hospitals is to make a deal. [The pharmaceutical company] has to give 15% of the [list] sales price [as a kickback] to the hospital, and another 20% to the [prescribing] doctor. If it's a specialist doctor, it can be even more.
>
> Hospital doctor, Malang

Those direct payments are added to the revenue a hospital can earn by selling expensive brands, illustrated in Figure 6.1.

Pharmacists and others also reported being incentivised to sell particular brands, not just on the basis of profit margins, but also because they could earn prizes, bonuses or discounts on stock by meeting certain sales targets.

Chapter 6 Pill pushers: Politics, money and the quality of medicine

> The sales people will offer some household appliance, like an oven or something. 'Ibu, take this many boxes of contraceptives for this many months, and you'll win this thing.'
>
> Village midwife, Malang

These inducements are prohibited, but commonplace—one of many discrepancies we found between de jure regulations and de facto practice. Producers and distributors also have many legal ways of promoting their products to pharmacists, who tend to focus not on the absolute price, but on the profit margin—the difference between buying price and selling price. Pharmacists try hard to increase their margins by acquiring products at deep discounts to the list price. Distributors, for their part, increase sales by pegging discounts to sales volume.

> I sometimes switch distributors if they are offering, maybe a bigger discount, then I'll take that, as long as it's profitable [laughs] ... Or if a principal [a sales representative direct from the market authorisation holder] comes—it's them that bring the promotional programs, if you buy this much, you get a discount of that much.
>
> Pharmacist, Malang

Volume discounts can be substantial. One chain pharmacy reported an additional 29% discount from a distributor providing 40,000 units of a specific INN medicine, compared with the price secured from a different distributor who supplied only 9,000 units of the identical medicine (same brand and dose form). Since the pharmacy sells the product at the same price regardless of source, this has a considerable influence on revenue.

Pharmacies providing medicines to JKN patients sometimes also sell the same products, sourced at e-catalogue prices, to non-JKN patients, earning many times the amount they would get if reimbursed by the public insurer. Table 6.3 shows the difference this makes to the bottom line, underlining the fact that maximising profits depends on finding the optimal combination of buying price, selling price and sales volume.

Other strategies to maximise profits include carrying products at a variety of price points so that you can meet the needs of a broader cross-section of potential customers; selling in bulk to frontline health care workers such as nurses and midwives who are not allowed to dispense de jure, but who de facto commonly sell medicines, especially in remote areas; and promoting products a patient doesn't really need.

> If a patient asks for paracetamol, we offer a branded version first. So that we're sure of making the most profit, if we give a generic, we'll give a vitamin combination, or if they've had fever, been tired, we'll sell them [herbal medicine] Imboost as well.
>
> Pharmacist, TTS

Table 6.3 Sales data for different brands of amlodipine 5 mg, from a single pharmacy that serves JKN and non-JKN patients, Nusa Tenggara Timur, 2021

	Buying price (from distributor) (rupiah)	Reimbursement/ selling price (rupiah)	Profit per unit (rupiah)	Annual sales volume (2019)	Total profit (rupiah)
E-catalogue INN, JKN patient	76	83	8	46,000	345,000
E-catalogue INN, non-JKN patient	76	1,300	1,225	28,000	34,286,000
Best-selling branded	2,000	2,800	800	200	160,000
Most profitable branded	6,500	9,000	2,500	170	425,000

JKN = Jaminan Kesehatan Nasional (National Health Insurance), INN = international non-proprietary name.

The result is a highly segmented market in which similar (and sometimes identical) medicines are sold at very different price points, depending largely on what the buyer can afford.

Figure 6.2 shows this variation across the 20 different brands of amlodipine 5 mg collected in our field surveys in East Java and NTT: there was a 128-fold price difference between the cheapest (Rp 60) and the most expensive pill (Rp 7,722) in our studies.

Companies, too, engage in segmentation, so that a single company often sells two or more versions of the same product. According to national regulations, the formulation of these 'twin' products must be identical; only the packaging and branding may differ. With differences in packaging and branding come differences in price. Figure 6.3 shows the maximum retail prices for these 'twin' products from a number of companies. Most make a branded version (the diamonds on the graph) as well as an INN generic (the circles); Company 7 makes branded twins, while for Company 6 we found triplets: two brands and an INN generic.

Some companies that wish to protect their 'brand value' but also wish to bid at rock-bottom prices for the large public market have adopted an additional segmentation strategy: they have created subsidiaries that make medicines for the public sector and at lower price points. By registering products under these subsidiaries, they get around the regulations that require identical formulations for 'twinned' medicines.

Figure 6.2 Variation in prices of amlodipine 5 mg: Malang and Nusa Tenggara Timur, 2021 (rupiah)

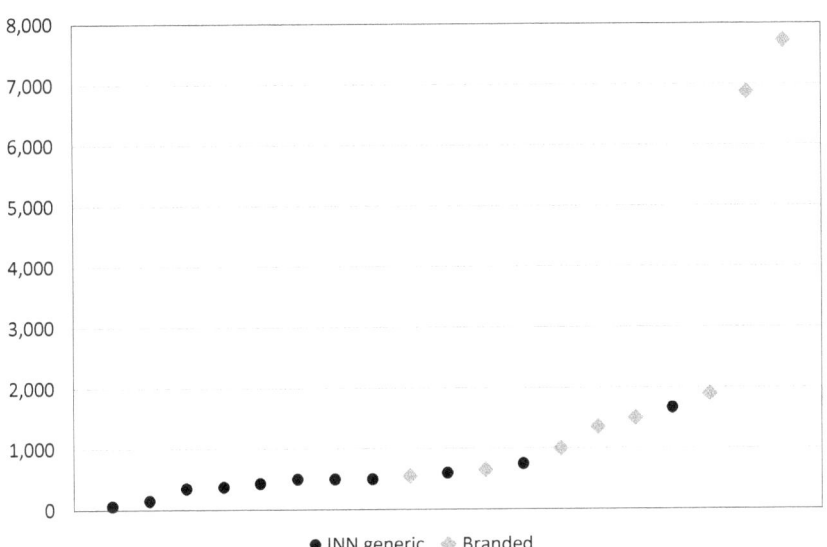

> Like [large private firm] Kalbe Farma; they sell [INN] generics only through their subsidiary [Hexpharm Jaya], while the state-owned companies concentrate on generics, and only sell branded products to mop up the mid-to-high end. If you look at the market, you see that Kalbe dominates. It's a successful strategy.
>
> Panel pharmacy, Kupang

We noted at the start of this section that health care providers (including pharmacists) can influence what brand of medicine a patient takes, and often also the price they pay for it. We found significant diversity in the price charged by different outlets for the identical product. But we note also that patient preference plays an important part. Many interviewees said that patients equated high price with high quality.

> It's like: you use the same petrol, but your motorbike is a different brand … It's just the tradition around here, patients prefer branded medicine to generics. Even though the medicine is the same, we get 'paracetamol doesn't suit me, only Sanmol [brand] works for me', though it's the same ingredients, and one is 25,000 [rupiah] and the other 85,000.
>
> Pharmacist, public sector 2, TTS

Some pharmacists say they set prices high simply to maintain trust.

Figure 6.3 Maximum permitted retail price (HET), amlodipine and amoxicillin, 2021 (rupiah). Prices are for the same molecule and dose, made by the same company

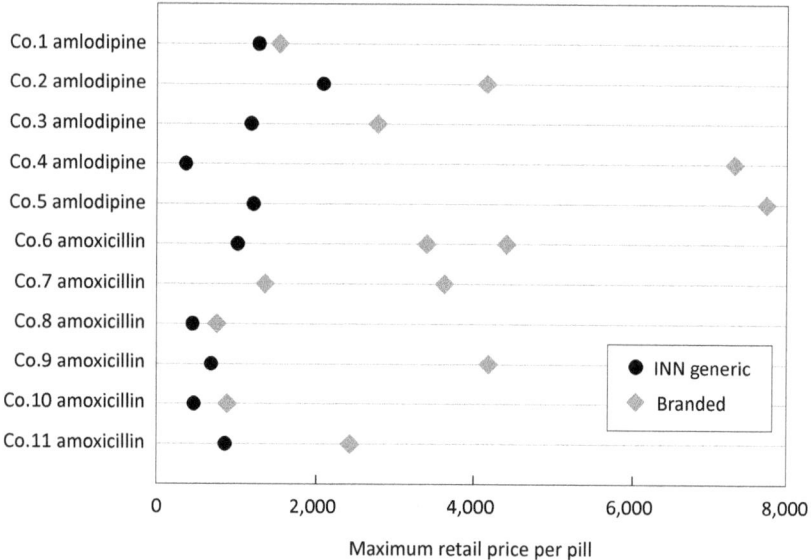

> [When we buy medicines at a large discount] we don't drop the selling price, because if it's too cheap patients don't trust the medicine, they think it's fake.
>
> Pharmacist, Kupang

Convenience also plays an important role.

> We only sell to regular [market] clients, we don't have anything at [JKN] prices. But rather than queuing up for ages, [JKN patients] will come to buy their medicines at the pharmacy.
>
> Pharmacist, Kupang

In short, many patients buy expensive medicines not because they have to, but because they choose to.

Discussion

The incentive structures described above arise when an increasingly socialised demand for medicine clashes with a staunchly profit-driven supply. The practices that result from this have implications for access to medicines and potentially also for their quality.

Chapter 6 Pill pushers: Politics, money and the quality of medicine

The Jokowi administration has invested considerable political capital in the expansion of socialised medicine through the JKN, a national health insurance scheme that is mandatory and thus theoretically universal, but that was planned with limited attention to financial sustainability. One response to JKN's structural deficit has been ongoing efforts at cost-containment in both medicine procurement and in payment for services.

By international standards, the prices that Indonesia's public health services pay for many essential medicines are now very low; health service providers complain that capitation fees and diagnosis-based reimbursement rates are also inadequate (PERSI 2019). Previous research has suggested that for-profit manufacturers and distributors (including state-owned enterprises) respond to low medicine prices principally in one of two ways, each of which threatens medicine quality. First, companies may choose to cut investment in quality assurance in order to bid low and win auctions, potentially leading to substandard medicines. Second (and alternatively), they may choose to withdraw from the public market, concentrating instead on higher-margin products for the private sector. This potentially creates shortages for public patients. At the same time, low reimbursement rates (which are supposed to include the provision of free medicines) constrain income for hospitals serving JKN patients. Health care providers are incentivised to maximise income by promoting demand for expensive products (Yuniarti et al. 2019). Patients may also equate expense with quality. Both health care providers and patients sometimes buy more expensive medicines from cheaper informal distribution channels where the risk of acquiring falsified medicines is greatest (Hasnida et al. 2021; Pisani et al. 2019).

The current study, which looks in greater detail at prices and incentives throughout the supply chain in both the public and the private sectors, provides a more nuanced picture.

We find that many manufacturers faced with low and falling prices in Indonesia's public market protect their profits by engaging in both of the above strategies simultaneously, through market segmentation. However, rather than compounding the risk to quality, this dual strategy may effectively decrease it. Companies can amortise the cost of a production line across all the brands that come off that line, so profits from the branded version sold at high prices in fancy packaging can subsidise any deficits when the same product is sold to the public system in plain packaging at a fraction of the price.

While the political promise of JKN is to provide free, publicly procured medicines to all Indonesians, not all patients yet have the paperwork, transportation options or patience to access public health services, nor are they sure of being offered free medicines when they do. Hospitals and other health care providers compensate for low earnings on JKN patients by seeking income elsewhere. They commonly 'upsell' patients, including JKN members, to more expensive versions of medicines (thus sometimes also earning incentive payments from pharmaceutical companies).

Patients who can't afford the medicines they are prescribed must choose between going untreated, assuming debt or trying to get the medicines at a discount, potentially acquiring falsified medicines from unlicensed vendors or online. However, as the public pharmacist from NTT noted, the upselling may not matter much for richer patients. Indeed, it may actually secure the quality of public sector medicines. Without cross-subsidising income from the 'regular' market, producers would find it hard to cover the cost of quality-assured production at current public procurement prices. By extension, greater effective coverage of JKN would likely require significantly more spending on medicines, not just because volumes would increase, but because the loss of cross-subsidy would mean prices for most medicines in the public market would have to rise if quality is to be maintained.

Indonesia's current 'mixed market' for medicine does not fulfil JKN's promise, but it does deliver medicines at price points that suit most family budgets. Attempts to procure ever-cheaper medicines for free distribution to all patients (including the richest 20% of Indonesians, who are currently the largest consumers of free inpatient care in Indonesia; Pratiwi et al. 2021) may well erode the quality of those medicines. Even as politicians promise all things to all people, policymakers might aim first to provide the poorest patients with access to affordable, quality-assured medicines. This could be achieved by concentrating resources on reducing supply chain incentives that create shortages of essential medicines for these patients, while addressing incentives in health care settings that expose them to upselling. While this study has pointed to many of these incentives, we were unable to interview manufacturers in any depth. Their perspectives, added to those of the distributors, health care providers and pharmacists interviewed here, would be valuable in devising feasible policy changes that maintain the robustness of the Indonesian pharmaceutical market while ensuring access for those who need it most.

We also found significant differences between regulation and practice, with many regulations poorly enforced. Paradoxically, this apparently lax enforcement (for example, turning a blind eye to sale of medicines by midwives, or failing to impose sanctions on e-catalogue distributors, who may themselves face arrears from public hospitals) was often a pragmatic response that balanced the needs of different constituencies across very diverse settings.

The medicine supply chain, from manufacture of active ingredients to consumption by patients in remote areas, is inherently complex. The diversity of responses in Indonesia to shifting incentives are, if anything, a sign that the Indonesian medicine market is rather robust. While some continue to call for tighter regulations to constrain prices while expanding provision of free medication for all, this study stands as a warning: be careful what you wish for.

Author contributions

The research was conceived by Elizabeth Pisani, who led the analysis and drafted the chapter. Relmbuss Biljers Fanda managed the study, carried out a literature review, conducted interviews and coordinated the market survey in NTT. Aksari Dewi conducted interviews and coordinated the market survey in Malang. Amalia Hasnida, Yunita Nugrahani and Mawaddati Rahmi participated with EP, RBF and AD in weekly data interpretation discussions between March 2020 and June 2021. All contributed actively to analysis, and to shaping this report. Ayuk Lawuningtyas Hariadini and Bachtiar Rifai Pratita Ihsan contributed to the implementation of the Malang work, under the supervision of Diana Lyrawati.

Acknowledgements

Elizabeth Pisani, Relmbuss Biljers Fanda and Yunita Nugrahani were supported by a grant from the Global Health Supply Chain Conference. Elizabeth Pisani received additional support from the Australian National Health and Medical Research Council, which also supported the participation of Aksari Dewi, Diana Lyrawati, Ayuk Lawuningtyas Hariadini and Bachtiar Rifai Pratita Ihsan, through a grant to the George Institute for Global Health. Amalia Hasnida was supported through a fellowship from the United States Pharmacopeia Quality Institute. We thank all participating institutions for sharing data to allow for cross-site analysis.

We are grateful for thought-provoking discussions and suggestions from our informal study advisory/validation group, all of whom participated voluntarily and in their personal capacities.

References

Anggriani, Yusi, Mohamed Izham M. Ibrahim, Sri Suryawati and Asrul A. Shafie. 2014. 'The impact of Indonesian generic medicine pricing policy on medicine prices'. *Journal of Generic Medicines* 10(3–4): 219–29. doi.org/10.1177/1741134314553605

Anggriani, Yusi, Hesty Utami Ramadaniati, Prih Sarnianto, Jenny Pontoan and Sri Suryawati. 2020. 'The impact of pharmaceutical policies on medicine procurement pricing in Indonesia under the implementation of Indonesia's social health insurance system'. *Value in Health Regional Issues* 21: 1–8. doi.org/10.1016/j.vhri.2019.05.005

Aspinall, Edward. 2014. 'Health care and democratization in Indonesia'. *Democratization* 21(5): 803–23. doi.org/10.1080/13510347.2013.873791

BPJS-K. 2021. *Laporan Pengelolaan Program Tahun 2020 & Laporan Keuangan Tahun 2020 (Auditan)* [Program Management Report 2020 & Financial Report 2020 (Audited)]. Jakarta: BPJS-K.

BPK (Badan Pemeriksa Keuangan, National Audit Agency). 2021. *Pendapat BPK – Pengelolaan Atas Penyelenggaraan Program Jaminan Kesehatan Nasional 2021* [BPK's Opinion – Management of the 2021 National Health Insurance Program Implementation]. Jakarta: BPK.

GP Farmasi. 2016. 'Kode Etik Usaha Farmasi' [Pharmaceutical Business Code of Ethics]. www.gpfarmasi.id/pages/kode-etik-usaha-farmasi

GP Farmasi. 2018. 'Hutang jatuh tempo obat & alkes JKN belum dibayar mencapai Rp. 3,5 T per Juli 2018' [The unpaid debt on JKN medicines & medical equipment reached Rp 3.5 trillion as of July 2018].

HAI (Health Action International). 2009. 'One-day snapshot of the price of ciprofloxacin 500'. Amsterdam.

Hasnida, Amalia, Maarten Olivier Kok and Elizabeth Pisani. 2021. 'Challenges in maintaining medicine quality while aiming for universal health coverage: A qualitative analysis from Indonesia'. *BMJ Global Health* 6(Suppl. 3): e003663. doi.org/10.1136/bmjgh-2020-003663

Kimura, Ehito. 2010. 'Proliferating provinces: Territorial politics in post-Suharto Indonesia'. *South East Asia Research* 18(3): 415–49. doi.org/10.5367/sear.2010.0005

Kristina, Susi, Hardika Aditama and Dwi Endarti. 2020. 'Evaluating accessibility of essential medicines in Indonesia: A survey on availability and prices in public and private health sectors'. *International Journal of Pharmaceutical Research* 12(2). doi.org/10.31838/ijpr/2020.12.02.0095

Mboi, Nafsiah. 2015. 'Indonesia: On the way to universal health care'. *Health Systems & Reform* 1(2): 91–97. doi.org/10.1080/23288604.2015.1020642

MoH (Ministry of Health). 2005. *The Prices People Have to Pay for Medicines in Indonesia*. Jakarta: Indonesian Government Ministry of Health with WHO Jakarta and Health Action International.

PERSI (Perhimpunan Rumah Sakit Seluruh Indonesia). 2019. *Buku Putih PERSI: Refleksi Perjalanan 5 Tahun Era Jaminan Kesehatan Nasional* [PERSI White Paper: Reflections on the First 5 Years of the National Health Insurance Scheme]. PERSI.

Pisani, Elizabeth, Maarten Oliver Kok and Kharisma Nugroho. 2017. 'Indonesia's road to universal health coverage: A political journey'. *Health Policy and Planning* 32(2): 267–76. doi.org/10.1093/heapol/czw120

Pisani, Elizabeth, Adina-Loredana Nistor, Amalia Hasnida, Koray Parmaksiz, Jingying Xu and Maarten Oliver Kok. 2019. 'Identifying market risk for substandard and falsified medicines: An analytic framework based on qualitative research in China, Indonesia, Turkey and Romania'. *Wellcome Open Research* 4: 70. doi.org/10.12688/wellcomeopenres.15236.1

Pratiwi, Agnes Bhakti, Hermawati Setiyaningsih, Maarten Olivier Kok, Trynke Hoekstra, Ali Ghufron Mukti and Elizabeth Pisani. 2021. 'Is Indonesia achieving universal health coverage? Secondary analysis of national data on insurance coverage, health spending and service availability'. *BMJ Open* 11(10): e050565. doi.org/10.1136/bmjopen-2021-050565

Putranto, Terawan Agus. 2019. 'Sambutan Menteri Kesehatan pada Upacara Hari Kesehatan Nasional 2019' [Message from the Minister of Health at the 2019 National Health Day Ceremony]. Indonesian Government Ministry of Health.

Rosser, Andrew, Ian Wilson and Priyambudi Sulistiyanto. 2011. *Leaders, Elites and Coalitions: The Politics of Free Public Services in Decentralised Indonesia*. Developmental Research Program Policy Paper No. 16. https://researchrepository.murdoch.edu.au/id/eprint/39744/

Tirtokoesnadi. 2020. 'Industri farmasi perlu perhatian BPJSK, Kemenkes, BPOM, Kemenkeu untuk menghadapi saat Covid-19/virus corona mewabah dan perkembangan industri farmasi kedepan' [BPJS Kesehatan, the Ministry of Health, the National Medicine Regulator and the Ministry of Finance should support the pharmaceutical industry during the COVID-19 pandemic and to assure the future development of the industry]. GP Farmasi.

Yuniarti, Endang, Yayi Suryo Prabandari, Erna Kristin and Sri Suryawati. 2019. 'Rationing for medicines by health care providers in Indonesia National Health Insurance system at hospital setting: A qualitative study'. *Journal of Pharmaceutical Policy and Practice* 12(1): 7. doi.org/10.1186/s40545-019-0170-5

PART 2

Health for all: Lessons and strategies

7 Navigating access to health care in Indonesia: A sociostructural analysis

I Nyoman Sutarsa

Ensuring timely access to quality health services is a basic human right. All people, regardless of their social location, race, economic circumstances, cultural background, sexual orientation or gender, should have equitable access to essential health services (WHO 2015a). From a government perspective, safeguarding responsive and appropriate access to essential health services is one of the key objectives of health systems (WHO 2000, 2007). In most instances, people interact with health systems as patients who require expert opinion and treatments about their health concerns. People's access to such services is influenced by at least three key dimensions of access: availability, affordability and acceptability (WHO 2015b). Availability refers to the physical presence and reach of the health facilities, workforce and services, whereas affordability refers to the ability of patients or communities more broadly to pay for the health services (ibid.). Acceptability deals with the sociocultural components of health services to ensure the delivery of quality, appropriate, timely and responsive health services (ibid.).

Inequitable access to health care is a recurring health system challenge in Indonesia, given the country's demographic, geographic, economic, sociocultural and political characteristics. The emergence of the COVID-19 pandemic in March 2020 has amplified existing access and health inequities within communities and between different population groups across Indonesia. As observed in other countries, the pandemic has led to disproportionate consequences, both mortality and morbidity, among socially and economically disadvantaged populations (Bambra et al. 2020; Dorn et al. 2020). The inequitable access to health care during the pandemic is exacerbated further by the interconnected systemic risks such as inequities in wealth, lack of social protection, unfair employment structure, food insecurity, and maldistribution of health infrastructure and resources (Bambra et al. 2020). For instance, existing government priorities and decisions embedded in sociopolitical infrastructure and economic forces have allowed the pandemic to discriminate against marginalised groups.

Ensuring access to affordable and comprehensive health services, therefore, requires interventions beyond the individual level to include these interrelated structural and political determinants of health. Designing new institutions and mechanisms to address the structural causes of access inequities requires critical examination of how problems and their solutions are framed. Inequitable access to health services must be dissected from multiple lenses: human rights, gender, sociocultural processes, political economy and health systems. Addressing access inequities to health care mandates different framing of the problems, moving away from individual level to sociostructural analysis.

This chapter explores the interconnected systemic risks or structural causes of access inequities, which are more visible during the COVID-19 pandemic. I draw on two case studies of transgender people living in Denpasar City and Jembrana district in navigating access to HIV services. These case studies explore the inequitable access to essential HIV-related services, from HIV testing to early treatment and social support, experienced by transgender people living in priority versus non-priority districts for HIV prevention and treatment in Bali Province. Through these case studies, this chapter discusses the intersection of various systems of oppression influencing people's access to health services and health outcomes. I argue the importance of the intersectionality approach to explain structural causes of access and health inequities, and the imperative of intersectional policy analysis in formulating solutions to promote social justice and health equity in Indonesia. Insights from these two case studies, along with the fundamentals of the intersectionality approach to unpack the notion of health inequities, are timely given that these intersections of vulnerabilities have been amplified by the COVID-19 pandemic.

COVID-19 pandemic: Exposing interconnected risks affecting people's access to health services

Many national initiatives exist to promote health equities in Indonesia, including the national health insurance scheme (Jaminan Kesehatan Nasional, JKN), which aims to address inequities in access to health services and outcomes among various segments of the population. Despite this scheme, the multidimensional risk associated with the COVID-19 pandemic has impacted certain population groups more than others. Recent literature from other countries has shown that social factors (e.g. geographical location, socioeconomic status, employment structure and barriers in accessing health services) (Aldridge et al. 2020; Kirby 2020) play a major contribution in explaining the inequitable effects of the pandemic among marginalised groups. Socially and economically disadvantaged groups find it challenging to effectively engage with health services and adhere to public health directions such as social distancing, self-isolation and practising good hand hygiene, due to their living arrangements and employment structure, a requirement to pay for regular testing on limited incomes, and lack of access to clean water and sanitation.

Similar observations can be made for Indonesia, the third-largest democracy in the world. For example, mortality rates have been particularly high in the elderly population, who make up the largest proportion of COVID-19 deaths. Of 135,861 deaths in Indonesia until 4 September 2021, the majority were among people aged more than 60 years (MoH 2021). This figure is consistent with global data. The presence of comorbidities in the elderly population has been attributed as the key factor leading to higher mortality rates among older people. The burden of chronic conditions including hypertension, pulmonary-related diseases, diabetes and cardiovascular risk is higher among those aged more than 60 years. However, studies have shown that after adjusting for comorbidities, various sociostructural issues emerge as key determining factors of higher mortality rates, including geographical location, poorer access to health services and socioeconomic status.

Similarly, people living in rural and geographically isolated areas across Indonesia will likely experience difficulties in accessing COVID-19-related services including vaccination, treatment or access to hospital. Geographical location is not just a physical description of an area for the purpose of public service, but includes gradients that separate people by different physical environments, social capital, cohesion and fragmentation, distribution of health facilities and resources, and the nature of health service delivery models. Rural areas across Indonesia, especially the eastern region of Indonesia, are relatively more deprived than urban settings in terms of income, employment, education, skills and training opportunities, access to health care, housing and living arrangements. Studies from other countries have found that morbidity and mortality rates due to the COVID-19 pandemic in the least-deprived areas were less than half of those in the most-deprived areas (Mishra et al. 2021). Rural populations in Indonesia face multiple challenges when dealing with the pandemic, for example, an ageing rural population, a higher proportion of chronic conditions, and poorer access to health services due to limited availability of health providers and maldistribution of health resources, making it more difficult for COVID patients to access appropriate, quality care in a timely manner.

There is also a close link between socioeconomic location and access to health services, and this link has been particularly prominent during the COVID-19 pandemic. It has been accepted globally that inequities in health are caused by many social determinants such as income, housing, education, employment and working conditions, and built environment. Global data reveal that mortality rates and hospitalisations due to COVID-19 are higher within those who are socially and economically disadvantaged (Muñoz-Price et al. 2020). These populations will likely continue working during the peaks of the pandemic and are more likely to live in overcrowded housing. Additionally, they tend to bear a higher burden of comorbidities, including chronic obstructive pulmonary disease, diabetes or other chronic conditions leading to a higher proportion of deaths (ibid.). In many circumstances, working from home is not feasible for these individuals given their employment structure, leading to increased exposure to the virus and a worsening overall prognosis of infection. This is also the case for more than 70 million informal workers in Indonesia (BPS 2019), who have been disproportionately affected by the COVID-19 pandemic and its control measures, especially self-isolation and social movement restrictions. The pandemic continues to have many negative implications on health outcomes that unfortunately are more visible among vulnerable groups of society. Hard public health measures of lockdown and self-isolation enacted by governments have put an extra strain on the most economically and socially marginalised groups in society. In turn, this can exacerbate the poor access to health services and health inequities for the underprivileged members of our society.

It is imperative to fully comprehend the root causes of access and health inequities if we are to take action to eliminate them. The COVID-19 pandemic has shown the significance of the consequences faced by those from disadvantaged communities and highlighted the predicament they face in the intersections of the pandemic and poverty. It exposes the longstanding structural causes of access and health inequities: precarious working conditions and employment structure, inequitable distribution of income and wealth, growing economic disparities, living arrangements, and social isolation and fragmentation. These systemic risks are interrelated with class, gender, education and other oppression systems that, during the pandemic, have amplified existing social vulnerabilities in society.

An intersectionality approach allows exploration of these complex interactions between systemic risks and multiple systems of oppression in explaining root causes of health inequities. Crenshaw (1991) uses intersectionality to describe the ways in which race and gender interact in shaping lived experiences of African American women related to employment opportunities. Intersections between sexism and racism converged in their daily experiences, and cannot be fully understood from a race or gender lens alone. Furthermore, intersectionality provides critical value to the analysis of multifaceted structural determinants that produce and sustain health and access inequities (Kapilashrami et al. 2015; Larson et al. 2016). Intersectionality focuses on the relationships and interactions between multiple factors and across multiple levels of society, to determine how health is shaped and distributed (Kapilashrami and Hankivsky 2018).

The pandemic presents as a window of opportunity to transform our collective understanding about access and health inequities. It allows examination of structural factors associated with health inequities and people's access to health services. It promotes a new way of framing the notion of access inequities from a structural perspective, highlighting that differences in access to health services are contributed by inequitable distribution of wealth, income and power, unsafe working environments and employment structure, and inequitable distribution of health facilities and resources. In other words, the pandemic reveals that people's access to health services is not random, but a product of multiple oppressions and privileges operating simultaneously at individual and community levels.

Structural causes of access inequities

The Commission on Social Determinants of Health maintains that access and health inequities are primarily caused by inequitable distribution of power, money and resources (CSDH 2008). The emergence of the COVID-19 pandemic has illustrated the 'toxic combination' of unfair economies and unjust social policies along with bad politics that promote social and health inequities (ibid.). Understanding what the future of a post-COVID-19 society could look like mandates a critical examination of structural determinants that drive access and health inequities among marginalised groups who live in the intersections of these systemic oppression systems.

Inequitable access to health services is a major determinant of lower health outcomes (Ottersen et al. 2014), including late diagnosis, high morbidity and even premature and preventable death. These effects are inequitably distributed and more pervasive among the poor and socially marginalised groups. To contextualise how access inequities affect the everyday life of people in Indonesia, I now turn my discussion to the lived experiences[1] of access inequities on the ground. As a point of departure, I outline the premature death of a male-to-female transgender person and place this narrative within the broader contexts of patriarchy, religious belief, risk population and health governance. These four perspectives co-create social exclusion and enhance structural and institutional barriers to accessing health services for socially marginalised groups.

Life from the margin: Asana and Vivi lived experiences

'Asana' was a 26-year-old transgender person from a small village in Jembrana district, one of the non-priority districts for HIV prevention and treatment in Bali Province due to the low prevalence of HIV and AIDS. She was a cheerful person, funny and often very loud. She was comfortable with her choice to live as a transgender person, although many people pitied her for her choice and decision. She told me that her family inherently disagreed with her choice, but they remained very supportive, especially her mother. A transgender person occupies an uneasy position in Balinese society, especially in a small village where Asana spent most of her life. Balinese society follows a patriarchal structure where men gain more privileges than women, for example, the line of family and inheritance. Coming from this perspective, her father and many people around her had blamed her for her choice. She was socially punished because she did not conform to societal expectations. She was perceived as deviant and socially sick for transferring her gender role from man to woman, and for some people this act is simply assumed to be amoral and a sin.

On 13 October 2016, Asana was admitted to the district hospital due to shortness of breath, and lung tuberculosis was suspected. As per hospital protocol, all suspected tuberculosis patients are tested for HIV. Asana was sent to the voluntary counselling and testing service, where rapid HIV testing was performed and came back positive. This information spread fast—most staff members at the health office and health providers at the Jembrana community health centre were informed about her HIV status. Health officials from the district health office insisted on performing contact tracing by obtaining sexual history information directly from Asana. From that day forward, Asana was no longer entitled to privacy. She was required to reveal her private life to bureaucratic entities because

---

1 These lived experiences were based in Bali Province during my fieldwork in 2017–2018, and were part of my PhD research.

she was perceived as a threat to the community. She became an object of surveillance, not only of public health but also moral surveillance. What is intriguing is that despite the potential public health threat from tuberculosis transmission, health officials were mainly concerned about the HIV transmission. The way health officials discussed what had happened to Asana represented their moral position towards transgender people and people living with HIV.

Asana encountered stigma and discrimination related to her HIV status and her gender non-conforming identity. Stigma and discrimination have been identified by many researchers as key barriers to accessing health services, leading to late diagnosis, delayed care-seeking, reduced adherence, increased severity and even premature death (Ford et al. 2004; Harapan et al. 2013; Kinsler et al. 2007; Mahajan et al. 2008). The lack of support from families or communities and the unavailability of peer support groups for Asana led to a lack of social support for care-seeking, prevention and treatment. This discrimination did not operate in silos but interacted in complex ways to create disparities and social inequities. At the time of my fieldwork in 2017, the outreach program for key population groups in Jembrana district received limited funding from the health office.

These fragments illustrate the intricate relationships between personal and societal values on morality and the notion of risk embedded in public health discourse. The rhetoric of moral pathology embedded in socioreligious belief and risk discourse have influenced political decisions around the allocation of health resources, target populations, program priorities, program implementation and simply which groups of people are allowed to be left behind. These two powerful structures—moral pathology and risk discourse—cohere in the exercise of control by bureaucrats over political and economic decisions, and constrain some people in exercising their choice, including Asana.

Asana's diagnosis had come too late. Her immune system and her physical condition were too weak to initiate antiretroviral treatment (ART), and she was never put on ART. She had side effects from her tuberculosis medications and could not continue them. A few months after her diagnosis, Asana died from respiratory failure due to suspected widespread (miliary) tuberculosis. If she had been living in Denpasar City where more support systems are available for transgender people, she would probably have had a better chance of being diagnosed earlier and could have started treatment sooner. The limited availability of outreach programs contributed to her late diagnosis. But also, her late diagnosis was a product of social neglect from health bureaucrats due to their decisions at political and economic levels.

Asana's premature and preventable death highlights how inequities in service availability between Denpasar City and Jembrana district affect access and use of HIV-related services among transgender people. There were no tailored programs or peer support programs that could help Asana navigate the complex HIV and AIDS care and service provision. She did not benefit from the implementation of ongoing support from external donors and local non-government organisations (NGOs), nor from political commitment of the provincial health office to provide comprehensive HIV services in the district.

To contrast the experience of Asana, Vivi is a 32-year-old male-to-female transgender person working as a project officer at a local NGO that provides HIV-related outreach and peer support for transgender people in Denpasar City and Badung district. Unfortunately, her NGO does not cover Jembrana district where Asana lived and died. Prior to her current role, Vivi worked as an outreach worker employed by a local NGO with funding from the Global Fund. As part of the HIV emergency response, twelve local NGOs have been established since the 1990s. Residing and working in Denpasar City, one of the priority districts for HIV prevention and treatment in Bali Province, Vivi has the privilege to be in regular contact with extensive social support groups and readily available health services including free HIV testing, free sexually transmissible infection (STI) services, and treatment for HIV and opportunistic infections. Since 2012, two transgender-and-gay-friendly health centres were established in Denpasar City to promote better linkages to early diagnosis and care. Vivi is now the coordinator of this initiative whose main task is inviting transgender people to undertake HIV and STI testing at the designated health centres.

Vivi contracted the virus seven years ago, and is now on regular HIV treatment. While still experiencing gender-based oppression, Vivi is located in Denpasar City with joined-up HIV-related services and social support granting her access to services she needs. Various HIV-related programs have been conducted in Denpasar City with funding from international NGOs, the HIV Cooperation Program for Indonesia, and the Global Fund. A strong emphasis on community-based HIV programs in Denpasar City has opened up economic opportunities for key population groups, including for transgender people, in securing various stable jobs (e.g. paid outreach worker, HIV counsellor, project officer). Availability of local NGOs in Denpasar City targeting multiple key population groups has resulted in reduced stigma against people living with HIV and AIDS. Similarly, better linkages between community-based programs, local NGOs and health services have created a safer environment for key population groups to access HIV-related health services that cater to their needs. Unfortunately, Asana and other transgender people who live in Jembrana district have no access to such privileges. Different types of HIV-related services are available in Denpasar City and Jembrana district, and they are disproportionately distributed. The lived experience of Asana in Jembrana district resembles stories of many individuals globally. Her suffering is indeed a result of processes involving various oppression systems and power configurations.

Asana's experience would have been completely different had she lived in Denpasar City. As a male-to-female transgender person in Jembrana district, she did not benefit from the joined-up service provision that is available in Denpasar City. Since the early days of the HIV epidemic, Denpasar City has been a priority area for HIV and AIDS programs, including community-based interventions for transgender people. In contrast to Jembrana district, many local NGOs were created in Denpasar City following the influx of bilateral and multilateral funding to Bali Province.

Ongoing support from donor agencies, higher fiscal capacity and stronger political commitment from local governments are several factors that facilitate better availability, service mix and readiness in Denpasar City. Decentralisation of HIV services to the district level in Indonesia means that districts with higher fiscal capacity, such as Denpasar City, along with stronger political commitment of local government and ongoing support from external donors, are better equipped to provide appropriate and timely services. By contrast, districts with low fiscal capacity such as Jembrana district have limited capacity to provide comprehensive HIV services. Prioritisation of donor interventions to high-prevalence districts has also contributed to inequitable service availability and readiness between priority and non-priority districts across Bali Province.

Access to health services can be partially explained through the lens of service availability. However, the real measure for access to health services is in the actual utilisation of services (Ensor and Cooper 2004; Gulliford et al. 2002). As can be observed from the lived experience of Asana, access to health services is also influenced by personal, financial, organisational, institutional and structural barriers to service utilisation (Coetzee et al. 2011; Ensor and Cooper 2004; Kagee et al. 2011). These barriers prevent service utilisation, especially for the economically disadvantaged and socially marginalised groups including transgender people within patriarchal society. This case study reveals that access inequities to essential health services are not random, but rather a systemic process stemming from political negotiations involving personal and societal values, political power and institutional arrangements. Locating comprehensive HIV services within priority districts may save more lives than placing those services in non-priority districts, and this decision is economically defensible. However, in doing so, it denies many people a fair chance at a significant benefit, and can lead to premature and preventable deaths. Control over decisions at political and economic levels by some influential actors have resulted in constraining exercise of choice at individual and community levels.

Analysis of social and structural determinants of access

A number of frameworks can be applied to explain why and how Asana was excluded, as well as the best scenario to move forward to redress these access inequities: for example, gender and sex-based analyses (Johnson et al. 2009), or conducting health equity impact assessments (Povall et al. 2013) to advance understanding of the different impacts of health system interventions in promoting inclusive and socially just health outcomes. While these frameworks allow identification of those who are benefiting the most and those who are excluded from the interventions, these frameworks fail to consider how and why different power structures shape and influence the operation of health systems, access to health care and use of health services.

Through comparing the experiences of Asana and Vivi in navigating health care in two different places and spatial contexts, it becomes apparent that transgender people do not fall into a single category but rather are complexly intertwined between class, social networks, economic structure, job stability, social norms and health care systems. There are huge differentials of privilege and oppression that affect their access to health services. Barriers to access to quality and appropriate health services are the direct results of complex factors including geographical location, access to economic opportunities and social networks. From Vivi and Asana's narratives, it can be argued that some transgender people experience greater stresses or burdens resulting from their social locations and existing power structures.

To move forward in addressing access inequities, I argue the urgent need to recognise multiple oppression systems and privileges at various levels. Access inequities are shaped by different factors and social dynamics operating simultaneously, where people can experience privilege and oppression at the same time depending on specific contexts. Actions to redress access and health inequities must be reoriented to reflect this intersectionality that links individual lived experiences and broader structural factors in order to understand how power relations are configured.

Returning to the experiences of Asana and Vivi, while still experiencing gender-based oppression, Vivi is situated in relatively privileged social, political, geographical and economic locations: the availability of various transgender-friendly health care facilities in Denpasar City; ongoing support from donor agencies and local NGOs creating political commitment from local government; readily available health services such as HIV testing, STI services and HIV treatment; extensive social networks and peer support groups; and access to economic opportunities and stable employment. These circumstances have allowed Vivi to be in regular contact with health services that cater to her needs. Asana's narrative is the opposite—the story of multiple and interconnected oppression from family, society, health officials and bureaucrats, resulting in her late diagnosis and premature death. By connecting the micro analysis of lived experiences and macro structural and political determinants, this analysis is able to disrupt the common belief that transgender people are a homogenous entity. They are in fact a diverse group with different needs, risks and predisposed variables.

Representing the whole population as rational beings and assuming that transgender people have similar needs and characteristics as the general population leads to the misrecognition of unique health needs and structural oppression experienced by transgender people. Similarly, treating the whole transgender population as a single group is insufficient because it ignores the intragroup diversity that often provides significant lessons for policy formulation, program design, service delivery models and policy implementation.

Various studies have identified intricate connections between access to health care, social factors, structural determinants and political determinants (Chapman and Berggren 2005; CSDH 2008; López and Gadsden 2016; Ottersen et al. 2014). My research corroborates these findings, indicating the need to disentangle these intersecting systemic risks to effectively redress access and health inequities. By applying an intersectional analysis, connections between individual attributes, institutional arrangements and structural determinants in a given sociohistorical context can be explicated. Such insights are important in any attempt to address social inequity and to promote social justice. An intersectional analysis provides practical benefits to health system processes in, for example, carefully designing the target population, recognising which populations should be protected by public health systems, or identifying what interventions should be promoted. It can also guide meaningful impact monitoring and evaluation of social policies and programs on different subpopulations, from the most disadvantaged through to the most privileged groups.

Addressing access and health inequities: An intersectionality approach

There are three broad areas where an intersectional analysis can shape equity-oriented health systems. First, intersectional analysis provides deep insights into the underlying causes of access inequities experienced by marginalised groups, whose lives are at the intersections of various systemic oppression systems. Reflecting on the lived experiences of Vivi and Asana, for example, though they may have suffered from the same disease and gender oppression, they had very different levels of resources at their disposal. Variations in the settings in which they lived, their access to social networks, their access to economic opportunities, interventions from donor agencies and the political will of local health bureaucrats all determined their ability to exercise choice at the individual level. Exposing the ways in which these complex intersections continue to shape access and health inequities within and between groups will guide the processes of developing more equitable health care for those in dire circumstances.

Second, the new framing of the policy problem will shift the primary focus of health system interventions. Reflecting on Asana's limited access to HIV care in Jembrana district, improving the availability of HIV services in primary care settings is insufficient without addressing the existing social structures and barriers, economic opportunities, social networks and institutional arrangements. Biomedical, public health, health care, social and structural interventions should be integrated to adequately and effectively redress inequities in access and health outcomes (Hankivsky et al. 2017).

Third, in providing health services to individuals, the conception of health must be situated within social relations, and locate health within society and communities beyond the individual bodies. Asana's late diagnosis in Jembrana district is a direct result of social neglect and structural violence, and led to her premature death. Drawing from Vivi's narrative and her social capital, improving access to health services requires collective action from individuals who share similar experiences, to demand for social and structural change. It is critical to adopt community-based and participatory approaches when designing health system interventions to ensure that all dimensions of risk, health needs and predisposed variables of marginalised groups are meaningfully taken into consideration.

The lived experience of Asana illustrates the complex nature of access and health inequities. Her late diagnosis and premature death were shaped by interactions between multiple social locations and levels of power, for example, institutions (family, society, governments, regulation and policies) and structures including patriarchy, gender norms and broader neoliberalism through the act of donor prioritisation to pursue efficiency. While the social determinants of health (SDH) framework recognises that access inequities arise from combinations of poor social policies, unfair economic arrangements and bad politics (CSDH 2008), this framework is less critical about competing political priorities, contested political ideologies and competing values underpinning political decisions (Lee 2015). Applying the SDH framework uncritically might conceal the nature of power asymmetries when examining causes of access and health inequities. There is a growing recognition of the role of power asymmetries in shaping health inequities (Ottersen et al. 2014), but also a growing demand to empirically study how power is expressed in health governance (Gore and Parker 2019; Sriram et al. 2018). Returning to the case of Asana in Jembrana district, her class position, gender, the patriarchal society in which she lived, and pervasive moral and religious values all increased the magnitude of social suffering and neglect that she experienced.

By attending to intersectionality in the complexities of access inequities to quality, timely and appropriate health services, we can see why programs and interventions that target the general population through mainstreaming HIV services into community health centres are failing to address the fact that those on the margins miss out. Health bureaucrats assume that predisposed and needs variables are equitably distributed across different groups. In fact, these risks are not evenly distributed. They are shaped by diverse structural and social determinants including gender, class, morality, social norms, religious values, and political and economic forces. Such narrow assumptions can conceal differentiated risks resulting from the unique social position and conditions of marginalised groups. For HIV services to be accessible by transgender people, those services must attend to the interconnected structural determinants that influence people's access to adequate economic opportunities, appropriate health and social care, and quality and friendly health services.

Asana's voice in Jembrana district gains no resonance from the health bureaucrats who have access to political power. In Denpasar City, by contrast, local NGOs supported by donor agencies (despite their economic interests) have effectively advocated for tailored programs for specific population groups—for example, by integrating outreach workers and peer support groups into health centres, leading to better access to timely and appropriate health services for marginalised groups. The strengths of shared experiences of many transgender people facilitated by the work of local NGOs and donor agencies has been a source of social capital that is beneficial to navigating access to health services. What we can observe from Asana's story is how the intersections of social, political and other structural systems work to exclude those who are different. The notion of risk and moral governance conflated in Asana's lived experience, creating structural and institutional barriers to access the health services she needed.

Drawing from the intersectionality perspective, several observations can be made by looking at Asana's experience. First, her social locations at the intersection of patriarchy structure, gender norms and risk group discourse underpinned by moral pathology rhetoric led to her exclusion and marginalisation from the public health system. These structural factors acted directly as structural determinants of health for Asana. Second, the exercise of control by health bureaucrats on the basis of risk group, moral pathology and socioreligious belief has justified the notion of horizontal equity as the legitimate goal of the public health system. This political decision has led to disregard for the vertical inequity experienced by socially marginalised individuals, including transgender people. Third, transgender people through the risk group discourse and moral pathology rhetoric are considered to be a social danger, socially sick and a deviant group. They become the subject of surveillance, not only public health and behaviour but also moral surveillance. They are constructed as an expendable population.

Taken together, these intersections of systemic risks have emerged as another source of disempowerment and have generated social, structural and institutional barriers to access quality, timely and appropriate health services for the marginalised population. To effectively address the needs of marginalised people in health systems, we cannot afford to address only the availability of services, but also need to confront the multilayered forms of oppression—including stigma, discrimination, social exclusion and job insecurity as a direct result of gender and class oppression—that often converge in the lives of marginalised groups. As the systems of gender norms under patriarchy, class, moral governance and risk group discourse converge, intervention strategies to improve equity of access must take into account different needs, risks and predisposed variables. An intersectional analysis can enhance our understanding of not only who is left behind, but also how and why. The analysis better reflects the dynamic nature of people's experiences, and their interactions with social contexts and systemic oppression systems. These insights are essential to charting new approaches to redress access inequities at various levels. Intersectionality promotes an understanding about access and health inequities by making visible the interconnected structures of power that produce social vulnerabilities. Intersectionality promotes an understanding of the dynamic nature of disadvantage and social neglect that permeates health care systems and affects people's lives and access to health services. Intersectionality also considers the interactions of various social locations and power structures that underpin them at multiple levels.

The notion of intersectionality can be used to guide the best policy options for marginalised people. An intersection analysis has transformational aims, seeking to give voice to those most excluded (Hankivsky 2012) by reorienting power relations to sustain more responsive and equitable health systems. It is grounded in a contextual analysis that probes beneath a single power mechanism to consider a range of power structures in order to better understand who is excluded and by what mechanisms they are excluded (Hankivsky and Christoffersen 2008). An intersectional analysis can guide actions towards eliminating access and health inequities by interrogating the intersections between different social categories and revealing the dynamics of power structures.

Conclusion

The risk group narrative in HIV discourse in Indonesia promoted by public health institutions frames key population groups as 'social danger' and 'the others'. These constructions have effectively enhanced stigma and discrimination experienced by key population groups, including the transgender population as illustrated in this chapter, and has created structural barriers for key population groups to access HIV care. In patriarchal and cultural-religious society like Bali Province, the discourse of good citizens has governed how the society is organised based on certain moral expectations. By aligning risk group discourse and the good citizen narratives, both rooted in a good/bad moral rhetoric, health bureaucrats have made decisions about resource allocation, target populations and program implementation that disqualify socially marginalised people from accessing health services. Reinforcing the discourse of risk groups perpetuates the assumption that HIV is experienced in homogenous ways within key population groups. This ignores the fact that risk groups are differently affected by risk environments rooted in institutional and structural determinants of health, and their capacity to access HIV care or navigate health care more broadly is impeded by the structural factors. These factors have converged in shaping lived experiences of access and health inequities. This chapter argues that without deep reflexivity to situate access and health inequities within proximal and systemic risks, policy problems and the interventions will be framed in a reductionist manner leading to inadequate and fragmented actions. Applying an intersectional analysis allows better reflection on the different experiences of populations and in turn improves ways to formulate health and policy problems and solutions.

Inequitable access to essential health services is not random, but rather a systemic process mediated by institutional arrangements, sociopolitical determinants of health and the ways society is organised. With the emergence of the COVID-19 pandemic, the interconnected systemic risks affecting people's access to health care—inequities in wealth, lack of social protection, unfair employment structures, food insecurity, financial crises, health infrastructure and governance, and sociocultural processes—are becoming more visible than before. Ensuring access to affordable and comprehensive health services, therefore, requires interventions beyond the individual level to include these interrelated structural and political determinants of health. Designing new institutions and mechanisms to address the structural causes of access inequities requires critical examination of how problems and their solutions are framed. Inequitable access to health services must be dissected from multiple lenses: human rights, gender, sociocultural processes, political economy and health systems. With clear articulation from diverse perspectives, health leaders are more likely to make better decisions for promoting universal access to health services and the wellbeing of the population. The pandemic presents an opportunity for Indonesia, as a collective identity, to formulate transformation strategies that promote social justice, protection and accountability.

References

Aldridge, Robert W., Dan Lewer, Srinivasa V. Katikireddi, Rohini Mathur, Neha Pathak, et al. 2020. 'Black, Asian and minority ethnic groups in England are at increased risk of death from COVID-19: Indirect standardisation of NHS mortality data'. *Wellcome Open Research* 5(88). doi.org/10.12688/wellcomeopenres.15922.2

Bambra, Clare, Ryan Riordan, John Ford and Fiona Matthews. 2020. 'The COVID-19 pandemic and health inequalities'. *Journal of Epidemiology and Community Health* 74(11): 964–68. doi.org/10.1136/jech-2020-214401

BPS (Badan Pusat Statistik, Statistics Indonesia). 2019. *Sektor Informal Mendominasi Pekerjaan di Indonesia 2015–2019* [Informal Sector Dominates Employment in Indonesia 2015–2019]. https://databoks.katadata.co.id/datapublish/2019/10/21/sektor-informal-mendominasi-pekerjaan-di-indonesia-2015-2019

Chapman, Rachel R. and Jean R. Berggren. 2005. 'Radical contextualization: Contributions to an anthropology of racial/ethnic health disparities'. *Health: An Interdisciplinary Journal for the Social Study of Health, Illness and Medicine* 9(2): 145–67. doi.org/10.1177/1363459305050583

Coetzee, Bronwyne, Ashraf Kagee and Nadia Vermeulen. 2011. 'Structural barriers to adherence to antiretroviral therapy in a resource-constrained setting: The perspectives of health care providers'. *AIDS Care* 23(2): 146–51. doi.org/10.1080/09540121.2010.498874

Crenshaw, Kimberle. 1991. 'Mapping the margins: Intersectionality, identity politics, and violence against women of colour'. *Stanford Law Review* 43(6): 1241–99. doi.org/10.2307/1229039

CSDH (Commission on Social Determinants of Health). 2008. *Closing the Gap in a Generation: Health Equity through Action on the Social Determinants of Health*. Geneva: World Health Organization.

Dorn, Aaron van, Rebecca E. Cooney and Miriam L. Sabin. 2020. 'COVID-19 exacerbating inequalities in the US'. *Lancet* 395(10232): 1243–44. doi.org/10.1016/S0140-6736(20)30893-X

Ensor, Tim and Stephanie Cooper. 2004. 'Overcoming barriers to health service access: Influencing the demand side'. *Health Policy and Planning* 19(2): 69–79. doi.org/10.1093/heapol/czh009

Ford, Kathleen, Dewa N. Wirawan, Gusti M. Sumantera, Anak A.S. Sawitri and Mandy Stahre. 2004. 'Voluntary HIV testing, disclosure, and stigma among injection drug users in Bali, Indonesia'. *AIDS Education and Prevention* 16(6): 487–98. doi.org/10.1521/aeap.16.6.487.53789

Gore, Radhika and Richard Parker. 2019. 'Analysing power and politics in health policies and systems'. *Global Public Health* 14(4): 481–88. doi.org/10.1080/17441692.2019.1575446

Gulliford, Martin, Jose Figueroa-Munoz, Myfanwy Morgan, David Hughes, Barry Gibson, et al. 2002. 'What does "access to health care" mean?' *Journal of Health Services Research & Policy* 7(3): 186–88. doi.org/10.1258/135581902760082517

Hankivsky, Olena. 2012. 'Women's health, men's health, and gender and health: Implications of intersectionality'. *Social Science & Medicine* 74(11): 1712–20. doi.org/10.1016/j.socscimed.2011.11.029

Hankivsky, Olena and Ashlee Christoffersen. 2008. 'Intersectionality and the determinants of health: A Canadian perspective'. *Critical Public Health* 18(3): 271–83. doi.org/10.1080/09581590802294296

Hankivsky, Olena, Lesley Doyal, Gillian Einstein, Ursula Kelly, Janet Shim, et al. 2017. 'The odd couple: Using biomedical and intersectional approaches to address health inequities'. *Global Health Action* 10(Suppl.2): 73–86. doi.org/10.1080/16549716.2017.1326686

Harapan, Harapan, Syarifah Feramuhawan, Hendra Kurniawan, Samsul Anwar, et al. 2013. 'HIV-related stigma and discrimination: A study of health care workers in Banda Aceh, Indonesia'. *Medical Journal of Indonesia* 22(1): 22–29. doi.org/10.13181/mji.v22i1.518

Johnson, Joy L., Lorraine Greaves and Robin Repta. 2009. 'Better science with sex and gender: Facilitating the use of a sex and gender-based analysis in health research'. *International Journal for Equity in Health* 8: 14. doi.org/10.1186/1475-9276-8-14

Kagee, A., R.H. Remien, A. Berkman, S. Hoffman, et al. 2011. 'Structural barriers to ART adherence in southern Africa: Challenges and potential ways forward'. *Global Public Health* 6(1): 83–97. doi.org/10.1080/17441691003796387

Kapilashrami, Anuj, Sarah Hill and Nasar Meer. 2015. 'What can health inequalities researchers learn from an intersectionality perspective? Understanding social dynamics with an inter-categorical approach?' *Social Theory & Health* 13(3–4): 288–307. doi.org/10.1057/sth.2015.16

Kapilashrami, Anuj and Olena Hankivsky. 2018. 'Intersectionality and why it matters to global health'. *Lancet* 391(10140): 2589–91. doi.org/10.1016/S0140-6736(18)31431-4

Kinsler, Janni J., Mitchell D. Wong, Jennifer N. Sayles, Cynthia Davis and William E. Cunningham. 2007. 'The effect of perceived stigma from a health care provider on access to care among a low-income HIV-positive population'. *AIDS Patient Care and STDs* 21(8): 584–92. doi.org/10.1089/apc.2006.0202

Kirby, Tony. 2020. 'Evidence mounts on the disproportionate effect of COVID-19 on ethnic minorities'. *Lancet Respiratory Medicine* 8(6): 547–48. doi.org/10.1016/S2213-2600(20)30228-9

Larson, Elizabeth, Asha George, Rosemary Morgan and Tonia Poteat. 2016. '10 best resources on … intersectionality with an emphasis on low- and middle-income countries'. *Health Policy and Planning* 31(8): 964–69. doi.org/10.1093/heapol/czw020

Lee, Kelley. 2015. 'Revealing power in truth: Comment on "Knowledge, moral claims and the exercise of power in global health" '. *International Journal of Health Policy and Management* 4(4): 257–59. doi.org/10.15171/ijhpm.2015.42

López, Nancy and Vivian L. Gadsden. 2016. *Health Inequities, Social Determinants, and Intersectionality*. Washington, DC: National Academy of Medicine. doi.org/10.31478/201612a

Mahajan, Anish P., Jennifer N. Sayles, Vishal A. Patel, Robert H. Remien, Sharif Sawires, et al. 2008. 'Stigma in the HIV/AIDS epidemic: A review of the literature and recommendations for the way forward'. *AIDS* 22(Suppl.2): S67–79. doi.org/10.1097/01.aids.0000327438.13291.62

Mishra, Vaibhav, Golnoush Seyedzenouzi, Ahmad Almohtadi, Tasnim Chowdhury, Arwa Khashkhusha, et al. 2021. 'Health inequalities during COVID-19 and their effects on morbidity and mortality'. *Journal of Healthcare Leadership* 13: 19–26. doi.org/10.2147/JHL.S270175

MoH (Ministry of Health). 2021. Situasi Terkini Perkembangan Coronavirus Disease (COVID-19) di Indonesia [The Latest Situation in the Development of Coronavirus Disease (COVID-19) in Indonesia]. https://covid19.kemkes.go.id/dashboard/covid-19

Muñoz-Price, L. Silvia, Ann B. Nattinger, Frida Rivera, Ryan Hanson, Cameron G. Gmehlin, et al. 2020. 'Racial disparities in incidence and outcomes among patients with COVID-19'. *JAMA Network Open* 3(9): e2021892. doi.org/10.1001/jamanetworkopen.2020.21892

Ottersen, Ole Petter, Jashodhara Dasgupta, Chantal Blouin, Paulo Buss, Virasakdi Chongsuvivatwong, et al. 2014. 'The political origins of health inequity: Prospects for change'. *Lancet* 383(9917): 630–67. doi.org/10.1016/S0140-6736(13)62407-1

Povall, Susan L., Fiona A. Haigh, Debbie Abrahams and Alex Scott-Samuel. 2013. 'Health equity impact assessment'. *Health Promotion International* 29(4): 621–33. doi.org/10.1093/heapro/dat012

Sriram, Veena, Stephanie M. Topp, Marta Schaaf, Arima Mishra, Walter Flores, et al. 2018. '10 best resources on power in health policy and systems in low- and middle-income countries'. *Health Policy and Planning* 33(4): 611–21. doi.org/10.1093/heapol/czy008

WHO (World Health Organization). 2000. *The World Health Report 2000. Health Systems: Improving Performance*. Geneva: WHO.

WHO (World Health Organization). 2007. *Everybody's Business—Strengthening Health Systems to Improve Health Outcomes: WHO's Framework for Action*. Geneva: WHO.

WHO (World Health Organization). 2015a. Anchoring Universal Health Coverage in the Right to Health: What Difference Would It Make? Policy Brief. Geneva: WHO.

WHO (World Health Organization). 2015b. *Service Availability and Readiness Assessment (SARA): An Annual Monitoring System for Service Delivery—Reference Manual*. Geneva: WHO.

8 Impact of COVID-19 on maternal, neonatal and child health programs: A case study for health systems strengthening

Tiara Marthias and Yodi Mahendradhata

The COVID-19 pandemic has been a major unprecedented stress on health systems globally. By 30 September 2021, a total of 233.8 million cases of COVID-19 had been confirmed worldwide (WHO 2021). And with the death toll reaching more than 4.7 million as of September 2021 (ibid.), the pandemic has become the largest outbreak of an infectious disease in recent history. As countries respond to the pandemic, additional burdens of maintaining essential health services have been imposed on their health systems. The escalated demand for COVID-19 testing, contact tracing and isolation of cases, and managing severe cases in hospitals, has overwhelmed health care systems in both high and low- and middle-income countries (LMICs). In effect, the pandemic has redirected the focus and prioritisation of health systems, diverting much of the limited health resources to managing the pandemic.

Indonesia is also facing similar challenges in managing the COVID-19 pandemic while trying to maintain the performance of its health system. While the government has issued various programs and policies to mitigate the COVID-19 pandemic, the number of cases has fluctuated since the first case was confirmed on 1 March 2020. As seen in Figure 8.1, the number of daily new confirmed cases continued to rise from early in the pandemic, with higher caseloads observed following the 2021 new year holiday. While the case numbers declined slightly following the roll-out of the COVID-19 vaccination program in late January 2021 (MoH 2021),

Figure 8.1 Daily new confirmed COVID-19 cases in Indonesia (thousands)

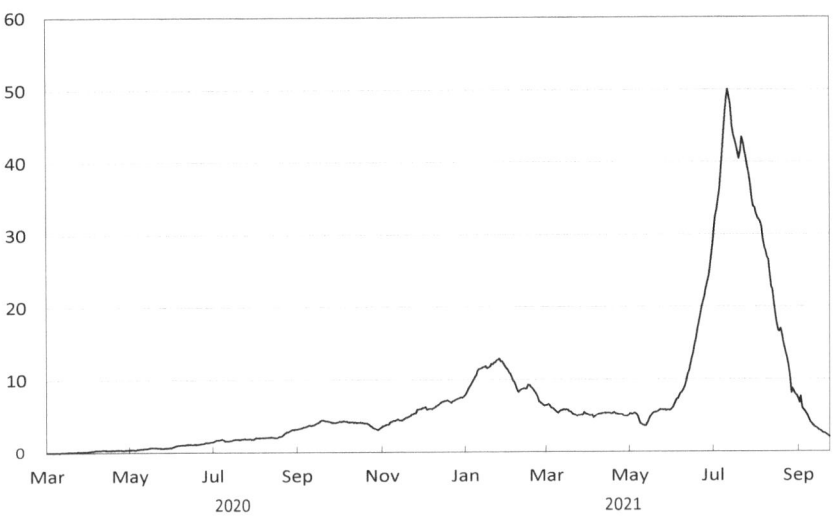

Source: Johns Hopkins University Center for Systems Science and Engineering, https://github.com/CSSEGISandData/COVID-19

Indonesia was severely affected by the Delta variant wave. And in mid-2021, Indonesia became the epicentre of the pandemic with more than 49,000 daily confirmed cases and a 2.6% fatality rate (Wibawa 2021). By the end of September 2021, the cumulative number of confirmed COVID-19 cases in Indonesia exceeded 4.2 million, with 141,000 deaths (WHO 2021).

In Indonesia and other LMICs, pandemic-induced disruptions to routine health care services threaten progress towards equitable health improvement. One health goal is to reduce maternal and child mortality, which is among the most sensitive indicators of development and functioning health systems. Even before the COVID-19 pandemic, Indonesia had a high burden of maternal and child mortality. Indonesia's current maternal mortality ratio is 177 per 100,000 live births, which is one of the highest in the Southeast Asia region (WHO 2020a). The neonatal mortality ratio, at 12.4 per 1,000 live births, is also comparably higher than in neighbouring countries such as Singapore (0.9) and Malaysia (4.6) (UN IGME 2020). Most maternal, neonatal and child health (MNCH) services require regular contact with routine health services. An overburdened health workforce and strained supply chains during the pandemic may impair the coverage of essential MNCH services, negatively affecting the outcomes of women's and children's health.

Previous studies have shown that health shocks, including pandemics, impair a health system's capacity to provide routine services (Abbas et al. 2020; Ly et al. 2016; Masresha et al. 2020; Saso et al. 2020; Shapira et al. 2021). This is due to an overburdened health workforce and strained health supplies. Health care–seeking behaviour may also be reduced due to fear of exposure among potential patients. This was the case during the Africa Ebola outbreak in 2013–2016, where women who believed that hospitals and other health facilities could be the source of infection were 30% less likely to deliver at a health facility (Ly et al. 2016). During the COVID-19 pandemic, lockdown policies have also affected population mobility and the ability to pay for health services due to reduced income. For instance, in a study in Nigeria, Siwatu et al. (2020) found a 79% reduction in household income between April and May 2020 compared with mid-March income levels.

The response to the COVID-19 pandemic has also inadvertently undermined the achievement of existing public health priorities, including MNCH programs. Based on the World Health Organization pulse survey conducted in May–July 2020, 90% of health officials in 105 countries stated some level of disruption to essential health services delivery due to the COVID-19 pandemic. Moreover, LMICs have reported more disruptions in a wide array of services compared with high-income countries. Shortages in health care workers and medical supplies have been cited as contributing factors to such disruptions (Saso et al. 2020). For the Indonesian context, however, there has been limited assessment of the impact of the COVID-19 pandemic on essential health services, including MNCH.

This study assesses the disruption to MNCH services in Indonesia during the COVID-19 pandemic, using routine health data. Understanding the impact of the pandemic on MNCH could also highlight existing health system challenges that have persisted during the pandemic. Our study also discusses how the impact of the pandemic on MNCH services highlights the importance of strengthening the health system to prepare for future major health shocks.

Methods

Data sources

To assess the impact of the COVID-19 pandemic on the use of essential MNCH services, we used routine health data procured from the Indonesian Ministry of Health database, District Health Information Software version 2 (DHIS2). The DHIS2 is designed to serve as an integrated health database that complies with various routine health service data, including reproductive, maternal and child health services. The DHIS2 covers data reporting from all 514 districts in Indonesia, inputted monthly to the system. The DHIS2 also includes a data validation feature, which allows the Ministry of Health to conduct data checks at the point of data input. We utilised DHIS2 data from January 2019 through to June 2021 with thirty data points for MNCH variables.

We also used COVID-19 data from the Our World in Data repository, which publishes key COVID-19 variables. For Indonesia, the COVID-19-related data published in Our World in Data were procured from the official Indonesian government COVID-19 dashboard (https://covid19.go.id/peta-sebaran) by the Johns Hopkins University Center for Systems Science and Engineering (https://github.com/CSSEGISandData/COVID-19). Further, the COVID-19 data were smoothed and presented as a 7-day rolling average. This approach was done to anticipate fluctuations in daily reporting. We included COVID-19 data from March 2020 (first confirmed case) until June 2021, or a total of fifteen data points for the COVID-19 variable.

Data processing

The DHIS2 data posed several challenges. First, information reported by district health offices may be incomplete. For instance, several districts have gaps in their data recording. To mitigate this, we excluded districts (8.9% of the districts) that had incomplete reporting of more than 20% of the data points. Second, data quality and timeliness of reporting varies across districts. Reports from district health offices and facilities are often done by hand and may include some reporting errors. Third, the COVID-19 pandemic may strain the availability of human resources at health facilities and cause reduced completeness and timeliness in reporting routine data. Thus, interpretation of the findings should be made with caution. To limit the threat to the reliability of the routine health data, we performed similar exponential smoothing across all MNCH service variables. The exponential smoothing method is a time-series forecasting used to produce predictions based on weighted averages of past observations while assigning decreasing weights for past observations. The more recent the observation, the higher the associated weight. Similar approaches have been applied to COVID-19-related studies (Seong and Lee 2021; Yonar et al. 2020; see also Holt 2004 and Winters 1960).

Variables and data analysis

The main study outcomes are the trends in selected key MNCH services. For maternal health services, we included (1) antenatal care (ANC) service, which includes the first ANC visit as well as at least four ANC visits; (2) facility delivery, described as all births that occurred at a health facility; and (3) postnatal check. Key variables for neonatal and child health services were (1) neonatal check and (2) complete immunisation for children under 5 years of age. To capture the burden of COVID-19 in Indonesia, we included the confirmed daily cases procured from the Our World in Data repository.

We plotted the trends of key MNCH services against the COVID-19 confirmed cases. Data are presented as a one-month average due to the fluctuations in daily data. The trends in both MNCH variables and COVID-19 confirmed cases show how the coverage of MNCH services may have been affected by the COVID-19 caseload.

We used absolute numbers of MNCH variables as well as confirmed COVID-19 cases and did not calculate the coverage of MNCH services as a function of the number of services divided by the target population (e.g. pregnant women or newborns), for several reasons. First is the unreliable monthly denominators at the district level. For instance, the number of pregnant women is usually unavailable at the district health office due to poor recording and population coverage and, in some cases, the numbers used are extrapolated from census data and the total fertility rate in a given district. This provides an approximation of the total number of pregnant women in one year. The monthly number of pregnant women is then calculated by dividing the estimated yearly number by twelve. If the estimated numbers are used, such crude approximation may mislead the level of services coverage as the number of pregnancies may fluctuate across months.

Second, as opposed to studies in high-income countries where the pandemic is predicted to decrease the fertility rate (or 'baby bust') (Aassve et al. 2021; Swift 2021; Yirka 2021), previous publications have suggested a possible increase in the number of pregnancies in LMICs. For instance, the UNFPA (2020) predicted that around 47 million women in LMICs would not be able to access modern contraceptives, which could result in 7 million unintended pregnancies. The decline in contraceptive coverage was also recorded by the Indonesian National Board of Family Planning (Badan Koordinasi Keluarga Berencana Nasional, BKKBN), which found active users of modern contraceptives decreased from 36 million in March to 26 million in April 2020 (BKKBN 2020). More recently, BKKBN reported an increase of around 300,000 births in January 2021 compared with the

Figure 8.2 Trends in antenatal care and facility delivery, and COVID-19 confirmed cases

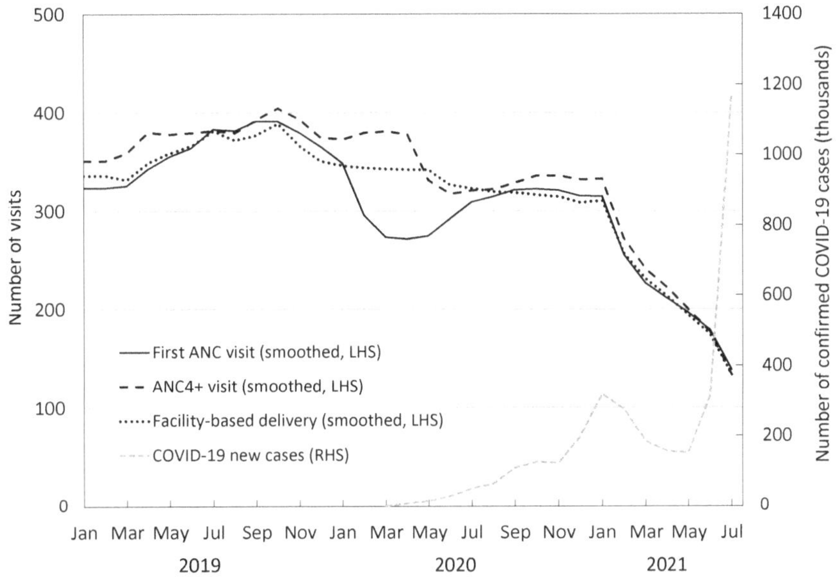

[Figure: Line graph showing First ANC visit (smoothed, LHS), ANC4+ visit (smoothed, LHS), Facility-based delivery (smoothed, LHS), and COVID-19 new cases (RHS) from Jan 2019 to Jul 2021. Left axis: Number of visits (0–500). Right axis: Number of confirmed COVID-19 cases (thousands) (0–1400).]

Source: Data analysed from DHIS2 Indonesia.

same period in 2020 (InfoPublik 2021), which were likely due to additional or unintended pregnancies that started around March–April 2020, or the early period of the pandemic. However, as there are no available routine data or updated census data on the actual numbers of pregnant women during the pandemic in Indonesia, we opted to use the absolute numbers of MNCH services utilisation.

Results

Figure 8.2 presents the trends in ANC first visit and at least four ANC visits (ANC4+) and deliveries at a health facility from January 2019 to June 2021. The COVID-19 data, depicted as one-month rolling confirmed new cases, was available from March 2020 to June 2021. The graph shows that the absolute numbers of ANC and ANC4+ visits and facility deliveries were relatively constant throughout 2019. We observed a decline in ANC services around February 2020, and the number of visits further declined following the first confirmed case of COVID-19 in March 2021. Interestingly, the levels of ANC4+ visits and facility deliveries remained relatively constant during the early period of the pandemic.

Figure 8.3 Trends in postnatal and neonatal care visits, and COVID-19 confirmed cases

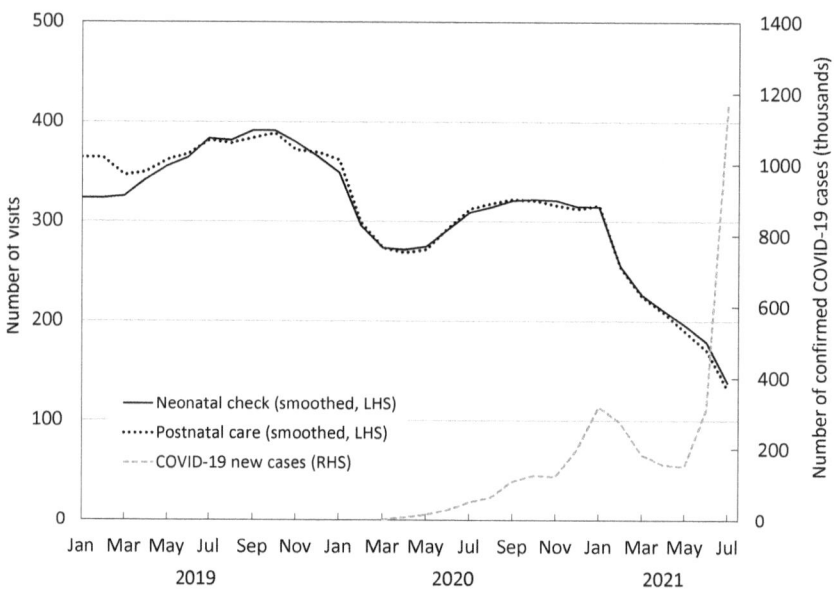

Source: Data analysed from DHIS2 Indonesia.

However, following the first main wave of COVID-19 post end-of-year holiday season, all three selected maternal health services experienced a significant decline. For instance, in December 2020, around 310,000 facility deliveries occurred across Indonesia, and only around 256,000 in February 2021. The absolute number further declined as COVID-19 case numbers increased. By June 2021, the last data point available, all three maternal health services remained in a steady decline.

As seen in Figure 8.3, reductions were observed in the number of postnatal and neonatal care visits around the early period of the pandemic. The number of services somewhat stabilised between June 2020 and January 2021. However, similar to ANC and ANC4+ visits and facility deliveries, the number of services plummeted following the increase in COVID-19 case numbers after the 2021 new year holiday season. Even after the COVID-19 case numbers decreased following the launch of the vaccination program in late January 2021, postnatal and neonatal care visits further decreased and did not recover throughout our last observation in June 2021.

We also analysed trends in child growth monitoring and complete immunisation visits for children aged under 5 years. As seen in Figure 8.4,

Figure 8.4 Trends in child growth monitoring and immunisation visits for children aged under 5 years, and COVID-19 confirmed cases

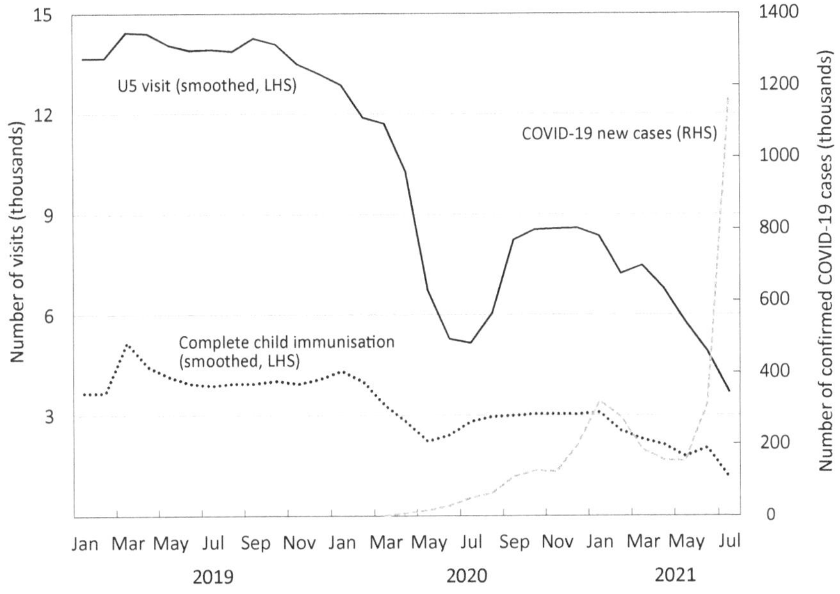

Source: Data analysed from DHIS2 Indonesia.

under-five growth monitoring visits plummeted around April–May 2020 after the first confirmed COVID-19 case in Indonesia. A slight decrease was also observed for complete under-five immunisation numbers. Following this, both child services remained stable until the end of 2020. However, similar to the maternal and neonatal health services, the numbers declined throughout the rest of 2021.

Discussion

Our assessment confirms reports of disruption to essential health services due to the COVID-19 pandemic. All maternal and child health services experienced some levels of decline due to the rising number of COVID-19 cases. The levels of disruption varied across the different types of services. For maternal health services, the absolute number of first ANC visits experienced a more significant decrease than ANC4+ visits or facility delivery. Services that occurred immediately after birth (postnatal care and neonatal visits) were disrupted during the pandemic's early period. And for child health services, the services that were most affected by the pandemic were the under-five growth monitoring visits. We also observed that during the first wave of the pandemic in Indonesia, following the 2021 new year holiday, the numbers for all types of maternal and child health services declined significantly, with no apparent recovery to our final observation in June 2021.

The disruptions to routine maternal and child health services revealed the limited capacity of the health care system to deliver essential health services during prolonged health emergencies. At the community level, a rapid assessment conducted by UNICEF Indonesia in 2020 found that around 76% of village health posts were closed and around 40% of home visits were suspended following the pandemic (UNICEF Indonesia 2020). The rapid assessment also revealed that health workers reported disruptions in several key reproductive, maternal and child health services, including family planning, child immunisation and other routine MNCH services. The suspension of services and closures of community health facilities were due to concerns for the community's safety, mobility restrictions imposed by the central and provincial governments, and health workers' own safety concerns (ibid.).

The pandemic has also strained public health resources at the primary care level, where health workers have been diverted to respond to COVID-19, away from their original main duties. For services that require routine contact with the target population, such as child growth monitoring, this diversion of resources has halted services that are important to address other critical health priorities, such as reducing childhood stunting in Indonesia. A previous study revealed that around 86% of districts that had high stunting prevalence in Indonesia reported significant disruption in child growth monitoring services (Center for Health Policy and Management UGM 2020), which was in line with our results. These disruptions threaten the progress in achieving stunting reduction to 14% in 2024 (BKKBN 2021).

The pandemic also exacerbated existing health system challenges in Indonesia. First is the distribution of human resources for health, depicted by the inadequate physician-to-population ratio and geographical disparities in the distribution of physicians. On average, Indonesia has 0.4 doctors per 1,000 head of population, which is lower than Malaysia (1.5), Thailand (0.8), Vietnam (0.8), the Philippines (0.6) and the average ratio for LMICs (1.2) (WHO 2020b). The availability of nurses and midwives is at 2.4 per 1,000 population, which is similar to the average of LMICs (2.5) but lower than Malaysia (3.5) and the Philippines (4.9). However, the distribution of health personnel within Indonesia is unequal. According to the latest data from the Ministry of Health, 62.5% of medical personnel were located in the Java–Bali region (where 59.1% of the population lives), particularly in large provinces in Java Island such as Jakarta, East Java and Central Java (MoH 2020). However, less densely populated areas including Kalimantan, Sulawesi and eastern Indonesia provinces have fewer health personnel. As seen in Figure 8.5, provinces with the highest ratio of physicians per 100,000 population were Jakarta (207.2), Yogyakarta (128.5) and Bali (121.2). All three provinces are in the Java–Bali region.

While using the ratio of health workers to population is useful for planning for health resources, a high ratio does not necessarily lead to better access to health services. This is particularly the case for Indonesian regions with a large landmass and low population density, which results in limited geographical access to health services. For instance, Papua province has a relatively high doctor to 100,000 population ratio at 32.4. However, its ratio of doctors to 1,000 square kilometres is extremely low at 3.4 compared to more developed provinces such as Jakarta (32,660), Yogyakarta (1,559) and Bali (899). Similarly, its midwives and *puskesmas* ratio to geographical area is one of the lowest in the country. This creates physical barriers in accessing services in provinces like Papua.

The second existing health system challenge is the limited health information system and the quality of health data. As observed from DHIS2 data alone, districts in underdeveloped regions had worse quality data with gaps in timeliness in data reporting. While the COVID-19 pandemic has increased the appreciation of integrated data systems, low reporting of services and health burden may have masked the actual health disparities across Indonesia's regions.

Third, decentralisation of the health system has impacted governance at all levels, including in planning and budgeting for health resources, the actual implementation of health programs, and in the monitoring and evaluation of those programs. The capacity of districts varied, where districts in well-developed regions in Indonesia have the means and technical capability to plan and budget for quality health service delivery. By contrast, districts located in provinces with weaker governance have suffered from inadequate planning and budgeting for health resources (Heywood and Choi 2010), resulting in lower-quality health service delivery.

Finally, Indonesia's expenditure on health has been historically inadequate. In 2018, health expenditure was only 2.8% of Indonesia's gross domestic product (GDP) and 8.5% of general government expenditure (World Bank 2020a). While public health expenditure per capita has increased from US$27 in 2004 to US$112 in 2018, the amount spent for health is significantly lower than in Malaysia ($427), Thailand ($276) or the Philippines ($137) (Hafez 2020; World Bank 2020a, 2020b). The low level of health investment has affected the adequacy and readiness of the

Figure 8.5 Distribution of physicians, 2020

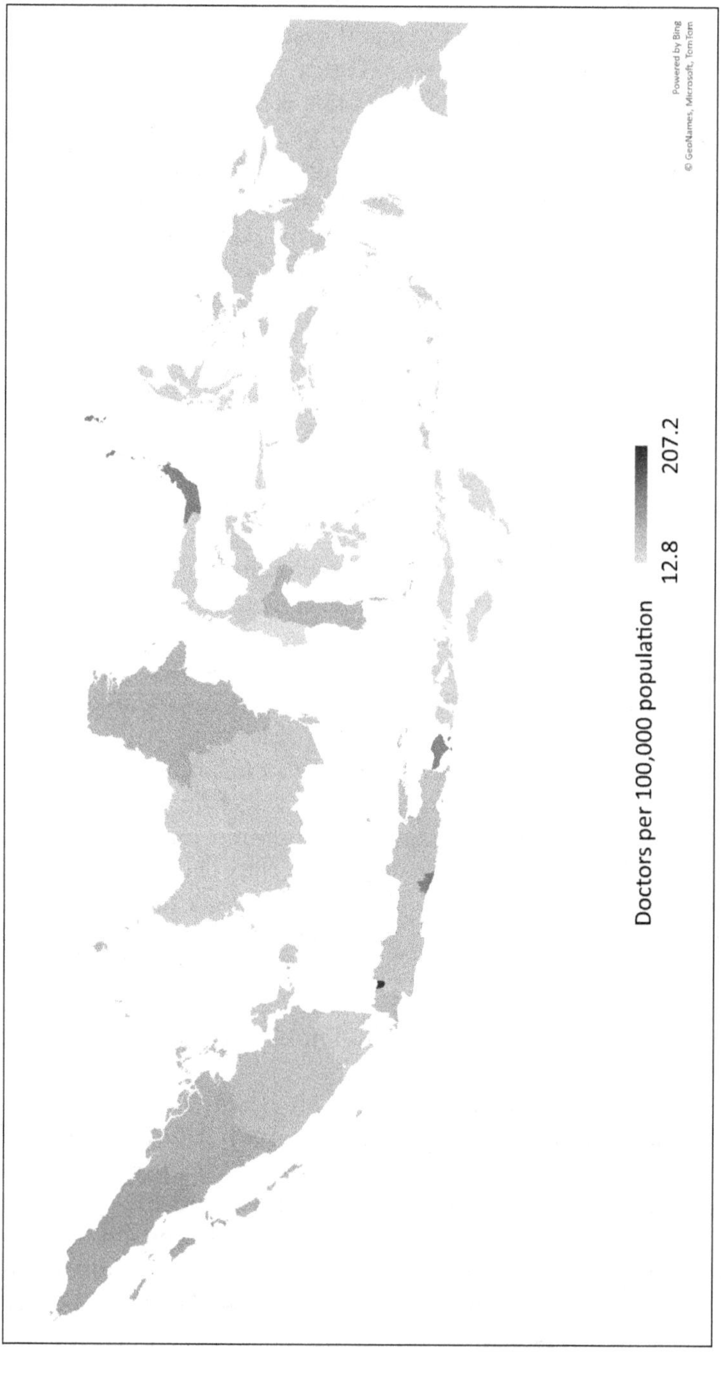

Source: Indonesia Health Profile, 2020; Indonesia Central Bureau of Statistics, 2020.

health care system to provide comprehensive, quality health services and prepare for health shocks such as a pandemic. Thus, increasing health expenditure in Indonesia is a key priority.

The effect of disruptions to essential health services also threatens the progress of other maternal and child health target indicators. A modelling study of the impact of the COVID-19 pandemic on maternal and newborn health in four LMICs, including Indonesia, estimated an additional 31,980 maternal deaths and 395,440 neonatal deaths over a 12-month period (Stein et al. 2020). Robust systems need to be in place to mitigate such adverse impacts. In the long run, Indonesia needs to reassess its health system capacity, identify gaps and build a more resilient health system.

Indonesia and other LMICs could learn from and adopt successful examples of maintaining the coverage of essential maternal and child health services during a large-scale emergency such as a pandemic. For instance, countries could develop context-specific solutions such as the maternity isolation ward that was established during the Ebola epidemic in Sierra Leone (Partners In Health 2020). Another solution is using telemedicine more effectively to ensure the delivery of routine health services (Tolu et al. 2021). Such initiatives have been proven to help ensure mothers and newborns are still able to access routine and emergency care needed.

However, the implementation of telemedicine would require a comprehensive legal basis, which is still lacking in Indonesia. During the COVID-19 pandemic, telemedicine was available only as an out-of-pocket service, mainly accessed by patients with good internet access and those with financial means. The national health insurance scheme, Jaminan Kesehatan Nasional (JKN), has not included telemedicine as a reimbursable service. The Ministry of Health has only recently planned to include telemedicine and home visits to be covered under the public insurance system. Thus, regulatory gaps need to be addressed to advance telemedicine implementation during and beyond the pandemic.

There are several caveats in this study that warrant cautious interpretation of the results. First is the use of routine health data that may pose issues in data quality, including in the completeness and integrity of the data recording and reporting, particularly in Indonesia and other LMICs (Lazuardi et al. 2021; Lemma et al. 2020; Mavimbe et al. 2005). While we have excluded data from districts with incomplete reporting of more than 20% of the data points, data quality issues may remain. The COVID-19 data is also influenced by the performance of tracing and tracking programs during the pandemic as well as the testing capacity that was very low during the early period of the pandemic. Second, the use of absolute numbers of MNCH services may limit the comparability of service coverage before and during the pandemic. However, as explained in the Methods section, there were no available quality data on actual number of pregnancies during the pandemic. Based on the estimation that there are likely additional pregnancies during the pandemic in Indonesia and other LMICs, our calculations might underestimate the true impact of the pandemic on MNCH services coverage. On the other hand, if the actual number of pregnancies during the pandemic is lower compared with the pre-pandemic period, the impact on MNCH services might not be as severe as we estimated.

In conclusion, the government needs to improve health care capacity holistically. Ensuring adequate and equitable distribution of human resources and health supplies still needs to be prioritised and addressed. Revamping financial investment in health, including ensuring sufficient financial protection for vulnerable groups, should also be prioritised. Finally, testing and implementing contextualised health innovations would support an effective pandemic response and create a more resilient health system.

References

Aassve, Arnstein, Nicolò Cavalli, Letizia Mencarini, Samuel Plach and Seth Sanders. 2021. 'Early assessment of the relationship between the COVID-19 pandemic and births in high-income countries'. *Proceedings of the National Academy of Sciences* 118(36): e2105709118. doi.org/10.1073/pnas.2105709118

Abbas, Dina F., Shafiq Mirzazada, Jill Durocher, Shahfaqir Pamiri, Meagan E. Byrne and Beverly Winikoff. 2020. 'Testing a home-based model of care using misoprostol for prevention and treatment of postpartum hemorrhage: Results from a randomized placebo-controlled trial conducted in Badakhshan province, Afghanistan'. *Reproductive Health* 17: 88. doi.org/10.1186/s12978-020-00933-8

BKKBN (Indonesia National Board of Family Planning). 2020. 'Threat of baby boom looms amid COVID-19 pandemonium'. BKKBN, 25 August. www.bkkbn.go.id/detailpost/threat-of-baby-boom-looms-amid-covid-19-pandemonium

BKKBN (Indonesia National Board of Family Planning). 2021. 'Indonesia cegah stunting'. BKKBN, 18 February. www.bkkbn.go.id/detailpost/indonesia-cegah-stunting

Center for Health Policy and Management UGM. 2020. 'E-monev for recovery of nutrition programs from the impact of the COVID-19 pandemic'. Gadjah Mada University, 17 December. https://pkgm.fk.ugm.ac.id/en/2020/12/17/e-monev-for-recovery-of-nutrition-programs-from-the-impact-of-the-covid-19-pandemic/

Hafez, Reem. 2020. 'Indonesia public expenditure review launch: Health'. World Bank. http://pubdocs.worldbank.org/en/384161592968065208/IDPER-Health.pdf

Heywood, Peter and Yoonjoung Choi. 2010. 'Health system performance at the district level in Indonesia after decentralization'. *BMC International Health and Human Rights* 10: 3. doi.org/10.1186/1472-698X-10-3

Holt, Charles C. 2004. 'Forecasting seasonals and trends by exponentially weighted moving averages'. *International Journal of Forecasting* 20(1): 5–10. doi.org/10.1016/j.ijforecast.2003.09.015

InfoPublik 2021. 'BKKBN soroti peningkatan angka kelahiran pada masa pandemi [BKKBN highlights an increase in the birth rate during the pandemic]'. InfoPublik, 23 January. https://infopublik.id/kategori/nusantara/504851/bkkbn-soroti-peningkatan-angka-kelahiran-pada-masa-pandemi

Lazuardi, Lutfan, Guardian Y. Sanjaya, Pungkas B. Ali, Renova G.M. Siahaan, Lia Achmad and Hanifah Wulandari. 2021. 'Interoperability of health digitalization: Case study on use of information technology for maternal and child health services in Indonesia'. *Business Information Systems* 1: 317–27. doi.org/10.52825/bis.v1i.53

Lemma, Seblewengel, Annika Janson, Lars-Åke Persson, Deepthi Wickremasinghe and Carina Källestål. 2020. 'Improving quality and use of routine health information system data in low- and middle-income countries: A scoping review'. *PLOS ONE* 15(10): e0239683. doi.org/10.1371/journal.pone.0239683

Ly, John, Vidiya Sathananthan, Thomas Griffiths, Zahir Kanjee, Avi Kenny, et al. 2016. 'Facility-based delivery during the Ebola virus disease epidemic in rural Liberia: Analysis from a cross-sectional, population-based household survey'. *PLOS Medicine* 13(8): e1002096. doi.org/10.1371/journal.pmed.1002096

Masresha, Balcha G., Richard Luce Jr, Goitom Weldegebriel, Reggis Katsande, Alex Gasasira and Richard Mihigo. 2020. 'The impact of a prolonged Ebola outbreak on measles elimination activities in Guinea, Liberia and Sierra Leone, 2014–2015'. *Pan African Medical Journal* 35(Suppl. 1). doi.org/10.11604/pamj.supp.2020.35.1.19059

Mavimbe, João C., Jørn Braa and Gunnar Bjune. 2005. 'Assessing immunization data quality from routine reports in Mozambique'. *BMC Public Health* 5: 108. doi.org/10.1186/1471-2458-5-108

MoH (Ministry of Health). 2020. *Profil Kesehatan Indonesia Tahun 2019* [Indonesia Health Profile 2019]. Jakarta: MoH. https://pusdatin.kemkes.go.id/resources/download/pusdatin/profil-kesehatan-indonesia/Profil-Kesehatan-indonesia-2019.pdf

MoH (Ministry of Health). 2021. 'Pelaksanaan vaksinasi COVID-19 di Indonesia membutuhkan waktu 15 bulan [Implementation of the COVID-19 vaccination in Indonesia takes 15 months]'. Sehat Negeriku, 3 January. https://sehatnegeriku.kemkes.go.id/baca/umum/20210103/2536122/pelaksanaan-vaksinasi-covid-19-indonesia-membutuhkan-waktu-15-bulan/

Partners In Health. 2020. 'Research: Maternal care methods can save lives, reduce infection amid Ebola'. Partners In Health, 21 January. www.pih.org/article/research-maternal-care-methods-can-save-lives-reduce-infection-amid-ebola

Saso, Anja, Helen Skirrow and Beate Kampmann. 2020. 'Impact of COVID-19 on immunization services for maternal and infant vaccines: Results of a survey conducted by Imprint—The Immunising Pregnant Women and Infants Network'. *Vaccines* 8(3): 556. doi.org/10.3390/vaccines8030556

Seong, Byeongchan and Kiseop Lee. 2021. 'Intervention analysis based on exponential smoothing methods: Applications to 9/11 and COVID-19 effects'. *Economic Modelling* 98: 290–301. doi.org/10.1016/j.econmod.2020.11.014

Shapira, Gil, Tashrik Ahmed, Salomé H.P. Drouard, Pablo A. Fernandez, Eeshani Kandpal, et al. 2021. 'Disruptions in maternal and child health service utilization during COVID-19: Analysis from eight sub-Saharan African countries'. *Health Policy and Planning* 36(7): 1140–51. doi.org/10.1093/heapol/czab064

Siwatu, Gbemisola O., Amparo Palacios-Lopez, Kevin R. McGee, Akuffo Amankwah, Tara Vishwanath and M. Abdul Azad. 2020. *Impact of COVID-19 on Nigerian Households: Baseline Results*. Washington, DC: World Bank.

Stein, Dorit, Kevin Ward and Catherine Cantelmo. 2020. 'Estimating the potential impact of COVID-19 on mothers and newborns in low- and middle-income countries'. *Health Policy Plus*. www.healthpolicyplus.com/covid-mnh-impacts.cfm

Swift, Diana. 2021. 'COVID-19 linked to baby bust in high-income countries'. *Medscape* 30 August. www.medscape.com/viewarticle/957530

Tolu, Lemi B., Garumma T. Feyissa and Wondimu G. Jeldu. 2021. 'Guidelines and best practice recommendations on reproductive health services provision amid COVID-19 pandemic: Scoping review'. *BMC Public Health* 21: 276. doi.org/10.1186/s12889-021-10346-2

UNFPA (United Nations Population Fund). 2020. *Impact of the COVID-19 Pandemic on Family Planning and Ending Gender-Based Violence, Female Genital Mutilation and Child Marriage*. Interim Technical Note, 27 April. UNFPA. www.unfpa.org/sites/default/files/resource-pdf/COVID-19_impact_brief_for_UNFPA_24_April_2020_1.pdf

UNICEF Indonesia. 2020. *Report of Rapid Health Assessment*. UNICEF Indonesia. www.unicef.org/indonesia/reports/report-rapid-health-assessment

UN IGME. 2020. 'Neonatal mortality'. UNICEF data. Accessed 11 September 2020. https://data.unicef.org/topic/child-survival/neonatal-mortality/

WHO (World Health Organization). 2020a. 'Maternal mortality: Situation – by country'. The Global Health Observatory, WHO. Accessed 30 August 2020. www.who.int/gho/maternal_health/mortality/maternal/en/

WHO (World Health Organization). 2020b. 'Physicians (per 1,000 people) – Indonesia, Philippines, Vietnam, Malaysia, Thailand, low & middle income'. Accessed 17 September 2020. https://data.worldbank.org/indicator/SH.MED.PHYS.ZS?locations=ID-PH-VN-MY-TH-XO

WHO (World Health Organization). 2021. 'WHO coronavirus (COVID-19) dashboard'. Accessed 29 October 2021. https://covid19.who.int

Wibawa, Tasha. 2021. 'Indonesia is the new epicentre of the COVID pandemic as the Delta variant surges and vaccination rates lag'. *ABC News*, 23 July. www.abc.net.au/news/2021-07-23/indonesia-covid-19-coronavirus-epicentre-lockdown-delta-variant/100310858

Winters, Peter R. 1960. 'Forecasting sales by exponentially weighted moving averages'. *Management Science* 6(3): 324–42. doi.org/10.1287/mnsc.6.3.324

World Bank. 2020a. 'Domestic general government health expenditure (% of general government expenditure) – Indonesia'. Accessed 15 October 2020. https://data.worldbank.org/indicator/SH.XPD.GHED.GE.ZS?locations=ID

World Bank. 2020b. *Indonesia Public Expenditure Review: Spending for Better Results*. Jakarta: World Bank. www.worldbank.org/en/country/indonesia/publication/indonesia-public-expenditure-review

Yirka, Bob. 2021. 'Pandemic led to lower birth rates in wealthy countries'. Phys.org, 31 August. https://phys.org/news/2021-08-pandemic-birth-wealthy-countries.html

Yonar, Harun, Aynur Yonar, Mustafa A. Tekindal and Melike Tekindal. 2020. 'Modeling and forecasting for the number of cases of the COVID-19 pandemic with the curve estimation models, the Box-Jenkins and exponential smoothing methods'. *Eurasian Journal of Medicine and Oncology* 4(2): 160–65. doi.org/10.14744/ejmo.2020.28273

9 Maternal health: Past, present and moving forward

Salut Muhidin and Jerico F. Pardosi

> Women are not dying because of untreatable diseases. They are dying because societies have yet to make the decision that their lives are worth saving: We have not yet valued women's lives and health highly enough.
>
> *Professor Mahmoud Fathalla*

We would like to begin this chapter by recalling an important message related to maternal health as quoted by the United Nations Secretary-General during the High-Level Forum on Accelerating Millennium Development Goals (MDGs-5) on 24 September 2013. He quoted a statement from Professor Mahmoud Fathalla, an international campaigner for safe motherhood and a founder of the Safe Motherhood Initiative. The key message of this quote is that no one should be left behind in health matters, including women and mothers. Our main question is then 'What about the progress of maternal health in Indonesia today?'.

This chapter attempts to answer that question by assessing how maternal health in Indonesia has changed over time and its potential trends in the future.

Maternal health commonly refers to the health of women during motherhood, starting from pregnancy, through to childbirth and the postnatal period. These are the most important stages during the parenthood experience. In actuality, maternal health starts when a woman enters adolescence, long before her motherhood period, and remains throughout a woman's reproductive life and beyond menopause. Moreover, maternal health does not stand alone. It is influenced by many factors, including women's living conditions, their early-age health status, as well as support from their family and partner. Therefore, maternal health–related issues should be a concern of societies at every level: micro (individual and family), meso (community) and macro (national and global).

At the macro level, maternal health has been a global priority as indicated in the United Nations MDGs (2000–2015) and subsequent Sustainable Development Goals (SDGs). Before then, the Safe Motherhood Initiative was introduced in 1987 at the Safe Motherhood Conference in Nairobi, Kenya (Sai and Measham 1992). Maternal health was covered in the fifth MDG, specifically a goal to 'reduce maternal mortality by 75 percent by 2015'. Most recently, maternal health is covered in the third goal—ensure healthy lives and wellbeing for all—of the seventeen SDGs. Specifically, Target 3.1 of reducing global maternal mortality includes programs in reproductive and maternal health. It also gives attention to the performance of whole health systems (that is, access to and distribution of health facilities and services). As a result, many programs related to maternal health have been widely adopted by many countries across the world, including Indonesia. An MDG Declaration was signed by Indonesia in 2000 with a commitment to reach a maternal mortality rate (MMR) of 102 per 100,000 live births by 2015. An SDG Declaration was signed in 2015 with a commitment to reach an MMR of 70 per 100,000 live births by 2030. This was an ambitious objective given that the estimated MMR in Indonesia was 236 per 100,000 live births in 2012 (BPS et al. 2013).

Over time, the government of Indonesia has applied several policies and programs focused on maternal health. In the early 1970s, family planning and safe motherhood programs were introduced. They were initially concentrated around Java and Bali, and eventually expanded to the whole country. To increase maternal health access such as basic antenatal care (ANC) at the village level, the government introduced Bidan Desa, or the village midwife training program, in the late 1980s. During that period, traditional birth attendants commonly helped mothers give birth at home, which often led to higher risks of maternal and neonatal deaths. Since then, more programs have been introduced, including the Suami Siaga or 'Alert Husband' campaign and the Bidan Siaga or 'Alert Midwives' campaign during the 1980s and 1990s and the Desa Siaga or 'Alert Village' campaign in the mid-2000s. These campaigns aimed to involve all societies at micro and meso levels (e.g. husbands, midwives and villages) in supporting mothers during their maternal period, and to reduce the risks of home births by encouraging mothers to use health facilities. To support the implementation of these programs, the government and private sector have established around 11,874 health facilities across the country (BPS 2022). These health facilities are dominated by polyclinics (75% or 8,905 units), followed by hospitals (2,617 general and 352 special maternal care). A quarter of a million *posyandu* (integrated health posts), which hold monthly gatherings at the community level, and approximately 10,000 *puskesmas* (community health centres) at the subdistrict level have been established throughout Indonesia's vast and sprawling archipelago (BPS 2022).

In addition to broad changes in the socioeconomic and demographic characteristics of the Indonesian population, these targeted programs have positively affected maternal health in Indonesia over time. The provision of better access to family planning services, for example, has contributed to a trend towards smaller families. At the same time, a decline in infant mortality has resulted in longer life expectancy. Nevertheless, other health indicators such as MMR and nutritional status have not reached their desired targets. Estimated MMRs during the past decade have consistently indicated rates between 200 and 350 maternal deaths per 100,000 live births (Utomo et al. 2021). A 2021 report from the Ministry of Health estimated MMR at 305 deaths per 100,000 live births in 2020 (MoH 2021). At the provincial level, however, there are stark variations in maternal mortality. The 2017 Indonesia Demographic and Health Survey (IDHS), for example, reported that MMR was 104 per 100,000 live births in Yogyakarta province while it was 307 per 100,000 live births in East Nusa Tenggara. Such dynamics have direct and indirect reciprocal relationships with sociopolitical transformation in the country.

In short, health in general is a basic human need. Referring to our opening quote that no one should be left behind, including a mother, it is important to have a better understanding of maternal health–related issues in Indonesia and their relationship to national development. This chapter will address those issues and is presented in two parts: first, the trends of maternal mortality and its determinants and, second, the utilisation and quality of maternal health services. Our analysis will consider regional variation and the link to broader socioeconomic development. A case study on three delay issues: (i) the decision to seek care, (ii) arrival at a health facility and (iii) the provision of adequate care, will be presented based on our latest empirical studies in the province of East Nusa Tenggara.

Maternal mortality

Maternal mortality is one of the main indicators that has traditionally been used to assess the progress of maternal health programs, typically measured by the MMR in every 100,000 live births per annum. Based on the World Health Organization's definition, MMR is the annual number of women's deaths due to any direct or indirect cause related to pregnancy or its management (excluding accidental or incidental causes) and childbirth, including the six-week postnatal period, irrespective of the duration and site of the pregnancy. Maternal deaths occur mostly due to complications of pregnancy or childbirth. As an indicator, MMR can also be used to assess the degree of public health, because of its sensitivity to the improvement of health services, both in terms of accessibility and quality.

In an overview of MMRs in Indonesia from 1990 to 2015, Sutrisna (2018) indicates that MMRs and targets vary according to different data sources and estimation methods. Based on data from the IDHS and from the intercensal survey, Supas (Survei Penduduk antar Sensus), there was a reduction in maternal mortality during the period 1990–2015, from 390 to 305 women's deaths per 100,000 live births (MoH 2021). This rate is higher than the estimated global MMR (211 per 100,000 live births in 2017) and other countries in Southeast Asia (WHO 2019). The estimated MMRs in 2017 for Southeast Asian countries were 20 for Thailand, 23 for Brunei, 40 for Malaysia, 54 for Vietnam and 114 for the Philippines (ibid.). The World Bank (2010) estimated a much more optimistic decline in MMR in Indonesia, from 419 in 1990 to 126 per 100,000 live births in 2015. The World Bank's estimate seems to follow the trend of MDG/SDG targets, which is to reduce deaths to 102 per 100,000 live births by 2015. Indonesia did not achieve that target, although there is a trend of decline in maternal mortality over time. Hull and Hosseini-Chavoshi (2018) argue that the Indonesian MMR is still high and is plagued with systemic under-reporting, especially at the district level.

At the regional level, MMRs vary among the provinces in Indonesia. It is not surprising because Indonesia is an archipelago country with diversities in regional socioeconomic, demographic and historical experience. Figure 9.1 shows the MMR in Indonesian provinces based on indirect estimates from the 2010 population census. The commonly used data of the IDHS cannot be used to provide the estimates because of the small sample size of the survey and limitations of the measuring method. Provinces in Java, Bali and western Indonesia have relatively lower MMRs (less than 200 per 100,000 live births) than provinces in the rest of Indonesia. For example, Bali and Jakarta have MMRs of 47 and 73 deaths per 100,000 live births, respectively. Meanwhile, MMRs are high in the eastern part of Indonesia. The provinces of Gorontalo in northern Sulawesi and East Nusa Tenggara have the highest MMRs, approximately 371 and 340 deaths per 100,000 live births, respectively.

Several studies conclude that the levels of MMR have been influenced by a number of factors. Ronsmans and colleagues (2006), for example, indicate that having higher levels of household income, women's education,

Figure 9.1 Maternal mortality rate by province (per 100,000 live births)

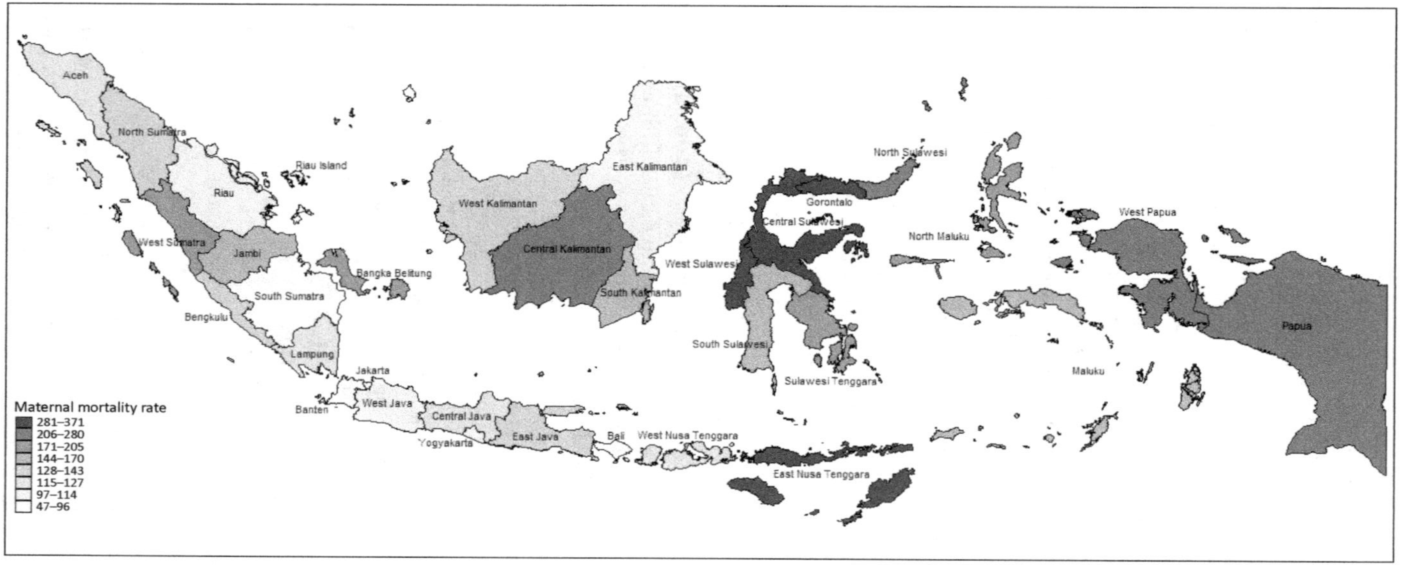

Source: Cameron et al. (2019).

urbanisation, household wealth and women's health status contribute to lower MMRs. In their recent study on Indonesian maternal mortality, Cameron et al. (2019) point out that the difference in regional maternal mortality is partially affected by access to and characteristics of health services (23%). The most important contributors are the number of doctors working at the community health centre (8.6%), the number of doctors in the village (6.9%) and distance to the nearest hospital (5.9%). Other studies investigate the link between reductions in Indonesian maternal mortality and the levels of contraceptive use (Utomo et al. 2021). Their study shows that around 38–43% of reduction in maternal deaths from 1970 to 2017 was attributed to contraceptive use. Furthermore, maternal mortality also depends on health system effectiveness in addressing health risks to women during their pregnancy.

In terms of causes of deaths, the annual health reports published by the Indonesian Ministry of Health indicate that severe bleeding after childbirth, high blood pressure during pregnancy, and infections are the leading causes of maternal deaths in Indonesia (Table 9.1). In the 2020 report, for example, severe bleeding and high blood pressure accounted for 28% and 24% of maternal deaths, respectively. At the provincial levels, maternal deaths caused by severe bleeding varied from as low as 7% in Bali to as high as 42% in East Nusa Tenggara. Most of these deaths are preventable and occur in resource-poor settings. We will come back to this point in more detail once we present the case study of maternal health in East Nusa Tenggara towards the end of this chapter.

Maternal health services

Ensuring that every woman can use and access quality maternal health services is essential to maintaining and improving the health of mothers and to reducing maternal mortality. Maternal health services include ANC for pregnant women, delivery assistance by trained health workers in proper health facilities, postnatal care for mothers and babies, referral systems in case of complications, and family planning services pre- and post-delivery. In this section, we will focus on the first two services.

Use of antenatal care services

Based on a World Health Organization recommendation and adopted by the Indonesian Ministry of Health, pregnant women should receive at least four or more antenatal care (ANC4+) visits during pregnancy. The visits should include at least one visit during the first trimester, one visit during the second trimester and two visits during the third trimester. The ANC services are useful for monitoring and maintaining

Table 9.1 Causes of maternal deaths by province, 2020

Province	Causes of maternal deaths (%)				
	HAE	HYP	INF	BCD	MD
Aceh	34.7	19.7	6.4	1.2	2.3
North Sumatra	35.8	27.3	1.6	4.3	0.5
West Sumatra	26.4	18.4	4.0	0.0	7.2
Riau	34.9	20.9	4.7	2.3	2.3
Jambi	37.1	27.4	4.8	0.0	0.0
South Sumatra	32.8	30.5	3.1	6.3	3.1
Bengkulu	40.6	15.6	0.0	9.4	3.1
Lampung	38.3	20.9	1.7	8.7	0.9
Bangka Belitung Islands	15.4	46.2	3.8	0.0	0.0
Riau Islands	18.4	31.6	0.0	0.0	2.6
DKI Jakarta	22.2	21.4	4.3	12.8	0.9
West Java	27.7	28.7	3.8	9.8	3.5
Central Java	17.2	24.0	4.2	4.3	1.9
DI Yogyakarta	17.5	15.0	17.5	0.0	0.0
East Java	22.5	26.0	5.8	0.5	5.1
Banten	26.0	26.9	2.1	9.9	0.4
Bali	7.1	23.2	0.0	8.9	5.4
West Nusa Tenggara	31.1	25.4	6.6	4.9	9.0
East Nusa Tenggara	41.7	13.2	4.6	4.6	0.0
West Kalimantan	34.8	22.6	4.3	4.3	7.0
Central Kalimantan	35.3	25.0	4.4	1.5	4.4
South Kalimantan	29.9	27.8	4.1	2.1	12.4
East Kalimantan	32.6	27.2	5.4	1.1	3.3
North Kalimantan	16.7	22.2	0.0	5.6	5.6
North Sulawesi	31.3	20.8	2.1	20.8	0.0
Central Sulawesi	39.5	17.3	6.2	3.7	0.0
South Sulawesi	33.1	22.6	7.5	3.0	4.5
South East Sulawesi	41.0	13.1	4.9	1.6	4.9
Gorontalo	19.6	21.4	5.4	0.0	0.0
West Sulawesi	23.9	30.4	2.2	0.0	0.0
Maluku	51.4	10.0	8.6	12.9	1.4
North Maluku	38.5	15.4	7.7	2.6	2.6
West Papua	37.0	11.0	8.2	0.0	0.0
Papua	34.7	13.9	15.3	2.8	1.4
Indonesia	28.6	23.9	4.6	4.9	3.1

Note: HAE = haemorrhage, HYP = hypertension during pregnancy, INF = infection, BCD = blood circulation system disorder, MD = metabolic disorder, CD = cardiovascular disease.
Source: MoH (2021).

Table 9.1 (continued)

Province	Causes of maternal deaths (%)			Total deaths (number)
	CD	COVID-19	Others	
Aceh	0.0	0.0	35.8	173
North Sumatra	0.0	0.0	30.5	187
West Sumatra	0.0	0.0	44.0	125
Riau	0.0	0.0	34.9	129
Jambi	0.0	0.0	30.6	62
South Sumatra	0.0	0.0	24.2	128
Bengkulu	0.0	0.0	31.3	32
Lampung	0.0	0.0	29.6	115
Bangka Belitung Islands	0.0	0.0	34.6	26
Riau Islands	0.0	0.0	47.4	38
DKI Jakarta	0.0	0.0	38.5	117
West Java	0.0	0.0	26.6	745
Central Java	0.0	0.0	48.5	530
DI Yogyakarta	20.0	5.0	25.0	40
East Java	0.0	0.0	40.0	565
Banten	0.0	0.0	34.7	242
Bali	0.0	0.0	55.4	56
West Nusa Tenggara	0.0	0.0	23.0	122
East Nusa Tenggara	0.0	0.0	35.8	151
West Kalimantan	0.0	0.0	27.0	115
Central Kalimantan	0.0	0.0	29.4	68
South Kalimantan	0.0	0.0	23.7	97
East Kalimantan	0.0	0.0	30.4	92
North Kalimantan	0.0	11.1	38.9	18
North Sulawesi	0.0	0.0	25.0	48
Central Sulawesi	0.0	0.0	33.3	81
South Sulawesi	0.0	0.8	28.6	133
South East Sulawesi	0.0	0.0	34.4	61
Gorontalo	0.0	0.0	53.6	56
West Sulawesi	0.0	0.0	43.5	46
Maluku	0.0	0.0	15.7	70
North Maluku	0.0	0.0	33.3	39
West Papua	34.2	0.0	9.6	73
Papua	0.0	0.0	31.9	72
Indonesia	0.7	0.1	34.0	4,652

Figure 9.2 Proportion of four or more antenatal care visits (ANC4+) by province, 2020

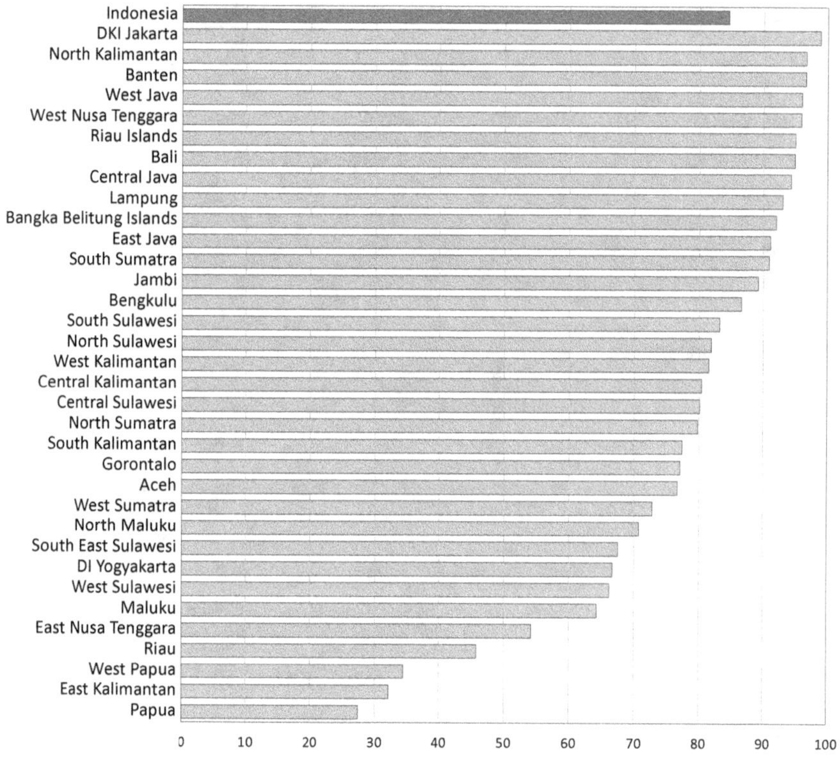

Province	
Indonesia	
DKI Jakarta	
North Kalimantan	
Banten	
West Java	
West Nusa Tenggara	
Riau Islands	
Bali	
Central Java	
Lampung	
Bangka Belitung Islands	
East Java	
South Sumatra	
Jambi	
Bengkulu	
South Sulawesi	
North Sulawesi	
West Kalimantan	
Central Kalimantan	
Central Sulawesi	
North Sumatra	
South Kalimantan	
Gorontalo	
Aceh	
West Sumatra	
North Maluku	
South East Sulawesi	
DI Yogyakarta	
West Sulawesi	
Maluku	
East Nusa Tenggara	
Riau	
West Papua	
East Kalimantan	
Papua	

Source: MoH (2021).

the health and safety of the mother and the fetus. ANC can detect possible complications of pregnancy and take necessary action, as well as prepare for a healthy birth.

Figure 9.2 shows the proportion of women with at least four ANC visits during their pregnancy at provincial level in Indonesia. In 2020, the national average of ANC4+ visits was about 85% with 40% of provinces having higher than national levels. Jakarta province had the highest proportion (98.9%) of ANC4+ services. Five provinces (East Nusa Tenggara, Riau, West Papua, East Kalimantan and Papua) had ANC4+ visits of less than 55%. Women in Papua province had 27.5% of ANC4+ visits (MoH 2021).

Using 2017 IDHS data, Laksono et al. (2020) evaluated regional disparities in ANC utilisation. Their study found that provinces in Java, Bali, Kalimantan and southern parts of Sumatra had relatively higher levels in the use of ANC services (more than 85%) than provinces in the rest of Indonesia. However, the utilisation of ANC visits by pregnant women in Indonesia is still unsatisfactory and needs to be improved. Laksono et al. (2020) also indicated that increased use of ANC services in Indonesia was linked to factors including older age of mothers, higher levels of education for mothers, lower birth parity, wealth status and health insurance. Women from older age groups have a higher likelihood of receiving ANC4+ visits than those in younger age groups. Women with higher levels of education have a better chance of making ANC4+ visits than those without higher levels of education. The probability of receiving ANC4+ visits decreases with increasing birth order and increases with the higher wealth status of a woman. Women from richer families are significantly more likely to receive ANC4+ visits than mothers from poor families. Furthermore, women who have health insurance tend to have more ANC4+ visits than those who do not have insurance.

Use of health facilities and assistance by trained health workers

As discussed earlier, many women, particularly in less-developed regions, are still dying every year because of complications during pregnancy and childbirth. Most of these deaths are preventable and occur in resource-poor settings. At the same time, some women still prefer to give birth at home or be assisted by a traditional birth attendant. Giving birth at home or at a non-health facility where adequate medical emergency support is usually unavailable can lead to a higher risk of maternal death, especially where blood loss (haemorrhage) is involved. In the absence of adequate medical equipment, even well-trained health workers might not be able to provide adequate medical care once they face an emergency during childbirth. Safety is therefore considered as the main reason to promote health facility births and assistance by trained health workers. Figure 9.3 shows the distribution of health facility births across Indonesia.

The use of health facilities for giving birth in Indonesia is relatively satisfactory with many provinces having reached 70% or more. Some provinces, however, still have low levels of health facility births. These provinces include Maluku (31.4%), West Papua (34.7%), East Kalimantan (35.1%), Papua (44.6%) and Riau (49.2%). In remote areas and islands, the implications for timely transport to an emergency health facility are self-evident and a highly challenging issue in Indonesia. In East Nusa Tenggara province with 60.5% of health facility births, for example, pregnant women who are in their last gestational stage and live far from health facilities are supported with a program called Rumah Tunggu, or waiting house (Muhidin et al. 2020). These women are advised to come to a waiting house

Figure 9.3 Proportion of health facility births by province, 2020

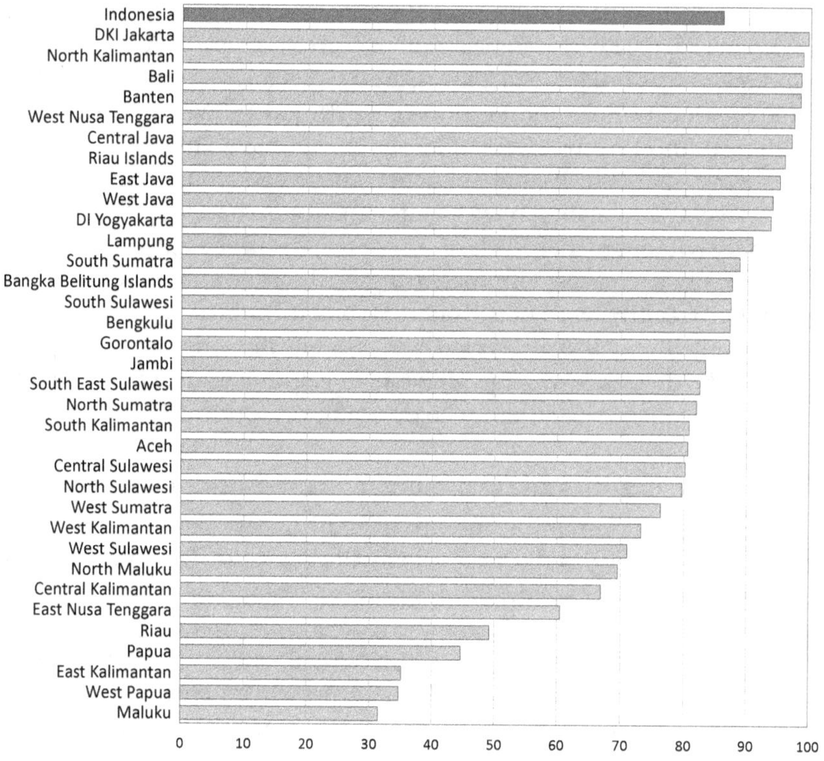

Province	
Indonesia	
DKI Jakarta	
North Kalimantan	
Bali	
Banten	
West Nusa Tenggara	
Central Java	
Riau Islands	
East Java	
West Java	
DI Yogyakarta	
Lampung	
South Sumatra	
Bangka Belitung Islands	
South Sulawesi	
Bengkulu	
Gorontalo	
Jambi	
South East Sulawesi	
North Sumatra	
South Kalimantan	
Aceh	
Central Sulawesi	
North Sulawesi	
West Sumatra	
West Kalimantan	
West Sulawesi	
North Maluku	
Central Kalimantan	
East Nusa Tenggara	
Riau	
Papua	
East Kalimantan	
West Papua	
Maluku	

Source: MoH (2021).

located close to a health facility within 2 to 7 days of the estimated due date of their child, as 90% of maternal deaths in East Nusa Tenggara occur during this time period (MoH 2002). A study by Pranata et al. (2021) argues that disparities in the quantity and quality of health care between urban and rural areas in Indonesia is adding to the challenges for women in giving health facility births. Higher urbanisation has also contributed to a higher level of health facility utilisation (Efendi et al. 2019).

Table 9.2 shows a significant link between the use of health facilities and births attended by trained or skilled health workers, including obstetricians, gynaecologists, general practitioners, nurses and midwives. In all provinces with higher levels of health facility births, attendance by skilled health workers is also higher. Surprisingly, the levels of skilled birth attendants are also high in provinces with low levels of births occurring at health facilities. The provinces of Riau and East Kalimantan with 49% and 35% of births occurring at health facilities, respectively, have 80.5% and 86.7% of births attended by skilled health personnel.

Muhidin et al. (2020) point out that the cost of giving birth at health facilities, especially in a hospital, is a challenge for many Indonesian families. The government of Indonesia has introduced health insurance for the poor—Jamkesmas (Jaminan Kesehatan Masyarakat)—that provides free primary health care services including maternity care at community health centres. In 2011, the Ministry of Health added a maternity benefit insurance, Jampersal (Jaminan Persalinan), for all pregnant women. Knowledge and awareness of these insurance schemes has unfortunately not reached all families across Indonesia.

Culture and tradition can also be part of the explanation for women who want to have births at home or assistance from traditional birth attendants (Agus et al. 2012; Wulandari and Whelan 2011). Pregnancy and delivery have traditionally been considered normal phenomena and giving birth at home and getting help from skilled health workers or traditional birth attendants is more convenient. Familiarity with the home environment and the feeling of close emotional support and practical assistance during pregnancy and after delivery also contribute to such practices. Traditional birth attendants are often valued and influential members of the community, thus they would be effective in encouraging community members to seek better health services and facilities to improve maternal health.

Case study of delays in East Nusa Tenggara

Following global trends in health development, such as SDG targets, Indonesia has implemented several programs to improve maternal health in general and to reduce maternal mortality. The programs have reduced mortality rates overall, but results at the subnational level have been variable. Accordingly, the government has made strong commitments to address this challenging issue, paying more attention to regions where mortality rates are still high. In this section, we present a case study from the province of East Nusa Tenggara, which still experiences high levels of maternal mortality.

Maternal health in East Nusa Tenggara

East Nusa Tenggara has experienced high rates of maternal mortality for several decades. In 2002 and 2012, for example, the IDHS reported MMRs as high as 554 deaths and 307 deaths per 100,000 live births, respectively (BPS et al. 2003, 2013). The national figure in 2012 was 236 per 100,000 live

Table 9.2 Distribution of birth attendants by province, 2020

	Pregnant women—ANC visit			Postpartum mother	
Province	1st visit (%)	4th visit (%)	Total (number)	Skilled birth attendant (%)	Institutional births (%)
Aceh	89.6	76.7	126,085	83.7	80.6
North Sumatra	85.6	79.8	329,118	83.2	81.9
West Sumatra	83.2	72.8	119,518	75.8	76.3
Riau	83.7	45.8	170,854	80.5	49.2
Jambi	99.4	89.2	71,970	92.1	83.3
South Sumatra	94.2	90.9	174,076	91.9	88.8
Bengkulu	93.6	86.6	40,609	88.1	87.3
Lampung	93.7	93.0	162,463	92.3	90.8
Bangka Belitung Islands	92.0	92.0	30,224	90.3	87.6
Riau Islands	99.8	95.0	44,625	97.0	95.9
DKI Jakarta	100.6	98.9	179,452	99.6	99.6
West Java	101.8	96.0	955,411	95.0	94.0
Central Java	99.7	94.3	575,082	98.6	97.0
DI Yogyakarta	76.7	66.7	59,422	93.7	93.7
East Java	97.7	91.1	618,207	97.0	95.1
Banten	100.4	94.4	267,628	108.3	98.4
Bali	101.4	94.9	70,859	98.6	98.5
West Nusa Tenggara	105.0	95.9	112,725	97.8	97.4
East Nusa Tenggara	68.6	54.2	154,663	64.0	60.5
West Kalimantan	91.0	81.5	109,316	81.2	73.2
Central Kalimantan	89.3	80.4	59,161	81.4	66.9
South Kalimantan	80.8	77.4	87,583	86.0	80.8
East Kalimantan	89.5	32.2	82,512	86.7	35.1
North Kalimantan	108.8	96.7	13,361	103.7	98.8
North Sulawesi	94.8	81.9	44,546	83.3	79.7
Central Sulawesi	89.7	80.1	68,716	82.3	80.2
South Sulawesi	91.5	83.2	183,791	88.3	87.4
South East Sulawesi	85.9	67.5	69,018	86.9	82.4
Gorontalo	–	77.1	26,283	–	87.2
West Sulawesi	76.7	66.2	36,337	49.0	76.8
Maluku	78.6	64.3	49,283	46.7	31.3
North Maluku	86.0	70.7	32,210	75.4	69.5
West Papua	57.0	34.5	24,189	48.2	34.7
Papua	59.1	27.5	78,487	49.8	44.6
Indonesia	93.2	84.5	5,227,784	89.8	86.1

Source: MoH (2021).

Table 9.2 (continued)

Province	Postpartum mother			
	1st postnatal visit (%)	Complete postnatal service (%)	Receiving vitamin A (%)	Total (number)
Aceh	83.1	77.9	82.0	120,354
North Sumatra	84.0	77.5	78.3	314,158
West Sumatra	76.9	74.3	76.9	114,086
Riau	81.1	73.0	80.2	163,088
Jambi	93.2	91.1	93.1	68,698
South Sumatra	91.8	88.4	90.7	166,164
Bengkulu	88.0	83.3	87.6	38,763
Lampung	92.3	89.6	90.3	155,079
Bangka Belitung Islands	90.2	88.7	90.6	28,850
Riau Islands	970.4	90.7	96.7	42,596
DKI Jakarta	99.6	98.6	99.4	171,295
West Java	97.1	95.5	97.4	922,883
Central Java	96.7	95.6	97.0	548,942
DI Yogyakarta	93.6	88.9	92.7	43,775
East Java	97.2	95.5	80.0	590,106
Banten	102.2	122.9	106.5	249,736
Bali	98.6	96.9	98.2	67,638
West Nusa Tenggara	96.9	96.9	97.3	107,601
East Nusa Tenggara	65.7	62.2	65.2	147,633
West Kalimantan	84.2	80.5	84.2	104,347
Central Kalimantan	85.4	81.0	85.8	56,472
South Kalimantan	84.0	81.2	84.3	83,602
East Kalimantan	87.3	80.0	80.6	78,762
North Kalimantan	104.1	99.2	103.4	12,753
North Sulawesi	81.7	79.6	81.6	42,521
Central Sulawesi	83.0	78.6	81.1	65,592
South Sulawesi	88.3	85.4	87.8	175,437
South East Sulawesi	87.9	83.6	86.2	58,917
Gorontalo	–	–	–	25,089
West Sulawesi	50.3	73.2	78.9	34,686
Maluku	49.1	44.7	47.7	47,043
North Maluku	78.1	76.5	76.1	30,746
West Papua	36.6	30.7	33.9	23,090
Papua	38.9	31.5	37.0	74,920
Indonesia	97.2	88.3	87.5	4,975,422

births. The lack of proper or quality health care at the front line or at the village level has been claimed as the main reason. As a matter of fact, there has been an effort to provide at least one *bidan* (professionally trained health worker) or midwife in each village to deal with ANC in East Nusa Tenggara. Nevertheless, many women are still dying every year due to complications during pregnancy, delivery and after delivery, especially among those who have births at home or at non-health facilities. Based on IDHS data, the proportion of mothers who gave birth at home was 78% in 2007 and 57% in 2012. Most were assisted by *dukun beranak*, traditional birth attendants (43% and 30%, respectively).

Having a low proportion of births assisted by health personnel, and high rates of maternal and neonatal mortality, in 2009 the government of East Nusa Tenggara introduced a program called Revolusi Kesehatan Ibu dan Anak (Revolusi KIA), or Mother and Child Health Revolution (Dinas Kesehatan Provinsi 2012). It is a provincial-wide program that has been applied in all 22 districts in East Nusa Tenggara and ratified in Provincial Act No. 42/2009. Revolusi KIA is defined as an effort to rapidly reduce maternal and neonatal deaths in revolutionary ways and encourage health facility births. Figure 9.4 illustrates how the program has been implemented for ensuring women have health facility births. It is a continuous monitoring program from when women have their first ANC visit with a midwife either at a village health centre or at home. Among disadvantaged and remote communities, Revolusi KIA encourages pregnant women who are ready to give birth to be safely brought to a *rumah tunggu* or maternity waiting house that is located close to adequate health facilities. It includes a *puskesmas* if the delivery is predicted to require only basic neonatal care or emergency obstetric care, or hospital if the delivery is predicted to require more comprehensive neonatal care or emergency.

Since the Revolusi KIA program was implemented there have been some improvements in health indicators, as presented in Table 9.3. Annual reports published by the provincial health office show that health facility births in East Nusa Tenggara significantly increased from 44.9% in 2009 to 93.5% in 2016. Figures from the IDHS also confirm this situation; the proportion of East Nusa Tenggara health facility births increased from 35.6% in 2012 to 65.8% in 2017 (BPS et al. 2003, 2013). At the district level, however, progress is variable. Table 9.3 indicates that having a higher proportion of health facility births does not always lead to lower maternal mortality. In Flores Island, for example, three districts had the same proportion of health facility births (98% in Lembata, Flores Timur and Nagekeo in 2016), but their maternal deaths per 100,000 live births were different in each district: 187 deaths in Lembata, 152 in Flores Timur

Table 9.3 Percentage of health facility births and maternal deaths in East Nusa Tenggara by district, 2009 and 2016

District	Urban pop. 2015 (%)	Health facility births (%)			Maternal deaths (per 100,000 live births)		
		2009	2016	Diff.	2009	2016	Diff.
Timor Island							
Kupang City	96.0	78.51	99.28	20.77	208	59	149
Kupang District	6.7	15.43	90.47	75.04	287	258	29
Timor Tengah Selatan	9.1	21.47	86.68	65.21	531	326	205
Timor Tengah Utara	13.8	53.62	96.14	42.53	402	135	267
Belu	22.1	62.7	91.64	28.94	262	113	149
Malaka	21.1	n.a.	97.65	n.a.	n.a.	116	n.a.
Flores Island							
Alor	22.7	36.09	89.68	53.59	356	468	-112
Lembata	18.1	83.53	98.37	14.84	174	187	-13
Flores Timur	20.9	69.12	98.38	29.27	307	152	155
Sikka	19.8	84.09	94.14	10.06	183	249	-66
Ende	32.2	80.52	94.14	13.62	249	317	-68
Nagekeo	0.0	89.3	98.21	8.91	288	149	139
Ngada	14.1	73.32	96.76	23.45	242	216	26
Manggarai Timur	0.0	13.37	84.25	70.87	463	250	213
Manggarai	25.7	20.29	91.2	70.91	254	113	141
Manggarai Barat	9.7	20.06	90.04	69.98	255	224	31
Sumba Island							
Sumba Barat Daya	8.1	13.76	95.19	81.43	288	195	93
Sumba Barat	19.7	48.35	96.77	48.42	105	184	-79
Sumba Tengah	0.0	21.08	95.13	74.06	269	160	109
Sumba Timur	21.0	43.06	97.66	54.6	249	268	-19
Rote Ndao	6.9	7.77	92.78	85.01	420	328	92
Sabu Raijua	0.0	n.a.	93.06	n.a.	n.a.	704	n.a.
East Nusa Tenggara (total)	20.5	44.92	93.45	48.53	304	209	95

Note. This table was created using data from East Nusa Tenggara Provincial Health Office reports from 2007 to 2017. n.a. = not available.

Figure 9.4 Maternity care and referral system (Revolusi KIA) in East Nusa Tenggara province

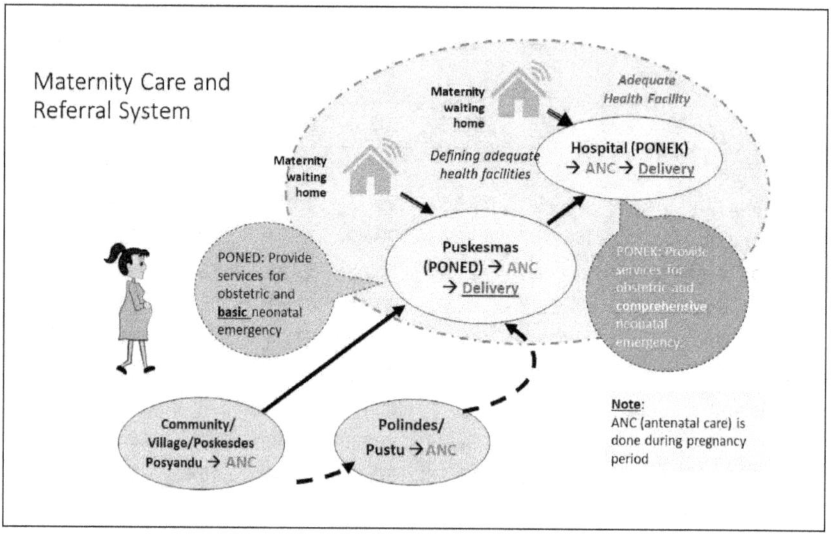

Source: Dinas Kesehatan Provinsi (2012).

and 149 in Nagekeo. These data indicate that not all women give birth at adequate health facilities. In the next section we will elaborate how and why these variable results occurred in East Nusa Tenggara.

Three delays model

To better understand the varying maternal mortality at subdistrict level in East Nusa Tenggara, we propose a 'three delays model'. Figure 9.5 shows the three delays model, which includes (1) delay in decision-making to seek care, (2) delay in reaching a health facility and (3) delay in receiving adequate care. Thaddeus and Maine (1994) suggested the three delays model by recognising barriers in accessing timely obstetric care during pregnancy, delivery and after delivery. The model has been widely used across less-developed countries to find potential solutions in preventing any delays that could lead to maternal and child mortality.

1. Delay in making decision

The first delay is the delay in seeking care or treatment for women, and is influenced by the decision-making process. Key factors include low socioeconomic status of the woman or her family, the woman's status

Figure 9.5   Three delays model for maternal care

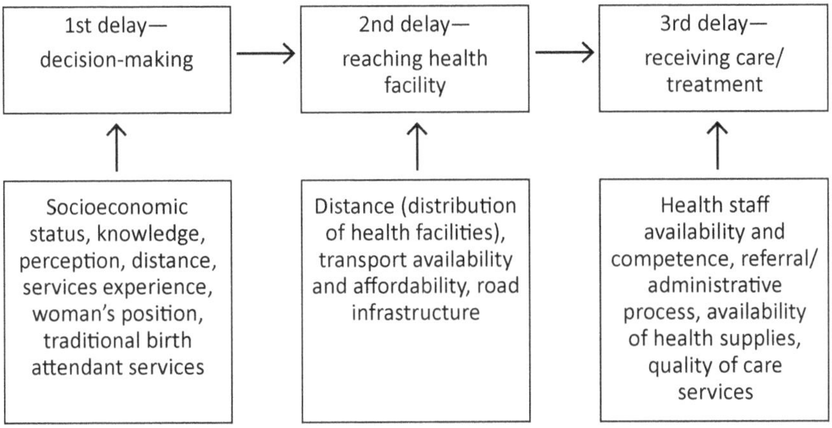

```
┌─────────────────┐      ┌─────────────────┐      ┌─────────────────┐
│    1st delay—   │ ───▶ │    2nd delay—   │ ───▶ │    3rd delay—   │
│ decision-making │      │ reaching health │      │ receiving care/ │
│                 │      │     facility    │      │    treatment    │
└─────────────────┘      └─────────────────┘      └─────────────────┘
         ▲                        ▲                        ▲
         │                        │                        │
┌─────────────────┐      ┌─────────────────┐      ┌─────────────────┐
│  Socioeconomic  │      │    Distance     │      │   Health staff  │
│ status, knowledge│     │  (distribution  │      │ availability and│
│ perception,     │      │ of health       │      │ competence,     │
│ distance,       │      │ facilities),    │      │ referral/       │
│ services        │      │ transport       │      │ administrative  │
│ experience,     │      │ availability    │      │ process,        │
│ woman's position│      │ and             │      │ availability    │
│ traditional     │      │ affordability,  │      │ of health       │
│ birth attendant │      │ road            │      │ supplies,       │
│ services        │      │ infrastructure  │      │ quality of care │
│                 │      │                 │      │ services        │
└─────────────────┘      └─────────────────┘      └─────────────────┘
```

Source: Thaddeus and Maine (1994).

in the community, inadequate knowledge of danger signs, previous experience with health care services and distance to the health facility.

Several studies (e.g. Muhidin et al. 2019, 2020; Pardosi et al. 2015) have shown that receiving and accessing maternal health care or services in East Nusa Tenggara is also part of the decision-making process. It includes decisions on how and with whom to have ANC, and the number of children (unwanted pregnancy). Decision-making not only involves women but also often their extended family, such as their husband or partner and parents. Earlier studies suggest that many women in this province still lack knowledge of the danger signs of pregnancy and illness, including awareness of the symptoms (Pardosi et al. 2015), especially those from low socioeconomic backgrounds. Such situations can lead to delays in making decisions if any health emergencies arise.

As in many Asian countries, the Indonesian population and East Nusa Tenggara community are dominated by a patriarchal family structure. Husbands or males are typically the head of family and hold economic and decision-making power. Thus, sometimes women do not have the power to choose a health facility birth. Also challenging is that a father's knowledge and engagement with regard to their partner's pregnancies and birth stages is generally superficial. Women's positions in the community need to receive more respect and women should be given more opportunities for making decisions on maternal health care services.

2. Delay in reaching health facility

The second delay is the delay in reaching a health facility. Key factors relate mainly to accessibility, including physical distance to the closest health facility; transportation availability and affordability, particularly for rural and remote areas; and road conditions.

In the context of East Nusa Tenggara, this second delay focuses on economic and physical access/geographic barriers. Indeed, access to health services is still a big challenge, given the vastness of the region, which consists of 22 districts, 3,270 villages and more than 566 islands with three main islands (Sumba, Flores and Timor). Most people (80%) live in rural areas. The uneven distribution of accessible health facilities within a fair distance is evident in East Nusa Tenggara. In a remote area, for example, reaching the closest village health post could take at least 6–7 hours by boat. Reaching further health facilities relies on transport availability, which is often costly and limited (public transport, for example, is available once a week or fortnight during market days) (Muhidin et al. 2019, 2020).

The delay in reaching a health facility is also strongly related to the delay in recognising the problem. If the mother or family members have better knowledge about pregnancy or delivery complications, then the mothers could travel earlier to health facilities to receive proper care.

3. Delay in receiving care

The third delay is focused on the performance of the health system relating to health staff availability; supplies availability (equipment, blood and medicines); health staff competence; referral processing time including administrative processes; and quality of care (respectful care to mothers and families).

The Revolusi KIA guidelines provided by the East Nusa Tenggara Provincial Health Office recommend the use of an adequate health facility for women giving birth. An adequate health facility has three requirements. First, it should have five *bidan* or midwives who have been trained on obstetric neonates (i.e. normal and emergency delivery). Second, it should have five *perawat* or nurses who have been fully trained on obstetric neonates, basic cardiac support and asphyxia. Third, it should have at least one other health staff member who has been trained based on his or her competencies, including a dentist or a laboratory technician.

Figure 9.6 shows that not all districts in East Nusa Tenggara have adequate health facilities, especially in rural areas. Using three categories of places for women giving birth: adequate health facility, inadequate health facility and no health facility or home, some districts have successful stories while others do not. In Flores Timur district, for

Figure 9.6 Proportion of health facility births in East Nusa Tenggara by district, 2012

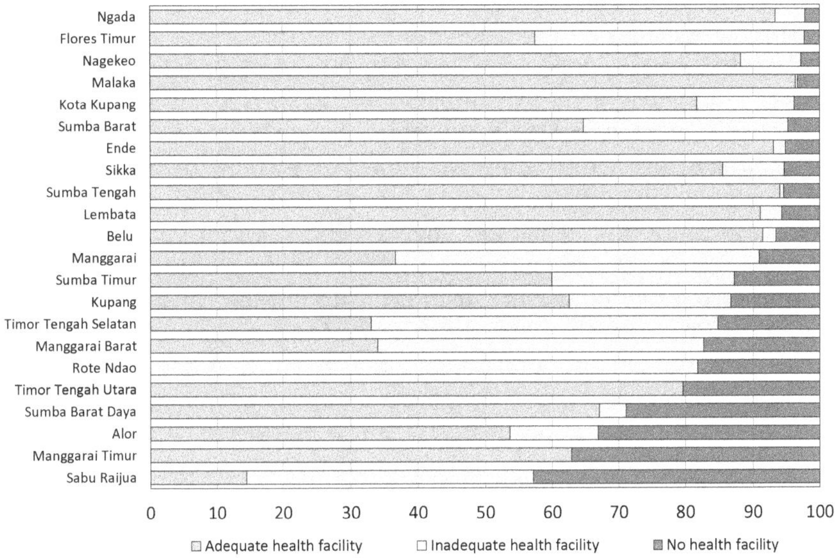

[Bar chart showing districts: Ngada, Flores Timur, Nagekeo, Malaka, Kota Kupang, Sumba Barat, Ende, Sikka, Sumba Tengah, Lembata, Belu, Manggarai, Sumba Timur, Kupang, Timor Tengah Selatan, Manggarai Barat, Rote Ndao, Timor Tengah Utara, Sumba Barat Daya, Alor, Manggarai Timur, Sabu Raijua; x-axis 0–100; categories: Adequate health facility, Inadequate health facility, No health facility]

Source: Dinas Kesehatan Provinsi (2012).

example, about 57% of births occurred at adequate health facilities, 40% occurred at inadequate health facilities and 2% occurred at home. In Nagekeo district, on the other hand, the majority of births occurred at adequate health facilities (88%). Hence, the issue of limited availability of doctors and obstetricians during emergency obstetric complications is still evident in this region. It also suggests that underutilisation of health services can be due to a misalignment between health care provision and socioeconomic context.

Among pregnant women with higher risks of blood loss and other complications during and after delivery, a delay in receiving treatment or care leads to a greater risk of maternal or neonatal death. A report from the Gadjah Mada University's Faculty of Medicine and East Nusa Tenggara Provincial Health Office (Dinas Kesehatan Provinsi 2012) indicates that common places where maternal and newborn deaths occur are between home and the health facility. Thus, a safe and systematic referral system is critical in order to bring mothers safely from their place of residence to health facilities and then to take them home safely.

4. Possible fourth delay?

The three delays model focuses mostly on women, families and health workers as well as health facilities. As stating at the beginning of this chapter, pregnancy and the motherhood experience is not just women's business. It needs support and assistance from the whole community, directly and indirectly. Acknowledging the strong influence of the community for maternal health outcomes, we can introduce a fourth delay factor that focuses on the timely support provided by the community to all women during pregnancy and motherhood.

Community involvement or engagement is relevant and important because maternal health outcomes can be affected by technical and moral support from the community. Technical support may include provision of transport or sufficient health insurance for a mother to give birth at a health facility. It is a moral obligation as the birth event is considered an extraordinary live event, for mother and baby as well as their family and wider community. Revolusi KIA can be considered as a community-based health intervention that involves active partnerships with multiple stakeholders within and across a community.

In the context of health programs, Farnsworth et al. (2014) recommend a level of shared leadership as an effective way to produce better outcomes in community engagement. They find that higher levels of community engagement occur when close collaboration and shared leadership is present in the community. Accordingly, maternal health outcomes might be improved by actively mobilising mothers and their families to use a health facility for childbirth through partnerships between local government and community organisations. Leaders or influential people in the community can also support health promotion that can lead to increased community engagement and practices towards better maternal health.

Conclusion

This chapter describes the progress of maternal health in Indonesia up to the present. Regional diversity in socioeconomic and demographic characteristics has significantly affected the progress for improving maternal health conditions across the country. Some regions have reached higher levels of maternal health development than others. In terms of ANC visits, women in some provinces may have four or more ANC visits, while others have fewer. The problem of birthing at non-health facilities is still faced by some provinces in the eastern part of Indonesia. Similarly, attendance at births by skilled health workers is reduced in the east. This heterogeneity reflects all kinds of development in health determinants across Indonesia.

Our case study on maternal health in East Nusa Tenggara province has added an important insight as to why MMR remains a significant challenge for health transition in Indonesia. The findings suggest a pressing need for adopting the continuum approach from the prenatal to postnatal period in preventing unnecessary delays and maternal deaths. Engaging the community in maternal health programs and services could contribute to greater survival of both mothers and newborns. Furthermore, identifying and tackling critical points of delay for mothers should be done continuously by recognising local support and resources.

Therefore, we propose the following IBU program for improving maternal health outcomes, particularly for eastern Indonesia. I is for 'Improving the quality of maternal health care services'. We recommend the government and relevant stakeholders increase health care services capacity by taking into account community voices and their involvement as part of strengthening existing health care services. Providing respectful care services and accessible and affordable health facilities in rural areas would be another priority to tackle preventable maternal deaths. Continuous health education should be promoted to increase the awareness of community and health care providers about health issues. Second, B is for 'Building trust between communities and health care providers'. This could be achieved by providing opportunities for communities to be part of planning, monitoring and evaluation, and supporting initiatives such as local ownership of maternity waiting homes. Third, U is for 'Understanding women's rights and needs by ensuring access for all women and their autonomy'. A greater involvement of women would be another key action to promote positive pregnancy and postnatal health outcomes. Communities and fathers should provide women with greater autonomy in making decisions about their health that would enhance survival outcomes for themselves and their children.

References

Agus, Yenita, Shigeko Horiuchi and Sarah E. Porter. 2012. 'Rural Indonesia women's traditional beliefs about antenatal care'. *BMC Research Notes* 5: 589. doi.org/10.1186/1756-0500-5-589

BPS (Badan Pusat Statistik, Statistics Indonesia). 2022. *Jumlah Sarana Kesehatan di Indonesia 2021* [Number of Health Facilities in Indonesia in 2021]. Jakarta: BPS.

BPS (Statistics Indonesia), BKKBN (National Population and Family Planning Board), Kementerian Kesehatan (Ministry of Health) and ORC Macro. 2003. *Indonesia Demographic and Health Survey 2002–2003*. Calverton MD: BPS, BKKBN, Kemenkes and ORC Macro. http://dhsprogram.com/pubs/pdf/FR147/FR147.pdf

BPS (Statistics Indonesia), BKKBN (National Population and Family Planning Board), Kementerian Kesehatan (Ministry of Health) and ICF International. 2013. *Indonesia Demographic and Health Survey 2012*. Jakarta: BPS, BKKBN, Kemenkes and ICF International. http://dhsprogram.com/pubs/pdf/FR275/FR275.pdf

Cameron, Lisa, Diana Contreras Suárez and Katy Cornwell. 2019. 'Understanding the determinants of maternal mortality: An observational study using the Indonesian population census'. *PLOS ONE* 14(6): e0217386. doi.org/10.1371/journal.pone.0217386

Dinas Kesehatan Provinsi (East Nusa Tenggara Provincial Health Office). 2012. *Pedoman Revolusi KIA di Provinsi NTT* [Guidance for the Mother and Child Health Revolution in East Nusa Tenggara province]. Dinas Kesehatan Provinsi.

Efendi Ferry, Ani Rihlatun Ni'mah, Setho Hadisuyatmana, Heri Kuswanto, Linlin Lindayani and Sarni Maniar Berliana. 2019. 'Determinants of facility-based childbirth in Indonesia'. *Scientific World Journal* 9694602. doi.org/10.1155/2019/9694602

Farnsworth, S. Katherine, Kirsten Böse, Olaoluwa Fajobi, Patricia Portela Souza, Anne Peniston, et al. 2014. 'Community engagement to enhance child survival and early development in low- and middle-income countries: An evidence review'. *Journal of Health Communication* 19(Suppl.1): 67–88.

Hull, Terence H. and Meimanat Hosseini-Chavoshi. 2018. 'Reproductive health and maternal mortality'. In *Routledge Handbook of Asian Demography*, edited by Zhongwei Zhao and Adrian C. Hayes, 131–50. London: Routledge. doi.org/10.4324/9781315148458-8

Laksono, Agung Dwi, Rukmini Rukmini and Ratna Dwi Wulandari. 2020. 'Regional disparities in antenatal care utilization in Indonesia'. *PLOS ONE* 15(2): e0224006. doi.org/10.1371/journal.pone.0224006

MoH (Ministry of Health). 2002. *Laporan Survey Kesehatan Rumah Tangga (SKRT) 2001: Studi Morbiditas dan Disabilitas* [Report of the National Household Health Survey 2001: Study of Morbidity and Disability]. Jakarta: MoH.

MoH (Ministry of Health). 2021. *Profil Kesehatan Indonesia Tahun 2020* [Indonesia Health Profile 2020]. Jakarta: MoH.

Muhidin Salut, Rachmalina Prasodjo, Maria Silalahi and Jerico F. Pardosi. 2019. 'Community engagement in maternal and newborn health in eastern Indonesia'. In *Global Health Leadership: Case Studies from the Asia-Pacific*, edited by Mellissa Withers and Judith McCool, 67–78. Cham: Springer Nature. doi.org/10.1007/978-3-319-95633-6_7

Muhidin Salut, Rachmalina Prasodjo, Maria Silalahi and Jerico F. Pardosi. 2020. 'Ensuring healthy lives: Saving lives at birth in Indonesia'. In *Industry and Higher Education: Case Studies for Sustainable Futures*, edited by Leigh Wood, Lay Peng Tan, Yvonne A. Breyer and Sally Hawse, 45–72. Singapore: Springer. doi.org/10.1007/978-981-15-0874-5_3

Pardosi, Jerico F., Nick Parr and Salut Muhidin. 2015. 'Inequity issues and mothers' pregnancy, delivery and early-age survival experiences in Ende district, Indonesia'. *Journal of Biosocial Science* 47(6): 780–802. doi.org/10.1017/S0021932014000522

Pranata, Angga Kresna, Andri Setiya Wahyudi, Lukman Handoyo and Ferry Efendi. 2021. 'Determinants of birthplace among middle- to lower-class women in Indonesia: A study using the Indonesian Demographic and Health Survey'. *PLOS ONE* 16(10): e0259417. doi.org/10.1371/journal.pone.0259417

Ronsmans, Carine, Wendy J. Graham and Lancet Maternal Survival Series Steering Group. 2006. 'Maternal mortality: Who, when, where, and why'. *Lancet* 368(9542): 1189–200. doi.org/10.1016/S0140-6736(06)69380-X

Sai, Fred T. and Diana M. Measham. 1992. 'Safe Motherhood Initiative: Getting our priorities straight'. *The Lancet* 339(8791): 478–80. doi.org/10.1016/0140-6736(92)91072-G

Sutrisna, Aang. 2018. 'Desk review of maternal, neonatal and child health in Indonesia'. Online paper in Academia.edu. www.academia.edu/44031705/Desk_Review_of_Maternal_Neonatal_and_Child_Health_in_Indonesia

Thaddeus, Sereen and Deborah Maine. 1994. 'Too far to walk: Maternal mortality in context'. *Social Science & Medicine* 38(8): 1091–110. doi.org/10.1016/0277-9536(94)90226-7

Utomo, Budi, Purwa Kurnia Sucahya, Nohan Arum Romadlona, Annette Sachs Robertson, Riznawaty Imma Aryanty and Robert Joseph Magnani. 2021. 'The impact of family planning on maternal mortality in Indonesia: What future contribution can be expected?' *Population Health Metrics* 19: 2. doi.org/10.1186/s12963-020-00245-w

WHO (World Health Organization). 2019. *Trends in Maternal Mortality 2000 to 2017: Estimates by WHO, UNICEF, UNFPA, World Bank Group and the United Nations Population Division*. Geneva: WHO.

World Bank. 2010. '… and then she died': Indonesia Maternal Health Assessment. World Bank. https://openknowledge.worldbank.org/handle/10986/2837

Wulandari, Luh Putu Lila and Anna Klinken Whelan. 2011. 'Beliefs, attitudes and behaviours of pregnant women in Bali'. *Midwifery* 27(6): 867–71. doi.org/10.1016/j.midw.2010.09.005

10 Disability in Indonesia: What can we learn from the available data?

Diana Contreras Suárez and Lisa Cameron

Disability can occur at any time during life—from birth to old age. It can be caused by a multitude of factors from poor nutrition to violence to poor health care. It can be mild or severe, and it could potentially affect a wide range of functional areas: mobility, vision, hearing, communication, psychosocial function limitations, etc. (Adioetomo et al. 2014: 2)

For many of us, the concept of disability is at once familiar and unknown. While it is common when considering disability to think of a woman in a wheelchair or a man who is blind, it is less usual to recall that 'disability [also] encompasses the child born with a congenital condition such as cerebral palsy ... the young soldier who loses his leg to a landmine, ... the middle-aged woman with severe arthritis, [and] the older person with dementia, among many others' (WHO and World Bank 2011: 7). In addition, the diversity of disability extends well beyond the type of health impairment to factors including severity, duration, age, age of onset, gender and income. For disabilities can be mild or severe, temporary or permanent, and can affect all people, whether they are young or old, men or women, rich or poor. Significantly, some factors appear to be more common than others (for example, disability tends to be more prevalent among women, older adults and the poor) but each set of circumstances gives rise to different needs and experiences, which are further influenced by the physical and cultural environment in which a person lives. Notably, around the world, and in developing countries in particular, this wide variation in the experiences and challenges faced by people with disabilities (PwD) and their families, and the policies and programs that could best support them, are still poorly understood, largely as a consequence of a lack of reliable, comparable data.

Indonesia recently passed Law No. 8/2016. This law follows the ratification of the United Nations Convention on the Rights of Persons with Disabilities in 2011 and commits the Indonesian government to the eradication of discrimination against PwD and to actively work to support and provide services to this segment of the population.[1] It also espouses the principle that public programs be inclusive and accessible to PwD.[2] This chapter seeks to use Indonesia's statistical resources to establish a baseline from which progress in disability inclusiveness can be measured and, when possible, present a description on how it has changed over time.

Defining and measuring disability

Around the world there are estimated to be one billion PwD, 80% of whom are thought to live in developing countries (ILO 2015). But what does this mean? What is it to be a person with a disability? The answer is more complex than it seems. For example, does someone who is unable to walk have a disability? What if their inability to walk is only temporary? Or if they are unable to walk long distances, but short distances are okay? Or, even if they cannot use their legs, they have a wheelchair so they are still able to get around? Does that make a difference? How about if, although they are very mobile in their wheelchair, they are unable to go down rough and potholed streets, or enter offices where the doorways are narrow or there are steps at the entrance?

The traditional approach to thinking about disability reflected the medical model, which focused on the health impairment (Mitra et al. 2011). Under this approach, people were considered to have a disability if they had a health condition, such as being unable to see or hear or communicate, regardless of whether they were restricted in their life activities (ibid.). This means that a person who did not have the use of their legs would be considered disabled. However, over time it increasingly came to be recognised that a person's environment has a significant influence on

---

1 Changing attitudes about disability is at the heart of allowing PwD to develop their full potential. Dibley and Tsaputra (2019) provide an overview of how the law came about and how its implementation is based in the principle of guaranteeing rights for PwD and providing similar opportunities as for any other group in the Indonesian population.
2 In *Development for All*, DFAT (2015) lays out the guiding principles for the Australian aid program in addressing the key challenges of disability-inclusive development in the Asia-Pacific.

the extent to which their impairment affects their capacity to participate in community life. The idea that disability is a product of barriers in the social environment (rather than an individual's characteristics) is captured in the social model of disability (ibid.), which reflects the view that although a person may be unable to walk, if their environment was accommodating (e.g. if they had a wheelchair or prosthetic limb, an accessible school or workplace, and a supportive community) their ability to carry out day-to-day activities may not be severely restricted.

The most current thinking on disability integrates the medical and social models into a bio-psychosocial framework called the International Classification of Functioning, Disability and Health (ICF) (Figure 10.1), which was developed by the World Health Organization (WHO) in 2001 (Mitra et al. 2011). This model reflects the notion that people are disabled by 'the interaction between their health condition and the environment' (ibid.: ii). In other words, it is a health impairment in conjunction with an environment that poses barriers for a person with that health impairment that creates a disability; the health impairment or the environment alone does not. In this approach, a person who must use a wheelchair in a town in which many streets and buildings are not wheelchair-friendly and there is little public transport may have severe difficulty moving around and thus be considered to have a disability. However, if that person lived in an area where the streets were smooth, buildings had wide doorways, ramps and elevators, and buses were wheelchair-accessible, they may have only mild difficulty moving around and no longer be classed as

Figure 10.1 Representation of the International Classification of Functioning, Disability and Health

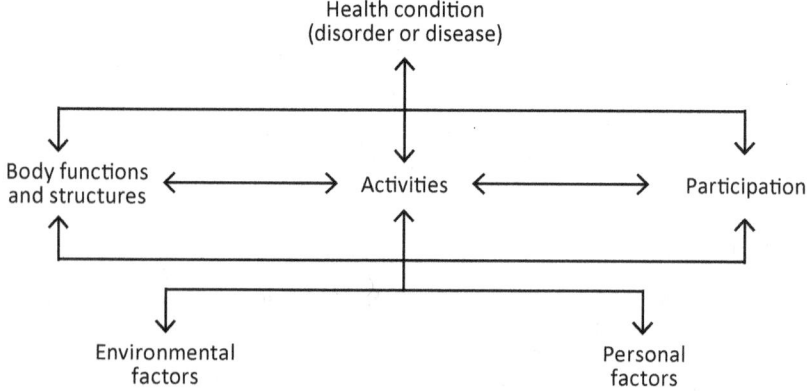

Source: WHO and World Bank (2011).

disabled. This means that two people with the same health impairment in different locations may have different disability statuses (Mitra et al. 2011).

The substantial scope for variation in approaches to defining and measuring disability poses considerable challenges. This is because even relatively small differences in the way disability is assessed (including how disability questions are phrased, whether they are asked by a trained interviewer, and which disability thresholds are used) can have a very large impact on the final statistics (ILO 2007), with the effect that the results of different studies may appear to be conflicting and cannot be easily compared.[3] By way of example, consider the global prevalence of moderate and severe disability in children aged 0–14 years. The WHO and the World Bank (2011) report a prevalence rate of 5.1%, while Mizunoya et al. (2016) estimate a rate of 1.4%. How can this discrepancy be explained? Is one study right and the other wrong? Has substantial progress been made in recent years? Or did the studies measure different things? In this case it appears there were important definitional and methodological differences between the studies, including that the WHO and World Bank analysis drew on a much broader dataset that took into account pain and discomfort, anxiety and depression, and cognition and social participation (Mizunoya et al. 2016). Therefore, the results of these studies are not strictly comparable.

Measuring disability is complex. In recognition of the challenges caused by inconsistent methods and approaches, the United Nations Statistical Commission established the Washington Group on Disability Statistics (Washington Group, WG) in 2001 to promote international cooperation in disability measurement to allow comparability across countries (ILO 2007; Mitra et al. 2011). The WG's recommendations are based on the ICF and provide a short set questionnaire which is designed for use in censuses and other large data collection efforts. Due to the complexity of disability measurement, the WG short set questions are not designed to measure all aspects of difficulty in functioning that people may experience, but rather those domains of functioning that are likely to identify the majority of people at risk of participation restrictions. The functioning difficulties included are:

- difficulty seeing, even if wearing glasses
- difficulty hearing, even if using a hearing aid
- difficulty walking or climbing steps

---

3 It is even necessary to be cautious when comparing the results for different countries based on a single standard, since interpretations of disability vary across countries and surveys (Mizunoya et al. 2016).

- difficulty remembering or concentrating
- difficulty (with self-care such us) washing all over or dressing
- difficulty communicating (using your usual language), for example understanding or being understood.

Respondents are asked to indicate whether in each domain they have 'no difficulty', 'some difficulty', 'a lot of difficulty' or 'cannot do at all'. These domains are then qualified as generating no limitation, moderate limitation or severe limitation.

However, despite the fact that the WG's recommendations have become 'one of the most widely accepted and internationally tested tools' (Mizunoya et al. 2016: 10), they are still far from universally used. Indonesia is not the exception. While data collection in Indonesia has gradually been getting closer to the WG, questionnaires differ in terms of the questions included to measure disability. This is true even across years within nationally representative surveys. Some surveys take a more medical model approach by attempting to identify sufferers of particular medical conditions associated with disability (e.g. blindness, deafness, brain damage). Some surveys use both the WG approach and the medical model. Appendix table A10.1 provides details on the specific questions used in each of the surveys used in this chapter. The differences in methodology mean that the prevalence estimates from each of the datasets are not directly comparable to each other, and mostly difficult to be comparable across time.

Data sources

Population Census 2010

The Population Census 2010 aims to provide information on all households in Indonesia in 2010. This survey follows the WG short set methodology, except that it combines the remembering/concentrating and the communicating domains (which are separate in the WG short set questions). The allowed responses about the level of difficulty also differ slightly from the four-level responses in the WG recommendation. Respondents indicate for each functioning domain whether they have 'no difficulty', 'a little (*sedikit*) difficulty', or 'severe (*parah*) difficulty'.

Susenas

The Indonesian National Socioeconomic Survey (Survei Sosio-Ekonomi Nasional, Susenas) is a nationally representative household survey that collects information on household characteristics and composition, education, health, main activities and fertility for ever-married women.

The questionnaire consists of core questions which are asked every year and a module. The modules ask specialised questions on particular topics and rotate in and out of the survey every three years. Questions on disability are included in the 'Social, culture and education' module that was implemented in 2000, 2003, 2006, 2009 and 2012. By 2018 the disability questions were reintroduced in the core questionnaire, but the information was collected only from individuals aged 2 or more.[4]

The 2000, 2003 and 2009 survey rounds measure disability using the medical model definition. They ask whether the person is blind, deaf, speech-impaired, and so on with the response being 'yes' or 'no'. It has been recognised that this measure excludes people with mild health impairments who might find it difficult to function in the community, and so produces a lower bound of the incidence of disability. Susenas 2006 also uses the medical model of disability but includes a different array of descriptions of medical conditions; for example, it asks whether the respondent has vision difficulties, rather than whether they are blind (see Appendix table A10.1). It also collects an additional set of questions on functioning that differ from the WG questions. Allowed responses to the question of whether such difficulties are experienced are 'yes' or 'no'. Susenas 2012 follows the WG more closely. It asks questions about the WG functioning domains but the response categories differ from that recommended by the WG. Allowed responses are 'no', 'modest' and 'severe'. Finally, Susenas 2018 includes the six WG function domains and the recommended four WG categories of 'no', 'some', 'a lot' and 'cannot do at all'. However, this round asked the set of questions only to individuals aged 2 or older.

Although Susenas collects information on disability in six non-consecutive survey rounds between 2000 and 2018, the changes in the questionnaire make it unsuitable for examining trends across time. For example, even though the survey questions on disability are the same in 2000, 2003 and 2009, using the medical definition in these years generates very low estimates of disability prevalence (less than 1% of the population) and so is also unsuitable to identify temporal trends or variations.

Sakernas

The National Labour Force Survey (Survei Angkatan Kerja Nasional, Sakernas) is a nationwide survey that collects information on the labour market characteristics of all working-age individuals (aged 15 and over). This survey is conducted annually and is predominantly used

---

4 In 2020 questions about disability were again included in the core questionnaire. Those data are not included in the current chapter.

to construct labour market statistics. The 2016 Sakernas included some questions designed to identify disability. It used a combination of the medical definition and functioning difficulties. Allowed responses were 'no difficulty', 'some difficulty' or 'severe difficulty'.[5]

Indonesia Family Life Survey

The Indonesia Family Life Survey (IFLS) is a multi-topic longitudinal survey that started in 1993 and has been following the same people for more than 20 years. The sample is representative of 83% of the Indonesian population living in 13 of the 27 provinces in the country (mostly in western Indonesia). For this analysis we use the latest round, which was conducted in 2014. This is a rich source of information and asks individuals aged 15 and older about their health and physical condition. It allows an identification of individuals with disabilities using a medical definition of disability. Unlike the other surveys, it asks if a health practitioner (doctor, nurse, midwife, etc.) has diagnosed each condition with the allowed responses being 'yes' or 'no'.[6]

The survey also includes a section on difficulties with physical functioning (walking, squatting, carrying, standing, reaching), daily living (dressing, bathing, getting up, eating, toileting) and activities of daily living (shopping, cooking, chores, managing money, medicines). We do not include these in this analysis as although they follow the spirit of the WG they are very different from the measures included in the census and other surveys, making them difficult to compare.

Disability prevalence

We start with an examination of the differences in prevalence rates across different data sources.[7] Figure 10.2 presents the proportion of people that each survey identifies as living with disability. In 2000, 2003 and 2009 Susenas used a medical model definition that asked if people were blind, deaf, mute, speech-impaired, or had a learning or physical disability. Using this approach to disability we calculate that around 0.8% of the population has one of those conditions. This measure, however, does not

---

5 Sakernas 2016 and Susenas 2018 asked about disability in a similar way. We will include some comparisons over time adjusting Susenas data to the specific questions and the population used in Sakernas to allow a comparison.
6 The medical diagnostic generates a lower bound of the disability prevalence as it does not include people who have not been diagnosed, for example, if they do not have medical access.
7 We use sample weights in the estimation of the prevalence in all the surveys.

Chapter 10 Disability in Indonesia: What can we learn from the available data?

Figure 10.2 Prevalence of disability in different surveys (%)

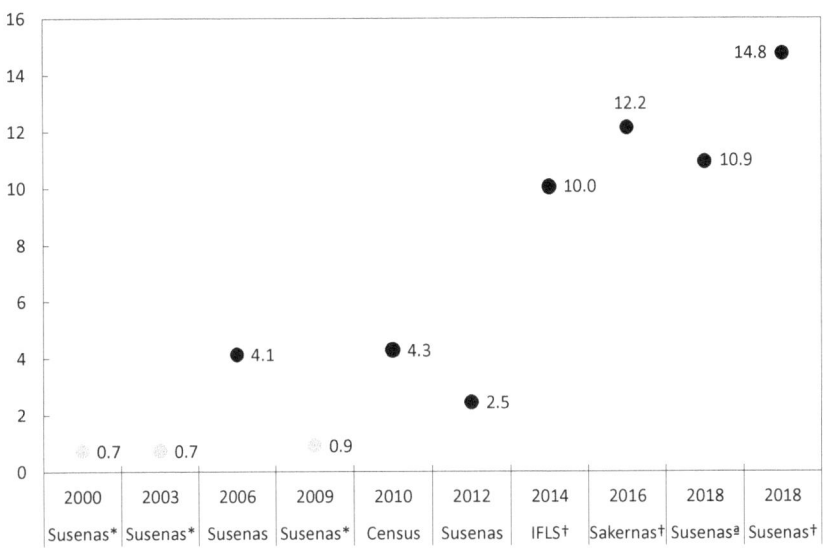

Note: * Represents surveys that used the medical definition of disability (grey dots). † The sample does not include children under age 15. ᵃ The sample does not include children under age 2. WG-like definition in black dots.

Source: Authors' calculations using sample weights in Susenas, IFLS and Sakernas.

include people who have other difficulties and does not exclude people who have a difficulty but with an assistive device can function in the community (as suggested by the WG). Susenas 2006, 2012 and 2018, the Census 2010, the IFLS 2014 and Sakernas 2016 use a definition more in line with the WG. Despite that, we find they generate significantly different estimates in terms of disability prevalence.

From the census and Susenas 2006 and 2012, we estimate that the proportion of the population with a functional disability is between 2.5% and 5%. The census disability prevalence rate is 4.3%, or 10,150,719 people with a disability, where disability is defined as having a little or severe difficulty in one or more of the functioning domains. This is at odds with surveys conducted after 2012 where the estimated prevalence is between 10% and 15%.[8] Adioetomo et al. (2014) use data from Riskesdas

---

8 This is more in line with other estimates obtained in the 2007 Riskesdas. If only moderate and severe disabilities are included, the 2007 Riskesdas suggests a disability prevalence rate of around 11% (Adioetomo et al. 2014).

(Riset Kesehatan Dasar, Basic Health Research) 2007 and estimated the prevalence of disability in Indonesia to also be between 10% and 15%, which they suggest may be a conservative estimate. The discrepancies in the estimated prevalence of disability are likely to be the result of differences in the way the surveys were implemented, even though they applied approaches consistent with the WG's recommendations.

Figures 10.3 and 10.4 show how people living with a disability are distributed across Indonesia. Gorontalo and North Sulawesi have the highest prevalence rates of the country at above 6%. The next highest prevalence provinces are Central Sulawesi, South Sulawesi and East Nusa Tenggara, with rates between 5% and 6%. Surprisingly, Papua, West Papua and Riau Island have low prevalence—below 3%—while other provinces like Jakarta or Yogyakarta, where a more supportive environment would be expected, do not have particularly low rates.[9] Disability in Indonesia is concentrated slightly more in rural areas (4.6%) compared to urban areas (3.9%).[10] This is consistent with the findings of Adioetomo et al. (2014) for Indonesia, and of Mitra et al. (2011) who find that disability is higher in rural areas in most of the fifteen developing countries they study.[11]

Figure 10.3 shows the provinces that have higher percentages of the population living with a disability. Figure 10.4 presents the distribution of the number of people affected, which provides some indication of the provinces where more resources (in absolute terms) may be required to support PwD. The map shows that the greatest number of people living with a disability are concentrated in Java, North Sumatra and South Sulawesi.[12] The eastern part of the country has the lowest number of PwD. We find that in relative and absolute terms Papua and West Papua have the lowest incidence of disability. Adioetomo et al. (2014) similarly find that disability prevalence is relatively low in these two provinces, based on analysis of the Riskesdas 2007 data.

---

9   We calculate a correlation of 0.56 between the prevalence rate generated by the Census 2010 and Susenas 2012 and a correlation of 0.76 between the Census and Susenas 2018, indicating a similar pattern.
10 The provinces that have the highest proportion of PwD in their rural areas are North Sulawesi, South Sulawesi, Gorontalo, West Sumatra and Riau Island.
11 Utomo et al. (2019) find that fertility decline and out-migration has created pockets of ageing in rural Indonesia. This can be one explanation for the difference in disability prevalence between urban and rural areas.
12 Using data from Susenas 2018 we also find these regions to have the highest numbers of PwD, but magnitudes are higher.

Chapter 10 Disability in Indonesia: What can we learn from the available data?   181

Figure 10.3 Prevalence of people with disability, by province

Source: Census 2010, authors' calculations.

Figure 10.4 Number of people with disability, by province

Source: Census 2010, authors' calculations.

Chapter 10 Disability in Indonesia: What can we learn from the available data? 183

Figure 10.5 shows how the number of PwD are distributed across the different functioning domains. Vision difficulties are consistently the most prevalent limiting aspect across different surveys. However, severe difficulties are relatively evenly distributed across the types of difficulties. It is common that people experience more than one type of disability. Forty per cent of PwD have more than one type of limitation. Therefore, total disabilities do not equate to number of people but, rather, indicate the type of disability that is more prevalent. While the WG short set of questions by themselves explicitly address limitations only in undertaking basic activities, they are designed for analysis with other information in a way that incorporates the full bio-psychosocial model of disability.[13]

Causes of disability

The Susenas surveys in their various versions enquire about the cause of disability. Knowing the cause of disability is informative, as it helps to determine what disabilities may be possible to prevent. For example, a congenital condition is less likely to be prevented, while a disability that is a result of an accident or disease can possibly be diminished or avoided. Figure 10.6 shows that 60% of disabilities are caused by diseases and 16% are caused by accidents.[14] Malnutrition is reported as being the cause of disability only 1.8% of the time. This may reflect that malnourishment often leads to other diseases which may be reported as the cause of the disability. Congenital disorders account for 17% of disabilities.

In Susenas 2012 people reported that vision difficulties are often caused by diseases and accidents (in 88% of cases). Communication difficulties are often related to congenital causes (40%), while difficulties remembering or concentrating are often the result of an accident (39%) or stress (26%). Diseases and accidents also often cause walking difficulties (60% and 24% respectively) compared to 15% of walking difficulties as a result of congenital conditions. These difficulties caused by diseases are also more likely to be related to ageing.

---

13   www.washingtongroup-disability.com/washington-group-question-sets/short-set-of-disability-questions/
14   Susenas 2012 asks about accidents and natural disasters. Susenas 2003 asked about natural disasters and accidents separately and shows that the contribution of natural disasters to disability is small (2%). Although natural disasters are not likely to be a cause of disability, PwD are at a higher risk during natural disasters.

Figure 10.5 Types of disability as a share of total disabilities (%)

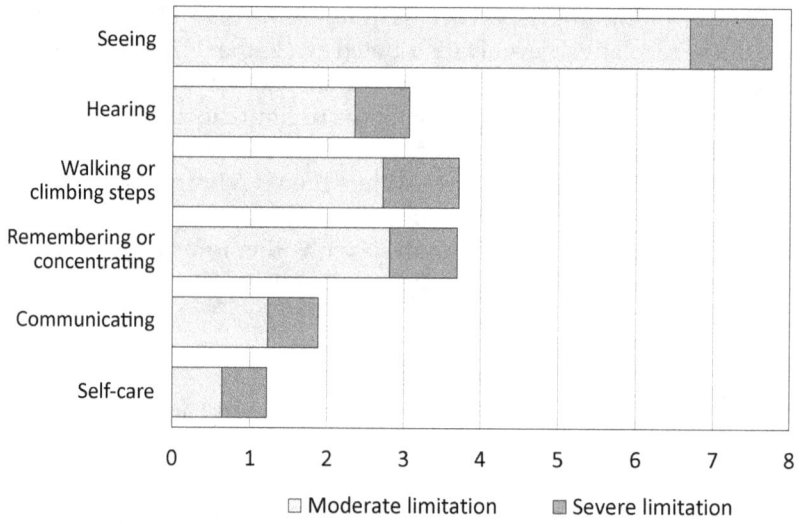

Note: Total disabilities are all the disabilities experienced by people. Since one person can experience more than one type, total disabilities do not equate to number of people.

Source: Susenas 2018, authors' calculations.

Figure 10.6 Causes of disability (%)

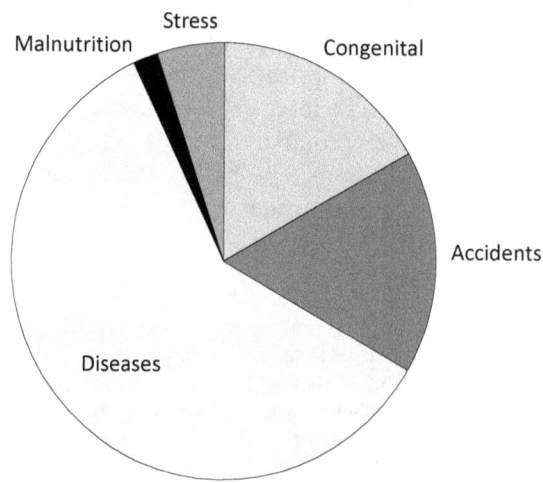

Source: Susenas 2012, authors' calculations using sample weights.

Figure 10.7 Total population distribution by age range and disability status (%)

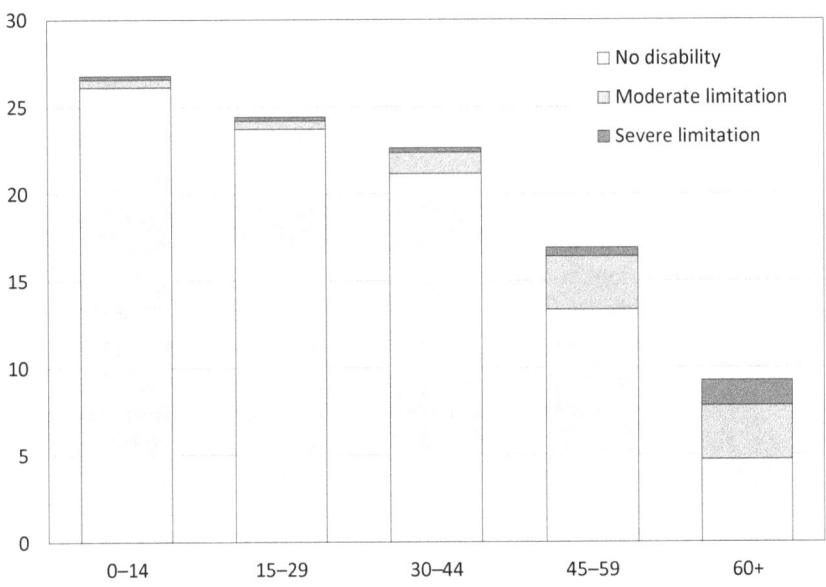

Source: Susenas 2018, authors' calculations. The percentage of disability for the ages 0–14 is a lower bound as data from ages 0 to 1 were not collected.

Figure 10.7 presents the age distribution of the total population in Indonesia and the proportion that has a disability. Indonesia is a young country, with 27% of the population aged between 0 and 14 years and 24% aged between 15 and 29. In these age groups 2% and 3% respectively are affected by a disability. In contrast, while people older than 60 comprise only 9% of the population, 49% of them are affected by a disability, indicating that most disability is concentrated among older adults.

Older adults (60+) constitute around half of the PwD population. When we examine the types of difficulties they face in Susenas 2018, we find that the most common limitation is having a vision problem—72% of older adults report difficulties seeing. A further 44% report hearing problems and 50% have difficulties walking and climbing stairs.

Finally, across the different surveys we find that disability prevalence does not vary markedly by gender. Census data show that the incidence of disability is similar for males and females—4.6% of women have a disability compared with 3.9% of men; and 54% of PwD are women. Figures from Susenas 2018 show a similar pattern: 55% of PwD are women, with a prevalence of 10% for men and 12% for women.

Assistive devices

Table 10.1 shows the proportion of people who indicate they do not have an assistive device, which they report needing by type of health impairment. For people with limited vision, 80% of those who report that they need glasses also report they do not have them and 28% of those who report they need a blind stick do not have one. This could be related to limited access to the cane itself but also to lack of access to appropriate training on how to use it. For those with hearing impairments who report that they need a hearing aid, 91% do not have one. Given that hearing is one of the most prevalent conditions (12% of PwD), improving access to and use of hearing aids has the potential to considerably improve the daily functioning of many people living with a disability. Access to prosthetics is also very low in Indonesia. For people with a difficulty using their arms, fingers, legs or with a physical deformity who need prosthetics, on average across these categories of disability less than 25% of people who could benefit from having a prosthetic are able to access one.

Table 10.1 Unmet demand for assistive devices

Health impairment	Assistive device needed	Unmet need (%)
Vision	Glasses	80
	Blind stick	28
Hearing	Hearing Aid	91
Speaking	Sign language	54
Using arms and fingers	Prosthetic	60
Using legs (walking)	Prosthetic	75
	Wheelchair	24
	Walking aid	28
Physical deformity	Prosthetic	90
	Wheelchair	25
	Walking aid	33
Paralysis	Wheelchair	11
	Walking aid	63
Chronic diseases	Breathing aid	31

Source: Susenas 2006, authors' calculations using sample weights.

Disability and education, labour market activity, health and access to services

Experiencing a disability is likely to impose restrictions in terms of access to public services. In this section we look at some areas where PwD are likely to be disadvantaged. Table 10.2 shows the difference between PwD and without a disability (Pw/oD) in different domains that are relevant at different periods over the life cycle. Educational attainment is lower among PwD. These differences could reflect, for example, that families decide not to send children with a disability to school as they are viewed as being unlikely to ever work or earn a reasonable living (demand-side factors), or a lack of access to education for children with a disability from families who do want to send their children to school (supply-side factors).[15] With the available data it is not possible to identify the main causes or whether the differences are driven by supply or demand factors.

If we look at school attendance, there is a 17 percentage point difference in school attendance between school-aged children with a moderate disability and those without a disability (62% versus 79%). There is an additional 30 percentage point difference between children with a moderate disability and children with a severe disability, with only 32% of school-aged children with a severe disability attending any school. It is thus likely that access to the labour market in the future will be severely limited for these individuals.

If we look at school participation by school level, we find that the gap in school attendance between children with a disability is larger for secondary school–aged children than for primary school–aged children. This is particularly true for those with a moderate disability. Having multiple disabilities is as restrictive as having a severe disability; only 37% of children with multiple disabilities attended school. Schools are often not equipped, nor prepared, to enrol children with a disability and this is even more so when children have multiple disabilities. We find that special schools (*sekolah luar biasa*, SLK) serve mainly this group of people with severe disabilities.[16] Finally, we also find a gap in government-provided support for schooling, with a lower proportion of children and young adults with a disability receiving the Smart Indonesia Program (Program Indonesia Pintar, PIP).

---

15 These are widely acknowledged by disability advocates as common occurrences in Indonesia (source: conversations with disability civil society organisations and other practitioners).
16 For more information on schools see Afrianty (2019).

Table 10.2 People with disability—access to education, health and the labour market

	Notes	PwD severe (1)	PwD moderate (2)	Pw/oD (3)	Diff (1–3)	Diff (2–3)
Years of education	1	2.8	4.4	6.5	−4	−2
		%	%	%		
Attending school, age 5 to 17		32	62	79	−47	−17
Attending school, age 5 to 12	2	29	65	84	−56	−19
Attending school, age 13 to 17	2	28	54	83	−54	−29
Attending school, age 18 to 25	2	3	14	16	−13	−2
Attending special school (*sekolah luar biasa*), age 5 to 17	3	17	4	0	17	4
Attending special school (*sekolah luar biasa*), age 18 to 25	3	13	1	0	13	1
Received PIP last year, age 5 to 17	3	10	15	18	−7	−3
Received PIP last year, age 18 to 24	3	1	2	3	−2	−1
Has birth certificate (age 2 to 17)	3	77	83	84	−6	0
Has national ID	1,3	80	86	89	−8	−2
Women's marriage before 16 (age 20 to 24)	3	1.6	3.2	2.6	−1.1	0.6
Women's marriage before 19 (age 20 to 24)	3	23	34	31	−7	3
Participating in the labour force 2010		28	61	66	−38	−5
Participating in the labour force 2016	4	25	67	70	−42	−3
Participating in the labour force 2018	3	42	69	69	−27	−1
Any health complaint last month 2012	2	53	46	20	33	26
Any health complaint last month 2018	3	54	47	26	28	21
Outpatient last month (for those with a health complaint)	1,3	62	57	50	12	7
Inpatient last year	1,3	11	6	3	7	3
Has health insurance	1,3	54	56	57	−3	−1
Has National Health Insurance (JKN)	1,3	52	53	53	−1	0

Notes: 1 = after controlling for age, 2 = Susenas 2012 using individual weights, 3 = Susenas 2018 using individual weights, 4 = Sakernas 2016 using individual weights. PwD = people with disability, Pw/oD = people without disability, Diff = difference, PIP = Program Indonesia Pintar (Smart Indonesia Program), JKN = Jaminan Kesehatan Nasional (National Health Insurance).

Source: Census 2010, unless otherwise stated. Authors' calculations. Differences are reported in percentage points.

Having a birth certificate is an official requirement for school enrolment and for accessing other services (although 22% of children attending school are reported to not have a birth certificate).[17] A lower proportion of children aged 2 to 17 with a disability have a birth certificate compared to Pw/oD at the same age. Difficulty in obtaining birth certificates may thus be a barrier to the educational participation of children with disabilities and their ability to access other public services. This pattern is also visible for the entire population with disability in relation to how many have a national ID card.

Poverty is one of the main drivers of child marriage in Indonesia and around the world; families marry their daughters with the hope that other households can better provide for them (Cameron et al. 2020). This is exacerbated for women with a moderate disability. Women aged 20 to 24 with moderate disabilities were more likely to be married as a child than any other group, while those with severe disabilities were less likely.

Participation in the labour market is also significantly lower for PwD.[18] The overall small difference between people with moderate disabilities and people with no disabilities (61% versus 66%) is mainly driven by those with moderate vision difficulties. If we exclude this group we find that only 38% of PwD are participating in the labour market (compared to 66% of Pw/oD). Most PwD work in the informal sector—in either household businesses or as household workers and predominantly in agriculture, retail and personal services. This reflects their limited economic opportunities.

Health is also poorer among people with a disability. Around 50% of PwD report health problems, which is 30 percentage points more than Pw/oD, and has remained similar across time. A higher prevalence of health problems among PwD leads to a higher demand for health care services. Utilisation of health care as outpatient and inpatient is indeed higher for PwD. In 2014, the government launched a national health care scheme, Jaminan Kesehatan Nasional (JKN).[19] Overall, we do not find large differences in access to health insurance between people with and without disabilities. However, we observe there is an important variation in access to and utilisation of health care across different age groups.

Figure 10.8 shows that children aged 2 to 14 across the entire population have a lower probability of holding health insurance. This is particularly

---

17 Calculated by the authors from Susenas 2018.
18 For this analysis we restrict the sample to those of working age (15 to 64 years).
19 The count of health care users includes those who reported having BPJS-K (Badan Penyelenggara Jaminan Sosial Kesehatan; Healthcare and Social Security Agency).

Figure 10.8 Access to health insurance (bars) and health complaints last month (lines) by age group (%)

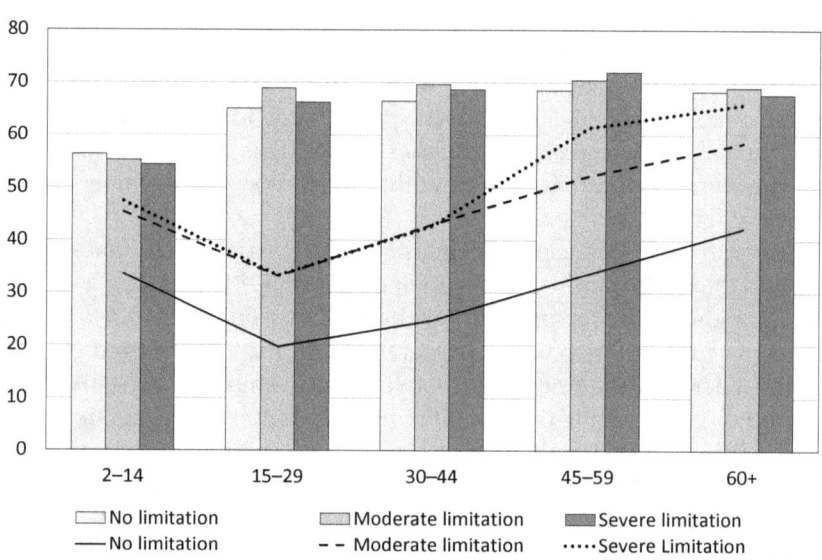

Source: Susenas 2018, authors' calculations.

problematic as medical attention during childhood is essential for longer-term health. We proxy health demand using health complaints, which are shown by the lines in Figure 10.8. Health demand follows a U-shape, where health issues are more prevalent during childhood and even higher for children with disabilities. As life progresses, health care demand decreases, then increases again as people get older. We observe that health issues increase for older adults, particularly for those with severe limitations. If a lower proportion of children have access to health care (because of not having health insurance) but the demand is high, there are two options—either more children are going without receiving the medical attention they need or their families are bearing the medical costs.

Comparing outpatient health care utilisation between those who have and those who do not have health insurance we calculate an outpatient utilisation rate of 78% for children without disabilities.[20] This means that 78% of children who required outpatient attention obtained it, but

---

20 Among children aged 2 to 14 without a disability who reported a health complaint the previous month and have health insurance, 31% went to an outpatient visit. Of those without health insurance, only 24% went to an outpatient visit. We calculate the outpatient utilisation rate as 24 ÷ 31 = 78%.

that their family had to cover the costs of the service. For children with moderate disability the rate is 74% and for children with severe disability it is 70%. If the rate for children without a disability is the baseline, we interpret the 8 percentage point difference between children with severe disabilities and without disabilities as the proportion of children that are not receiving the medical attention they need, while the majority of families are personally paying the cost of health care. As age increases, we find that the rate decreases and therefore that more people are going without the needed health care because of not having health insurance. For older adults, the rate is 34% for those without disabilities and 36% for those with severe limitations.[21] As poverty is associated with lower health status and health care demand, access to health insurance improves equity in health for PwD.

Families of people with disability

Having a disability affects the general wellbeing of the person who has the condition but its impact also extends to his or her family. Census data show that while 4.3% of the population faces a disability, 13.3% of households have a household member with a disability. This is more than 8 million households that have at least one person with a disability.[22] The disability of a household member likely imposes a cost on the household, for example, a higher share of expenditure on health and a reduction in the time the household is able to devote to economically productive activities because household members may need to devote time to the care of the person with a disability.[23] In this section, we describe differences between households with and without disabilities.

It is important to note that it is not clear whether poverty is a cause or a consequence of disability (or both) and more research is required in this area. However, it is likely that poverty is a risk factor for non-congenital disability. Chronically poor people are at risk of ill health and injuries which can lead to disability through a variety of routes. They often live in unsanitary and substandard housing conditions, are unable to afford nutritious foods, lack the ability to access clean water and basic sanitation,

---

21 The only exception of a decreasing rate is in individuals with severe disabilities aged 15 to 29 for whom the rate is 21%, the lowest among all groups.
22 If we follow the data from Susenas 2018 we calculate that 29% (around 20 million) of the households in Indonesia have at least one person with a disability.
23 Susenas 2006 shows that 38% of PwD need help in their daily activities at least occasionally.

are more likely to have unsafe or dangerous jobs, live in areas where there is a higher probability they will be victims of violence, or lack access to appropriate health care (Groce et al. 2011).

Table 10.3 presents some differences between households with a PwD and households without a PwD focusing on children, the caregiver and some general household aspects like expenditure and government support. For the smallest children in the house, we find only a small difference in having ever been breastfeed in PwD and Pw/oD households. In households with PwD, 76% of school-aged children attend school compared to 79% where there is no PwD, but we do not find a significant difference between the attendance of siblings of a PwD and children in households with no PwD.

In households where there is a PwD, 2% of children aged 5 to 9 are working. This represents approximately 450,000 children and double the proportion of children in households where there is no PwD. Children may be working to help supplement household income to meet the increased costs associated with the presence of a member with a disability and to compensate for adults' reduced ability to work because of caring responsibilities. Another possible explanation is that poor households are more likely to have a member with a disability and child labour is another expression of their poverty.

In households with a married couple, we look at the economic participation of the female spouse as she is most often the caregiver. We find a slightly lower rate of participation in households with a member with a disability compared to households without a PwD. In contrast, in households where the household head is a woman (divorced or widowed), the difference in participation rates is large. These households thus appear to be particularly vulnerable and disproportionately affected by the presence of a PwD and seem to have more time constraints due to caring responsibilities.

Consistent with the intertwining of poverty and disability, we find that households with a disability have a lower wealth index, are more food insecure and have lower total expenditure per capita. We find that using a definition of functional disability, expenditure per capita is 13% lower in households with a PwD compared to those without. However, if we use the health impairment definition of disability as incorporated in the 2009 Susenas, the difference is about 21% (result not shown). The health impairment definition captures the most severe cases of disability where more care is required, and a heavier burden is borne by families. In light of this large difference in expenditure per capita, social assistance payments to compensate these households for at least some of the extra costs they face is likely to significantly improve the wellbeing of these households.

Table 10.3 Household differences with disability status

	Notes	PwD (1)	Pw/oD (2)	Diff (1–2)
Children (%)				
Children ever breastfed, age 0 to 5	1	95	96	1
Children attending school, age 5 to 17		76	79	3
Siblings attending school, age 5 to 17		81	80	1
Child labour, age 5 to 9	1	2	1	1
Main caregiver (%)				
Female spouse participating in the labour force		49	50	1
Female head participating in the labour force		45	65	20
Household				
Wealth index (between 0 and 1)	4	0.17	0.21	−0.04
Monthly total expenditure per capita (rupiah)	2	303,204	346,999	−43,794
Monthly total expenditure per capita (rupiah)	3	383,722	485,307	−101,584
Food insecure (%)	4	30	21	−10
Receiving Rastra or BPNT (%)	4	42	33	−9
PKH (%)	4	10	8	−1
Has or receives social security (%)	4	11	11	0
Jaminan pension/veterans	4	8	6	−2
Old age pension	4	5	6	1
Work accident	4	5	7	2
Life insurance	4	4	5	1
Severance payment	4	2	3	1

Notes: 1 = Susenas 2003, 2 = Susenas 2006, 3 = Susenas 2009, 4 = Susenas 2018. PwD = people with disability, Pw/oD = people without disability, Diff = difference, Rastra = Rice Program, BPNT = Bantuan Pangan Non-Tunai (Non-Cash Food Subsidy Program), PKH = Program Keluarga Harapan (conditional cash transfers).

Source: Census 2010, unless otherwise stated. Authors' calculations. Monthly expenditure in current prices. All Susenas calculations include sample weights. Differences are reported in percentage points.

We also examine the differential access to government support and we find that households with a PwD are more likely to access poverty-targeted programs like non-cash food subsidies (Bantuan Pangan Non-Tunai, BPNT) or conditional cash transfers (Program Keluarga Harapan, PKH). It is not clear whether these programs have systematically incorporated disability as an additional targeting criterion and if they have tailored programs to support PwD.[24] In contrast, we find no difference in receiving other forms of social security, but we find there is a compositional effect. More households with a PwD receive Jaminan pension or a veterans' pension,[25] while other forms of social security that are linked to private sector employment are less prevalent for households with a disability. Overall, we observe that households with a PwD are on average poorer and seem to be more time constrained.

Conclusion

We find that in Indonesia disabilities impose considerable burdens on both people with a disability and their families. Providing educational, economic and infrastructure opportunities for PwD is a key aspect of their constitutional rights. Efforts directed at removing barriers to access education, training and job opportunities have the potential to generate large improvements in wellbeing. For example, access to assistive devices is a simple way to improve welfare in several domains.

The health sector has an important role in supporting those with disabilities. Increasing the proportion of children with disabilities who have access to appropriate health care through health insurance and quality care has the potential to ameliorate the negative effects of disability on the individual and their families. As we observe that disability increases with age, prevention of injury and disease that lead to disability needs to be more strongly considered in the health care provision of the country. Most of the disabilities reported are non-congenital and instead acquired or developed because of diseases and accidents. Some disabilities can thus be prevented by improved health service access and labour standards. Such action is likely to be cost effective as it will reduce the financial burden of

---

24 PKH incorporated disability as one of its targeting mechanisms after 2018. The difference we observe in the data is likely to be driven by differences in poverty rather than the presence of disability in the household, as not all households with a PwD receive it.

25 The Jaminan pension is a pension scheme for civil servants, armed forces and police that aims to ensure a minimum standard of living for those who retire or experience a permanent disability. It is likely that veterans experience disability as a result of their service and that this drives this difference.

disability treatment. For example, health service protocols could be put in place to identify children and adults at risk of acquiring a disability. Also, early diagnosis of low-level disabilities and early intervention can diminish the probability of increasing severity. Implementing regulations that establish minimum workplace standards will reduce the risk of workers acquiring permanent disabilities.

Finally, data on disability that are consistent over time and measure disability in accordance with international standards are vital. Consistency in data collection across time is essential to the study of progress with regard to disability inclusiveness. The need for high quality data on disability is especially pressing given the passing of Law No. 8/2016. Through this law, the Indonesian government has committed to improving the welfare of Indonesians with disabilities and their ability to participate in society. Data will allow progress against goals in key areas to be measured—such as educational attainment, economic opportunities, health and welfare. A system for monitoring implementation of the law and associated regulations and evaluating progress over time is vital to ensuring that the intent of the law becomes a reality.

References

Adioetomo, S.M., D. Mont and Irwanto. 2014. *Persons with Disabilities in Indonesia: Empirical Facts and Implications for Social Protection Policies*. Jakarta: Demographic Institute, Faculty of Economics, University of Indonesia in collaboration with Tim Nasional Percepatan Penanggulangan Kemiskinan (TNP2K).

Afrianty, Dina. 2019. 'Disability inclusion in Indonesia: The role of Islamic schools and universities in inclusive education reform'. In *Contentious Belonging: The Place of Minorities in Indonesia*, edited by Greg Fealy and Ronit Ricci, 95–110. Singapore: ISEAS Publishing. doi.org/10.1355/9789814843478-010

Cameron, Lisa, Diana Contreras Suárez and Susan Wieczkiewicz. 2020. *Consequences of Child Marriage in Indonesia*. Melbourne: Australia-Indonesia Partnership for Gender Equality and Women's Empowerment (MAMPU).

DFAT (Australian Government Department of Foreign Affairs and Trade). 2015. *Development for All 2015–2020: Strategy for Strengthening Disability-Inclusive Development in Australia's Aid Program*. Canberra: DFAT.

Dibley, Thushara and Antoni Tsaputra. 2019. 'Changing laws, changing attitudes: The place of people with disability in Indonesia'. In *Contentious Belonging: The Place of Minorities in Indonesia*, edited by Greg Fealy and Ronit Ricci, 77–94. Singapore: ISEAS Publishing. doi.org/10.1355/9789814843478-009

Groce, N., N. Bailey, R. Lang, J.F. Trani and M. Kett. 2011. 'Water and sanitation issues for persons with disabilities in low- and middle-income countries: A literature review and discussion of implications for global health and international development'. *Journal of Water and Health* 9(4): 617–27. doi.org/10.2166/wh.2011.198

ILO (International Labour Organization). 2007. *The Employment Situation of People with Disabilities: Towards Improved Statistical Information*. Geneva: International Labour Office.

ILO (International Labour Organization). 2015. *ILO and Disability Inclusion (GED/PARDEV)*. Geneva: International Labour Office.

Mitra, Sophie, Aleksandra Posarac and Brandon Vick. 2011. *Disability and Poverty in Developing Countries: A Snapshot from the World Health Survey*. SP Discussion Paper No. 1109. Washington, DC: World Bank. doi.org/10.1596/27369

Mizunoya, Suguru, Sophie Mitra and Izumi Yamasaki. 2016. *Towards Inclusive Education: The Impact of Disability on School Attendance in Developing Countries*. Innocenti Working Paper No. 2016-03. Florence: UNICEF. doi.org/10.2139/ssrn.2782430

Utomo, Ariane, Peter McDonald, Iwu Utomo, Nur Cahyadi and Robert Sparrow. 2019. 'Social engagement and the elderly in rural Indonesia'. *Social Science & Medicine* 229: 22–31. doi.org/10.1016/j.socscimed.2018.05.009

WHO (World Health Organization) and World Bank. 2011. *World Report on Disability*. Geneva: WHO.

Appendix table A10.1 Questions used by different Indonesian surveys to gather data on disability

Medical definition	Susenas 2000	Susenas 2003	Susenas 2006	Susenas 2009	Susenas 2012	Susenas 2018	Census 2010	IFLS 2014	Sakernas 2016
Blind	x	x		x					
Deaf	x	x		x					
Dumb	x	x		x					
Deaf and dumb	x	x		x					
Physical disability	x	x		x				x	
Learning disability	x	x		x					
Insane	x	x							
Physical and mental disability/multiple				x					
Other				x					
Brain damage								x	
Vision problem								x	
Hearing problem								x	
Speech impairment								x	
Autism								x	
Seeing			x						
Hearing			x						
Speaking			x						
Using arms, hands and fingers			x			x			
Using legs (walking, climbing stairs)			x						x

Appendix table A10.1 (continued)

Medical definition	Susenas						Census 2010	IFLS 2014	Sakernas 2016
	2000	2003	2006	2009	2012	2018			
Physical deformity			x						
Paralysis			x						
Chronic diseases			x						
Epilepsy			x						
Learning and understanding			x						
Mental retardation			x						x	
Mental disorder			x						
Level of disability distinction	Yes; No (allowing for only 2 medical conditions)	Yes; No (allowing for only 2 medical conditions)	Yes; No	Yes; No (allowing for only 2 medical conditions)					

Appendix table A10.1 (continued)

Difficulty in functioning definition	Susenas 2000	2003	2006	2009	2012	2018	Census 2010	IFLS 2014	Sakernas 2016
Communication and social activities such as speaking, understanding conversation			x						
Physical mobility such as waking up from sleep, moving around, long distance walking			x						
Sighting such as observation or looking at an object within 30 cm			x						
Difficulty seeing						x			x
Difficulty hearing						x			x
Difficulty seeing, even if wearing glasses					x		x		
Difficulty hearing, even if using a hearing aid					x		x		
Difficulty communicating (speech-impaired)					x				
Difficulty remembering or concentrating					x	x	x (and communicating)		
Difficulty walking or climbing steps					x	x	x		x
Talking and understanding/ communicating with others						x			x

Appendix table A10.1 (continued)

Difficulty in functioning definition	Susenas							Census	IFLS	Sakernas
	2000	2003	2006	2009	2012	2018		2010	2014	2016
Difficulty with self-care (eating, bathing, dressing, toilet)			x		x	x		x		
Difficulty controlling behaviour/ emotional						x				
Other (ex. remembering/ concentrating, behavioural/ emotional, self-care, etc.)										x
Level of disability distinction			Yes; No		No; Yes, modest (*ringan*); Yes, severe (*berat*)	Yes, always have difficulty; Yes, often have difficulty; Yes, have a little difficulty; No difficulty		No; A little (*sedikit*); Severe (*parah*)		No; Some (*sedikit/ sedang*); Severe (*parah*)
Other related questions										
Require help for daily activities			x							
Disability limits your interaction with the community				x						
Population	all	all	all	all	all	2+		all	15+	15+
Sample size	241,189	259,231	275,086	1,155,566	277,854	1,131,825		236,785,424	36,379	131,339

11 Out of the shadows: A brief introduction to mental health in Indonesia

Aliza Hunt, Sandersan Onie and Hans Pols

Mental illness has historically dwelt in the shadows of global health and international development. Only recently has it moved from the margins to become a central priority in both research and policy. Mental disorders account for a significant proportion of the worldwide non-fatal and overall disease burden, which includes death and disability. By 2030 the annual cost to the global economy is estimated to be as high as US$6 trillion (Ferrari et al. 2022; Marquez and Saxena 2016). Large middle- and low-income countries like Indonesia continue to confront a plethora of challenges in delivering adequate mental health care. This chapter is a brief introduction to how, and how well, Indonesia has met, and is currently meeting, that challenge. Specifically, using two vignettes (which are composite portraits based on actual experience), we clarify the current state of knowledge on mental health needs in association with existing infrastructure, including a preliminary sketch of the current legislative framework. We touch on the impact of the COVID-19 pandemic and conclude with a firm call to action. Without urgent reform, Indonesia's mental health system will continue to risk failing tens of millions of Indonesians with mental health issues.

Please note, although the following vignettes are not actual cases, they are composites of real people either met directly by the authors or appearing in recent Indonesian media. We caution readers that the following chapter contains confronting themes, and we urge our readership, if you experience any subsequent distress, to contact your local mental health care provider. Some links are provided at the end of this chapter. The other people included in the vignettes, together with their current roles in Indonesian mental health care and the institutions mentioned, are real and can also be contacted for mental health assistance.

Ahmed

Ahmed is 43. He farms a small plot of land in Kebumen, Central Java. He lives in a separate household to his wife and two children, who are currently attending junior secondary school. This separation is a result, he tells us, of 'his episodes'. They start the same time every year, in July, his birth month. I tried not to look down at the length of chain wound tightly around Ahmed's right ankle; the other end of the chain secured him to the dirty cement floor. He is now one of 30 shackled residents at the home of Mbah (grandfather) Marsiyo, who runs an informal institution for people like Ahmed.

Ahmed's first episode was in 2009. His wife was pregnant with their second child, finances were tight and flooding meant they lost their harvest. Ahmed was spending more and more time at the community watch post, playing cards and drinking coffee into the early hours. One day a neighbour found Ahmed sitting sprawled across the path, wearing only a sarong, with blood streaming down his forehead. He gripped a large bloody rock tightly in both hands. He was jerking awkwardly from side-to-side, muttering incoherently. The neighbour took him home to rest and get better. He did not.

A month later, Ahmed's strange behaviours continued. His wife had taken him to the local health care centre. Because the treatment he had received did not help much, the family also visited local healers, hypnotists and Chinese medicine specialists, and purchased over-the-counter *jamu* or traditional medicine; all of which soon exhausted their meagre funds. Finally, Ahmed was admitted to the mental hospital two hours away in Magelang where he was treated with Haloperidol, an antipsychotic medication commonly used in high-income countries in the 1960s. When Ahmed was released three weeks later, he seemed to have recovered and went back to work on his rice fields. Everything returned to normal, until the following July, when he suffered another episode.

Estimates based on the most recent Indonesian health survey, the 2018 Basic Health Survey (Riskesdas), indicate there are 450,000 families in

Figure 11.1 A resident at the home of Mbah Marsiyo

Source: Photo taken by Robert Ern-Yuan Guth (2015).

Indonesia with at least one member diagnosed with a psychotic illness; given the high level of stigma against mental illness and psychosocial disabilities, we suggest this number is much higher. Many of these people are subject to human rights abuses, such as being left to languish in cages, stocks or chains—practices referred to as *pasung*. According to Human Rights Watch (2016), this practice affects as many as 57,000 Indonesians who, like Ahmed, have experienced *pasung* at some point in their lives.

Aisyah

Aisyah, who is 20 years old, is originally from Banten. She was studying nursing at Universitas Indonesia in Jakarta and until her final year at university had been excelling at her studies. As courses went online in 2020, Aisyah appeared more and more distracted. She delayed returning to her home town in Banten and stayed on in her simple boarding house in North Jakarta. She wanted to be close to her policeman boyfriend who was stationed there. Shortly after, Aisyah was no longer seeing her boyfriend; his family had objected to the match.

Aisyah at first became withdrawn; her boarding house friend Susi related that Aisyah had barely emerged from her room in six weeks. Susi, who was an active member of Bipolar Care Indonesia, a mental health consumer group in Jakarta, gradually introduced Aisyah to an online mental health app and teleconferencing service. Aisyah began seeing an online psychologist and was prescribed antidepressant medication by her doctor. A few months later, however, Susi found Aisyah sobbing uncontrollably on the floor of the communal washroom. Her face was bruised and she was clutching her stomach. It turned out that Aisyah's boyfriend's family had found out that she was pregnant and had pressured her to take drastic steps. Aisyah could not stand the thought of having an abortion and, out of desperation, had overdosed on her antidepressant medication.

Aisyah's face was puffy and her breathing laboured as she lay surrounded by family on a tiny hospital bed. The doctors had just finished pumping her stomach and declared her stable. 'Accidental poisoning' was the official reason for her visit, although those there understood it was not. Compared to other global estimates, only a small number of Indonesians attempt suicide every year (2.6 per 100,000 people; WHO 2022). Most other Southeast Asian countries report having suicide rates at least twice that of Indonesia's. Moreover, if we consider these official statistics to be reliable, citizens in developed economies like Australia, Germany, New Zealand, the United States and Canada are at least four times more likely than Indonesians to die from suicide (ibid.).

Do Indonesians suicide much less frequently compared to citizens of other geographic regions? Currently, the actual number of suicide deaths in Indonesia is impossible to determine as there is no official national suicide registry and suicide numbers are taken primarily from police reports. In addition, due to stigma, police are rarely called or notified unless necessary. A recent situational analysis discovered that a death registry had been implemented in several provinces, and even with key flaws in its information pipeline, estimates were already higher than those in official reports (Onie et al. in prep). Even without explicit requests from family, doctors do what Aisyah's doctor did; they rarely write the real reason for a patient's visit, a phenomenon dubbed 'reporting stigma'. In addition, Indonesia's national health insurance scheme (Jaminan Kesehatan Nasional, JKN) does not cover injuries resulting from self-harm, and unnecessary problems arise for the hospital if patients cannot afford to pay (ibid.).

Globally, between four and six out of every ten individuals suiciding or attempting suicide have depression; nine out of ten have a psychiatric disorder (Hawton et al. 2013). According to national surveys using population-representative sampling and valid questionnaires about psychological symptoms in Indonesia, 26.23 million people—more than the population of Australia—suffer from clinically relevant psychological distress and 16.33 million likely meet the diagnostic criteria for a depressive disorder (calculated from Riskesdas data; BPPK 2018). Gotlib and Hammen's (2002) handbook suggests that the lifetime risk of suicide for those with depression is 20%, which is equivalent to over 3 million Indonesians. A more recent estimate based on a meta-analysis demonstrates that individuals with a major depression diagnosis (MDD) have a sevenfold increase in the risk of completed suicide compared to those without MDD (Cai et al. 2021).

Indonesia's mental health care system

Although there has recently been a shift in health care policy towards community-based outpatient models of care, Indonesia's 48 mental hospitals and 269 psychiatric wards in general hospitals are still the primary sources of care. Need continues to outstrip supply: eight provinces are without a mental hospital and three of these provinces are without a single psychiatrist (Pols 2020). The Indonesian Directorate of Mental Health and Illegal Drugs (Direktorat Keswa dan Napza) has concentrated its recent efforts in equipping primary health care centres (*puskesmas*) with mental health programs and personnel, including community-centred early detection. The mental health directorate aims to equip a quarter of all districts' (*kabupaten/kotamadya*) *puskesmas* with mental health capabilities by the end of 2024. Data from 2020 suggest 40% of Indonesia's 514 districts or six of its provinces have reached this target as at the last available reporting period (MoH 2021).

There are currently 1,212 registered psychiatrists, 3,189 clinical psychologists and 1,014 mental health nurses to service over 270 million people.[1] With the addition of other types of mental health workers, this amounts to approximately 3 mental health personnel per 100,000 people according to the most recent Indonesian mental health profile in the World Health Organization's Mental Health Atlas (WHO 2018). This is a little below the median rate for low-middle-income countries (3.8/100,000; WHO 2021). However, compared to high-income countries this amount is low: these countries have a median of over 62 mental health personnel per 100,000 population (WHO 2021). Indonesia also has a smattering of social workers (1.66/100,000) and has instituted mental health specialist training

---

[1] Bu Niken, Psychiatric Association Secretariat, personal communication, 2022; Pusat Data Strategis dan Statistik Ikatan Psikolog Klinis Indonesia (Center for Strategic and Statistical Data, Indonesian Association of Clinical Psychologists, https://data.ipkindonesia.or.id/, 21 April 2022); MoH (2017).

Figure 11.2 Mental health treatment pathways

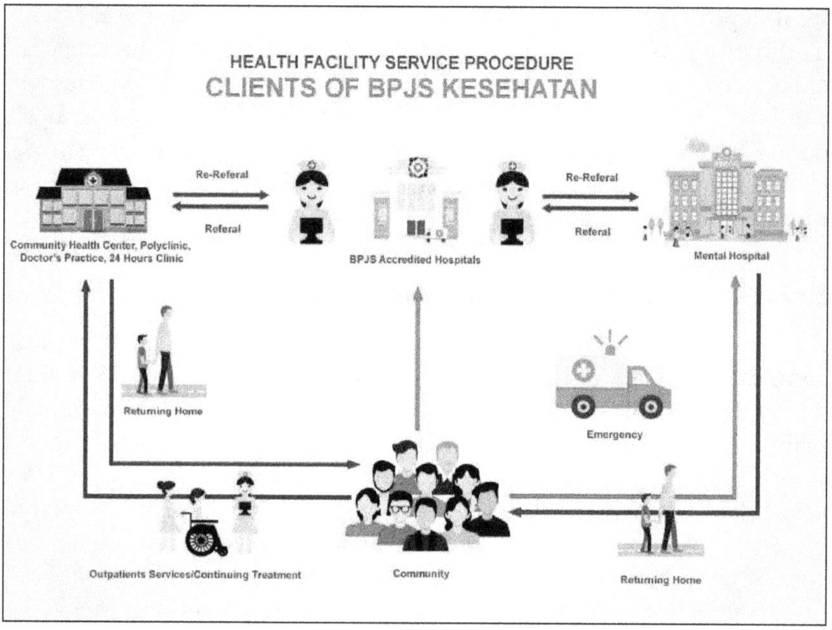

HEALTH FACILITY SERVICE PROCEDURE
CLIENTS OF BPJS KESEHATAN

- Community Health Center, Polyclinic, Doctor's Practice, 24 Hours Clinic — Re-Referal / Referal
- BPJS Accredited Hospitals — Re-Referal / Referal
- Mental Hospital
- Returning Home
- Emergency
- Outpatients Services/Continuing Treatment
- Community
- Returning Home

Source: Diagram adapted from the Indonesian Department of Health's Android application, Sehat Jiwa, launched for World Mental Health Day 2015 and later republished in Ministry of Health Regulation No. 54/2017.

for general practitioners (GPs) in certain regions.[2] Provinces like Aceh, Bali and Yogyakarta have lay community mental health advocates called *kader jiwa* who assist with mental health data collection, early detection and linking people with available services.

Intended treatment pathways in Indonesia are best demonstrated by the Indonesian Department of Health's infographic (Figure 11.2). Initial access is predominantly through primary care facilities including *puskesmas*, assisting *puskesmas* (*pustu*), polyclinics, army and police clinics, and family doctors using an outpatient model of care. Severe cases are then transferred to mental health–equipped district or private hospitals, or to mental hospitals. After a psychiatric patient has been treated for acute symptoms, they are ideally provided with outpatient care, which is coordinated by the *puskesmas*. This system, which is covered by JKN, is supplemented by other services not fully covered by this insurance scheme. These include residential and day-care facilities for individuals

---

2 Ministry of Social Affairs presentation to ASEAN, 2022.

with chronic conditions and rehabilitative services for reintegrating patients into the community, as well as outreach services, such as home visits by *puskesmas* staff and *kader jiwa*. Ideally, these services are implemented in a coordinated manner by trained professionals, and monitored, evaluated and funded through a combination of national and local budgetary allocations.

This treatment pathway was initially laid out in association with the historic 2014 mental health legislation (Law No. 18/2014) and clarified in the Ministry of Health's 2017 regulation for the management of *pasung* cases (Regulation No. 54/2017). Indonesia has a long history legislating how persons with a mental illness should be treated, which can be traced back to the Indonesian constitution and the 1966 mental health law (Law No. 3/1966). Unfortunately, the passing of the 2014 mental health law has not been followed up by an essential legislative mechanism that ensures the ministries responsible for its implementation enact their respective regulations.[3] This has resulted in inadequate coordination across ministries and lack of implementation of the mental health law, including the building of basic infrastructure and provision of mental health personnel. Very few of the targets set by the mental health law have been met nationally (Hunt et al. 2021).

The Directorate of Mental Health and Illegal Drugs was recently moved from Disease Prevention and Control (Pencegahan dan Pengendalian Penyakit, or P2P) in the Ministry of Health to the Public Health subsection, Kesehatan Masyarakat. Following the reallocation of most funding and resources in mental health during the emergency phase of the COVID-19 pandemic, the Ministry of Health had considered folding the entire mental health directorate in 2021.[4] Mental health issues were increasingly understood as cross-cutting and were proposed to be embedded across all health subsections. Aided by Indonesian mental health specialist advocates, the mental health directorate resisted attempts to close it and instead was moved. In addition, a new institution called the National Center for Mental Health was opened in February 2022 at Bogor mental hospital. The center is intended to provide a model for best practice, develop a coordinated network of mental health services and undertake mental health research (Ministry of Health Decision No. 741/2022).

---

3 N.R. Yusuf, former DPR (House of Representatives) member, personal communication, 2021.
4 I. Irmansyah, former director of Mental Health and Illegal Drugs, personal communication, 2022; Diana Setiyawati, head of Center for Public Mental Health at Universitas Gajah Mada, personal communication, 2022.

Mental health data

Budgetary allocations

The Ministry of Health's total budgetary allocation has hovered for some time at around 3% of GDP (MoH 2021). We have not seen any reports suggesting this amount increased significantly during the pandemic. This sum compares unfavourably to high-income countries such as Australia (about 10% of GDP), the United Kingdom (13%) and the United States (nearly 20% during the pandemic). Over the past several decades, only a small proportion of the health budget has been spent on mental health. Reports from the mental health directorate for the year ending 2020 suggest that less than 1% of the health budget is allocated for its use (P2P 2020). No integrated reporting on mental health expenditure currently exists, as additional funds are allocated across other ministries. For example, JKN obviously funds aspects of the population's mental health care and the Social Welfare Ministry handles budgets that fund residential care facilities and a nationwide ring of social workers called TKSK (*tenaga kesejahteraan sosial kecamatan*) who, among other tasks, respond to mental health crises cases in the community. The regional autonomy law also ensures provincial and district budgets can be allocated for mental health purposes and are in areas that prioritise mental health concerns (e.g. Aceh, Yogyakarta, Bali and Central Java). Actual funding in regencies is therefore highly variable, depending on the health priorities of the local districts. The lack of mental health expenditure data is part of a larger issue around the absence of an integrated system of mental health data.

National mental health reporting

The mental health directorate recently trialled a national mental health reporting system called Simkeswa (*sistem kesehatan jiwa*). However, the use of parallel systems of reporting persists—including the use of Google forms. Reporting needs to occur from community health workers all the way up through the various levels of government. The complexity of the current care system, which is embedded across different ministerial portfolios, adds to the challenges of arriving at a coherent picture of Indonesia's mental health needs, existing system and treatment gap. Data from the most recent Indonesian entry for the WHO's Mental Health Atlas (WHO 2018) have many missing fields, including details on subcategories of mental health professionals, information regarding inpatient and outpatient care (e.g. data on number of beds and total admissions to hospitals), total numbers with severe mental illness, and numbers treated. Many basic components of a functioning mental health system, such as state-run prevention and mental health promotion programs, and a national suicide prevention strategy, do not yet exist or exist at the subnational level and have gone undocumented at the central government level.

The absence of an integrated data system means that numbers of mental health personnel and details of current programming and facilities are held in many different databases across different ministries at different levels of government; other sources include private institutions. Sources often contradict each other. For example, prior to the COVID-19 pandemic in 2019, Human Rights Watch (2020) suggested the number of persons experiencing *pasung* was approximately 15,000 nationwide. The Indonesian Department of Health estimated only 5,200 *pasung* cases in the same year (Sulaiman and Efendi 2020). Reports from all sources suggest the number of *pasung* cases has increased during the pandemic, with fewer available social and economic resources within families and everyday stressors multiplying. The health department's estimations suggest there were 6,200 *pasung* cases by the end of 2020. A survey by advocacy organisation Perhimpunan Jiwa Sehat (PJS) sampled 190 social rehabilitation centres (*panti*) in 2021 and found nearly twice the Department of Health's estimate for the previous year (11,000 cases) in that sample alone. However, PJS defined *pasung* more broadly, including the use of restraints or confinement *and* forced sterilisation (CNN Indonesia 2022).

Under-reporting of mental health needs is complicated by differences in operationalised definitions and the lack of pan-professional standards for categorising mental health problems. A brief history reveals the tendency of Indonesian psychiatrists to rely on professional judgement to diagnose patients, while psychologists prefer using standardised tests (Hunt 2019). However, recently, there has been a move in psychiatric diagnostics towards a more evidence-based approach. This has meant psychiatrists and other mental health workers (e.g. nurses, *kader jiwa*) are increasingly using symptom screeners and diagnostic interviews that are favoured by high-income countries. Unfortunately, many of these diagnostic assessment aids have not been appropriately adapted to the Indonesian context. Even when adaptation has been done, these tools often continue to perform poorly in the unique Indonesian cultural context. Although mental health problems are universal, the way a syndrome presents can vary across cultural contexts and hence necessitate adaptation of diagnostic instruments (e.g. see Kirmayer and Jarvis 2007).

Recent estimates of depression prevalence in Indonesia based on the Riskesdas data rely on a structured psychiatric interview called the Mini International Neuropsychiatric Interview (MINI). The team from the National Institute of Health Research and Development, Banglitbangkes, validated this tool for use in Indonesia (Idaiani et al. 2019). The MINI instrument is good at screening out cases who were not depressed (80.8% accuracy). Unfortunately, it is not as good at identifying clinical depression: only 60.7% of people with depression were correctly identified within their sample. This instrument is currently used in the Riskesdas data series and suggests that 6.1% of the Indonesian population were depressed in 2018. This depression measurement tool is a new addition to the Riskesdas data series.

Indonesia has measured what is typically referred to as mental and emotional problems using a symptom screening tool called the Self-Report Questionnaire 20. This instrument has been adapted to the Indonesian population and previous research suggests it has performed well in classifying individuals with and without high levels of psychological distress (e.g. Idaiani et al. 2009). In 2018, 9.8% of the Indonesian population had high levels of psychological distress that would probably warrant a depression or anxiety diagnosis. This was up from 6.0% in 2013. Another large national survey, the Indonesia Family Life Survey (IFLS), found that 21.8% of the Indonesian population has depression, only a year after the Riskesdas 2013 survey (Peltzer and Pengpid 2018). The IFLS uses a short symptom screening tool called the Center for Epidemiological Studies Depression Scale (CES-D), which has not yet been formally validated with any Indonesian adult population. Although psychological distress and depression are not identical, they are related constructs and such variable prevalence estimates point to some issues around mental health measurement standards (see Hunt 2022 for an extended discussion). The absence of universal standards of assessment hampers efforts to provide a consistent picture of Indonesian mental health needs.

The treatment gap

Indonesia has made some strides towards building an effective mental health system. However, the concentration of facilities and trained personnel on Java, and to a lesser extent in Aceh and Bali, means that many geographic areas are without any mental health services. When facilities are offered, barriers of access persist. Facilities are often a long distance away, costly to attend and continuing treatment is expensive to finance. Community-based systems that work to destigmatise mental illness and encourage social support and treatment compliance are only offered in a limited number of areas. This has resulted in a significant number of highly vulnerable people with severe mental illness simply falling through the cracks and ending up as we found Ahmed, chained to the concrete floor in a community care facility.

A survey by Komnas HAM (National Commission on Human Rights) suggested that just over half of those diagnosed with a severe mental illness receive regular medication—one of the main reasons they did not continue to medicate was due to cost (Komnas HAM 2020). The health department reported that at most 4–5% of those with more severe mental emotional problems were being treated (MoH 2021). In addition, medications that are available in Indonesia to treat mental health problems are mostly first-generation antipsychotic and antidepressants that have more severe side effects; this is another problem for continuing treatment. The national insurance scheme has also been shown to inadequately cover patients' mental health treatment needs (Komnas HAM 2020). Finally, local idioms of ill-health lead patients to understand their mental illness as requiring only acute-phase medication, rather than a long-term or continuing course. So often patients choose to cease treatment when symptoms subside, only to relapse. Feeling as though the medication has failed them, they subsequently opt for alternative treatment approaches (Hunt et al. 2021).

Civil society, consumer groups and for-profit organisations

Over the past twenty years, there has been a greater movement in the non-government sector for mental health, both in the non-profit and commercial sectors. Here we discuss some of these groups, as well as the challenges they face.

One of the first groups that became active within mental health was the Indonesian Schizophrenia Support Community (KPSI), which was founded by Bagus Utomo in 2002. Bagus's brother has schizophrenia, and he and his mother had faced the challenges managing his symptoms for a long time before his brother received appropriate medical treatment. Through internet research, Bagus found information about schizophrenia, translated it into Indonesian and made it available on the internet. KPSI is currently active in many cities across Java and, to a lesser extent, elsewhere in Indonesia. It organises activities for individuals with schizophrenia and their family members, often in association with mental health professionals. It organises public health education, campaigns to reduce the stigma associated with mental illness, and brings individuals in need of medical treatment in contact with mental health professionals.

Like KPSI, several groups have emerged known for their public advocacy, training and awareness. In 2013, Bipolar Care Indonesia was founded by five individuals who had been diagnosed with bipolar disorder.[5] Their efforts include organising public forums on World Bipolar Day and providing information on bipolar disorder online. In that same year, Into the Light Indonesia was founded by Benny Prawira Siauw; this group focuses on suicide prevention among youth. It organises group activities and has training programs for the volunteers who participate in its activities. In association with the Indonesian Press Council, it has formulated guidelines for suicide reporting.

In addition, several groups not explicitly branded as mental health–related initiatives have also conducted mental health advocacy; this has allowed for a wider reach. For example, Rahasia Gadis (A Girl's Secret) is a non-profit organisation which boasts over 1 million followers on Instagram and is focused on peer support for women across the country. Other groups have emerged more recently that are better equipped with funding and international research expertise. Emotional Health for All (EHFA), founded by Dr Sandersan Onie and Dr Jessica Nilam, focuses on scalable approaches to suicide. EHFA has co-authored studies published in leading journals such as *Nature Human Behaviour* and *Proceedings of the National Academy of Sciences*, and represented Indonesia in the International Association for Suicide Prevention 2022 Asia Pacific Meeting for leading a national situational analysis with WHO Indonesia and the Ministry of Health (Nowogrodzki 2021).

However, several key issues plague these groups, which limit their effectiveness in creating a healthier country. First, there is often a disconnect between most of these groups and current research, largely due to Indonesia's lagging mental health and suicide research; thus, a vast majority of these groups focus primarily on advocacy and awareness, without realising the limitations of these awareness programs (Harvey 2022). Second, there is a disconnect with each other, resulting in many of these organisations repeating the same efforts.

There has also been an increase in commercial, for-profit organisations and start-ups that offer mental health services. For example, Ibunda (translated as Mother) focuses on free peer chat-based counselling, with a paid option for professional psychologists and psychiatrists. Riliv provides similar offerings, but focuses primarily on mindfulness and self-help. Ubah Stigma is a blend of these two models, advocating for mental health while working with psychologists. A key issue for these for-profit models is that they are competing with one another for a limited pool of psychologists. Thus, while they may improve access to services, this has not resulted in a net increase in Indonesia's psychological workforce.

---

5   www.bipolarcareindonesia.org

Many of these important groups feature prominently in the Indonesian mental health landscape, due in part to their inspirational stories and relatability. However, the non-government sector faces many challenges and can therefore not form the core of the country's mental health efforts. These organisations nonetheless provide additional services and support that meet the needs of many affected individuals.

And then came COVID-19 …

Indonesia's first COVID-19 case was recorded on 2 March 2020. Since then, over 6 million cases and more than 150,000 deaths have occurred.[6] Indonesia's response varied hugely from province to province as the central government attempted to avoid nationwide restrictions to protect people's economic security. As time went on and the virus spread, restrictions were introduced, called *pembatasan sosial berskala besar* (PSBB) or *pemberlakuan pembatasan kegiatan masyarakat* (PPKM). People were increasingly isolated as the middle classes started to work and study from home. Industries that required face-to-face interaction were decimated and people were increasingly out of work. At the same time, mental health infrastructure and personnel were 'repurposed' to respond to the pandemic. Psychologists, mental health nurses and community health workers were used for tracking, tracing and quarantining suspected COVID-19 cases. In addition, they were relied upon in their public health capacity to bust vaccine hoaxes, administer vaccines and to assist public compliance with government restrictions.[7] Suddenly, the few available resources for mental health and treating individuals with various chronic mental illnesses were no longer available.

A brief appraisal of the research around COVID-19 and mental health in Indonesia suggests an accepted position of increased mental health need. A much-quoted statistic is a 9% increase in mental health problems. This is taken from Swaperiksa, a self-check application developed by the Indonesian Psychiatric Association or PDSKJI (Penhimpunan Dokter Spesialis Kedokteran Jiwa Indonesia), where people fill in simple checklists for various psychological complaints to find out if they should seek psychological help.[8] Clearly, it is difficult to conclude whether there is an overall increase in mental health problems or whether there is merely an

---

6 https://covid19.go.id/peta-sebaran (accessed 5 May 2022).
7 I. Irmansyah, former director of Mental Health and Illegal Drugs, personal communication, 2022; Diana Setiyawati, head of Center for Public Mental Health at Universitas Gajah Mada, personal communication, 2022.
8 www.pdskji.org/phq.html

increase in the treatment gap, due to the repurposing of existing mental health services. Indonesians are incredibly resilient—as one of the authors, who is involved in a longitudinal research project studying the mental health of older Indonesians, has concluded. A story from one of the studies' samples during the 2021 Delta wave illustrated how COVID-19 was, at least for older Indonesians, just another pandemic among many that they had experienced. As one elderly person commented: 'Well [COVID] is nothing compared to the *wabah pes* where you got it in the morning and were dead by nightfall ... ha ha', referring to the bubonic plague that persisted in some areas in Indonesia until 1940.

What is clear is that the pandemic has resulted in an increase in mental health awareness. Our analysis of Google web searches demonstrated a five- to seven-fold increase in the rate of Indonesians searching on the term mental health in both English and Indonesian from 2018 to 2021. Other terms, which have historically had more traction in Indonesia such as *depresi* (depression in Indonesian), anxiety (in English), and stres(s) (in both languages) have also seen an increase in search popularity. A Google news analysis also shows a 1.36- to 3.67-fold increase in the popularity of these mental health terms for the same time period. High-profile suicide cases going viral on social media, such as that of Valeriblue who left a three-act play as a suicide note in English, have also ensured an increase in community awareness of mental health issues (Kartikasari 2022). More Indonesians than ever currently understand the importance of looking after their own and their communities' mental health.

Mbah Marsiyo and the Kebumen case study

When we first met Ahmed, he was chained to a cement floor at Mbah Marsiyo's home in Winong village, Mirip, Kebumen in Central Java. He was one of 60 people living at the home of Mbah Marsiyo who had experienced or were currently experiencing severe mental illness. About half of these were shackled using chains, while the other half roamed freely, caring for those who were restrained. Ahmed was housed in the main wing behind the house's courtyard, in a row of open concrete cells. 'The stench [was] nauseating at first, the ground littered with human waste. They [had] no bedding, no free access to water, no toilets, and nothing to occupy themselves with except each other' (Hunt et al. 2021: 7).

During the pandemic, an increasing number of patients were dropped off at Mbah Marsiyo's house, growing to over 80 residents. In August 2020, Ahmed was back at Mbah Marsiyo's after his latest relapse. As his physical condition worsened, he was transferred by the local *puskesmas* staff lead, nurse Tshui Sian, to Prembun hospital, a short distance from Winong village. *Puskesmas* involvement at Mbah Marsiyo's had begun back in 2013, following a visit from the local health office (Dinkes). Although Mbah Marsiyo's was a private dwelling, the then head of Dinkes managed to negotiate *puskesmas* provision of medication and supplementary meals for patients. More recently, after a long advocacy campaign that has seen the transformation of Kebumen into a mental health model district, patients are regularly transferred out of Mbah Marsiyo's by the *puskesmas* (Setiyawati 2020). They are taken to the new mental health wards in Rumah Sakit (RS) Prembun, RS Sudirman, or RS Muhammadiyah in Gombang, or mental hospitals further away.

The Kebumen government recognised that most of the residents of Mbah Marsiyo's were invisible. The previous area statistics on *pasung*, for instance, had completely ignored those in Mbah Marsiyo's house. In 2018 the Kebumen government enacted Law No. 15/2018 on Health Insurance and established a district-level insurance fund to plug gaps left by the inadequate coverage of mental health cases by the national scheme, JKN. By January 2022, government representatives were overcoming yet another of the major obstacles facing individuals with a severe mental illness in Indonesia. These individuals often do not have an identity card and are therefore not able to register for any type of health insurance. Representatives from the civil registration office came to Mbah Marsiyo's house and provided every resident with an identity card and full health insurance.[9]

Kebumen previously housed one of Indonesia's few mental health crisis care *puskesmas*. The facility offered a full community care program. Now, all 35 *puskesmas* in Kebumen have functioning mental health programs; there are three times as many psychiatrists as there were in 2015 and the numbers of other mental health workers are growing. There is even a scholarship program sponsored by the local government for one local nurse to attend Universitas Indonesia (Jakarta) to enrol in the mental health nursing subspeciality program. The government coordinating body for management of mental health problems, TPKJM (Tim Pelaksana Kesehatan Jiwa Masyarakat), now runs community volunteers called *tagana*, who are trained in mental health first aid by one of the area's psychiatrists; they respond to crisis cases and are paid an honorary sum of Rp 250,000 per month (A$25). Mental health literacy in government and community leaders is high.[10]

---

9   Interview with mental health advocate Ninik Supartini, 2022.
10 Ibid.

Mbah Marsiyo's informal institution continues to operate in parallel to other systems of care, including a recently opened government-run residential care facility (Panti Sosial Dosaraso). However, conditions have improved as mental health advocates Ninik Supartini and Dr Mahar have continued to work with passionate actors in the Kebumen government to fund renovations at Mbah Marsiyo's house. They have also worked closely with nurse Tshui Sian and others to establish subdistrict-level cooperatives to ensure continuous supply of adequate raw food ingredients and ready-made food, as well as equipping residents at Mbah Marsiyo's with the requisite cooking skills.

As for Ahmed, he recovered from his worsening physical condition at Prembun hospital. He was accommodated for some time at Mas Slamat's coffee plantation, where he learned how to raise goats. Mas Slamat runs his plantation as a rehabilitation centre to equip its residents with important life skills including animal husbandry. It is part of a local consumer group called Selaras Jiwa; other local consumer groups also operate in the area, for example, Kopigawa (Komunitas Peduli Kesehatan Jiwa), with the ethos of empowering those with mental illness through various types of skills development.[11]

When Ahmed arrived back in his village in 2021, he brought a goat with him to help supplement his income gained from rice farming. He now receives his medication from the local *puskesmas*. He lives in one of the 41 villages in Kebumen that have fully integrated mental health programming called Desa Siaga Sehat Jiwa. The high level of awareness of mental health issues in the village supports a compassionate inclusion of Ahmed in his broader community. He continues to attend the watch post regularly to chat with friends after Quranic readings have finished, particularly during the fasting month. He now volunteers as a mentor for Selaras Jiwa. His daughter is proud of her father and hopes to study mental health nursing when she finishes high school.

Slipping through the cracks

At this point, we return to visit Aisyah's family in Banten. Aisyah lost her baby during her suicide attempt and after someone leaked her personal story on Twitter, her family pulled her out of nursing school and forced her to return to the village in Banten. The gossip followed Aisyah home. People would stare at her or, worse, fall silent as she passed in the street and mutter after her in hushed tones. Her subdistrict is not among those

---

11 Interview with mental health advocate Ninik Supartini, 2022.

that had been resourced by the local Dinkes with a mental health clinic at the *puskesmas*, and her village is not equipped with integrated mental health programming (Desa Siaga Sehat Jiwa) that might have meant community mental health workers (*kader jiwa*) or crisis workers (*tagana*) could assist her.

Mental health literacy in her village is low, which corresponds to high levels of stigma. Not surprisingly, Aisyah felt ostracised from her community. Barred by her family from returning to Jakarta, she continued seeing her psychologist online for some time. However, her family blamed the Jakarta-based psychologist and prescribing doctor for Aisyah's suicide attempt—they had, after all, provided her with the medication that she had used when trying to take her own life. Consequently, her parents forbid her from seeing her counsellor and ensured her compliance by limiting her access to the internet. As an alternative, they took her to a local *imam*, who administered a method of spiritual healing called *ruqyah*; she was also seeing a local hypnotist. Cut off from her networks of existing social and clinical support, Aisyah's symptoms worsened. In December 2021, Aisyah had another suicide attempt; this time she was successful.

Summary and conclusion

The story of Aisyah highlights the dire consequences of inadequate systems of mental health care in the regions, as well as the important role online support systems can play in alleviating experiences of severe mental distress. These internet-based support groups have the capacity to offer spaces for unfiltered sharing and can improve access to mental health knowledge and link people with existing systems of professional care. However, nothing can fully replace face-to-face support from a trusted counsellor and/or friend nestled within integrated systems of community-based mental health care. Kebumen offers an excellent example of what a district can achieve when citizens prioritise mental health concerns.

Resource shortages, including mental health personnel and infrastructure, constitute the most concrete obstacles to Indonesians receiving adequate mental health care. Lack of political follow-through has left the mental health directorate and the new National Center for Mental Health hamstrung and lacking clarity around their respective roles in building Indonesia's mental health care system. The absence of, or conflicting nature of, Indonesia's mental health data, including knowledge on expenditure, existing mental health needs and facilities, and treatment gap, provides little additional insight into the complex task of building mental health systems. In some cases, civil society and local governments have succeeded in plugging gaps left by inadequate national-level leadership and policy implementation. However, evidence of a rising treatment gap during the COVID-19 pandemic heralds an urgent call to action.

Afterword

The authors of this chapter call for a repositioning of Indonesia's mental health priorities. Successfully building an efficacious mental health infrastructure requires a comprehensive legislative framework, which has not yet been achieved. This would then allow for the clarification of roles and responsibilities within national-level mental health–specific institutions and across other involved ministries. It would also signal the importance of mental health to lower levels of government and, theoretically, could free up much-needed funding.

We cannot overemphasise the importance of collecting reliable centralised data of culturally relevant, valid information on treatment needs, existing infrastructure and expenditure. These data would allow for the considered delivery of services to subpopulations most in need of help. We are encouraged by recent data projects being undertaken by universities and within government departments. However, we suggest the next few years offers unprecedented opportunity to collect valid and reliable mental health data.

The missing fields in the Indonesian entry of the WHO Mental Health Atlas must be remedied through population-representative sampling or, better still, a nationwide mental health census. This is something that has constituted an important precipitator of development for many high-income countries' mental health systems (e.g. Jorm 2011). The delay of the detailed module of the 2020 Indonesian Census to 2022–23 could feasibly still be utilised to complete this task. In addition, the existing survey of health facilities undertaken by Banglitbangkes needs only to include some choice questions on mental health infrastructure to supplement a national registry of mental health data, which could be housed at the existing Indonesian mental health directorate.

Important contacts

Australia

Lifeline: https://www.lifeline.org.au/131114

Suicide Call Back Service: 1300 659 467

Kids Helpline: 1800 55 1800

Indonesia

Sejiwa, HIMPSI mental health hotline: 118 ext 9

LISA Helpline: https://www.instagram.com/lisahelpline/?hl=en

Emotional Health for All: https://ehfa.id/help-and-support/

References

BPPK (Badan Penelitian dan Penembangan Kesehatan). 2018. *Laporan National Riskesdas 2018* [National Health Survey Report 2018]. Jakarta: Ministry of Health.

Cai, Hong, Xiao-Meng Xie, Qinge Zhang, Xiling Cui, Jing-Xia Lin, et al. 2021. 'Prevalence of suicidality in major depressive disorder: A systematic review and meta-analysis of comparative studies'. *Frontiers in Psychiatry* 12. doi.org/10.3389/fpsyt.2021.690130

CNN Indonesia. 2022. 'Masalah ODGJ: 11 ribu kasus pemasungan, sesak di panti' [ODGJ problems: 11,000 cases of shackling, overcrowding in nursing homes]. www.cnnindonesia.com/nasional/20210827203048-20-686571/masalah-odgj-11-ribu-kasus-pemasungan-sesak-di-panti

Ferrari, Alize J., Damian F. Santomauro, Ana M. Mantilla Herrera, Jamileh Shadid, Charlie Ashbaugh, et al. 2022. 'Global, regional, and national burden of 12 mental disorders in 204 countries and territories, 1990–2019: A systematic analysis for the Global Burden of Disease Study 2019'. *Lancet Psychiatry* 9(2): 137–50. doi.org/10.1016/S2215-0366(21)00395-3

Gotlib, Ian H. and Constance L. Hammen, eds. 2002. *Handbook of Depression*. New York: Guilford Press.

Harvey, Samuel. 2022. 'Do mental health awareness campaigns work? Let's look at the evidence'. Black Dog Institute. www.blackdoginstitute.org.au/news/do-mental-health-awareness-campaigns-work-lets-look-at-the-evidence

Hawton, Keith, Carolina Casañas I Comabella, Camilla Haw and Kate Saunders. 2013. 'Risk factors for suicide in individuals with depression: A systematic review'. *Journal of Affective Disorders* 147(1–3): 17–28. doi.org/10.1016/j.jad.2013.01.004

Human Rights Watch. 2016. *Living in Hell: Abuses against People with Psychosocial Disabilities in Indonesia*. Human Rights Watch. www.hrw.org/report/2016/03/20/living-hell/abuses-against-people-psychosocial-disabilities-indonesia

Human Rights Watch. 2020. *Living in Chains: Shackling of People with Psychosocial Disabilities Worldwide*. Human Rights Watch. www.hrw.org/report/2020/10/06/living-chains/shackling-people-psychosocial-disabilities-worldwide

Hunt, Aliza. 2019. 'Dari data menuju klinik: Memahami depresi di Indonesia' [From the data to the clinic: Understanding Indonesian depression]. In *Jiwa Sehat, Negara Kuat* [Healthy Mind, Strong Country], 72–88. Jakarta: Kompas.

Hunt, Aliza. 2022. 'Meaning behind the metrics of misery: Understanding prevalence estimates of poor mental health in two samples of older rural Indonesians'. Canberra: Australian National University.

Hunt, Aliza J., Robert Ern-Yuan Guth and Diana Setiyawati. 2021. 'Evaluating the Indonesia Free *Pasung* Movement: Understanding continuing use of restraint of the mentally ill in rural Java'. *Transcultural Psychiatry* 136346152110096. doi.org/10.1177/13634615211009626

Idaiani, Sri, S. Suhardi and A.Y. Kristanto. 2009. 'Analisis gejala gangguan mental emosional penduduk Indonesia' [An analysis of symptoms of mental emotional disorders in the Indonesian population]. *Majalah Kedokteran Indonesia* 59: 473–79.

Idaiani, Sri, R. Mubasyiroh and S. Isfandari. 2019. 'Validity and reliability of depression, anxiety and psychosis questionnaire of Mini International Neuropsychiatric Interview (MINI) in Indonesia'. *ASEAN Journal of Psychiatry*, December.

Jorm, Anthony F. 2011. 'The population impact of improvements in mental health services: The case of Australia'. *British Journal of Psychiatry* 199(6): 443–44. doi.org/10.1192/bjp.bp.111.097956

Kartikasari, Bunga. 2022. 'VIRAL MEDSOS kisah pemuda bunuh diri tinggalkan surat di Google Drive' [Going viral on social media: The story of a young suicide who left a note on Google Drive]. TribunJogja.com, 8 April. https://jogja.tribunnews.com/2022/04/08/viral-medsos-kisah-pemuda-bunuh-diri-tinggalkan-surat-di-google-drive

Kirmayer, Laurence J. and G. Eric Jarvis. 2007. 'Depression across cultures'. In *The American Psychiatric Publishing Textbook of Mood Disorders*, edited by Dan J. Stein, David J. Kupfer and Alan F. Schatzberg, 699–715. Washington, DC: APA Publishing.

Komnas HAM (Komisi Nasional Hak Asasi Manusia). 2020. *Kajian Pemenuhan Hak Atas Kesehatan Bagi Kelompok Rentan di Indonesia* [Study on the Fulfilment of the Right to Health for Vulnerable Groups in Indonesia]. Jakarta: Komnas HAM.

Marquez, Patricio V. and Shekhar Saxena. 2016. 'Making mental health a global priority'. *Cerebrum*, July–August.

MoH (Ministry of Health). 2017. 'Infodatin perawat; Pusat Data dan Informasi Kementerian Kesehatan RI' [Nurses; Center for Data and Information, Ministry of Health]. Jakarta: MoH.

MoH (Ministry of Health). 2021. *Profil Kesehatan Indonesia Tahun 2020* [Profile of Indonesian Health Trends 2020]. Jakarta: MoH.

Nowogrodzki, Anna. 2021. 'Global impacts of *Nature's* journalism and opinion'. *Nature*, 28 September. doi.org/10.1038/d41586-021-02652-x

Onie, Sanderson, A. Daswin, A. Taufik, J. Abraham and Diana Setiyawati. In prep. 'Situational analysis of suicide in Indonesia in 2022'.

P2P. 2020. *Laporan Kinerja Direktorat Jenderal Pencegahan dan Pengendalian Penyakit (P2P) 2020* [Performance Report of the Directorate General of Disease Prevention and Control (P2P) 2020]. Jakarta: Ministry of Health.

Peltzer, Karl and Supa Pengpid. 2018. 'High prevalence of depressive symptoms in a national sample of adults in Indonesia: Childhood adversity, sociodemographic factors and health risk behaviour'. *Asian Journal of Psychiatry* 33: 52–59. doi.org/10.1016/j.ajp.2018.03.017

Pols, Hans. 2020. 'The future of mental health care in Indonesia'. *Inside Indonesia* 141: July–September. www.insideindonesia.org/the-future-of-mental-health-care-in-indonesia-6

Setiyawati, Diana. 2020. 'Locals powering change'. *Inside Indonesia* 141: July–September. www.insideindonesia.org/locals-powering-change-3

Sulaiman, M. Reza and Dini Afrianti Efendi. 2020. '*Kemenkes sebut kasus pasung meningkat selama pandemi COVID-19, kok bisa?*' [Ministry of Health says *pasung* cases increase during the COVID-19 pandemic, how is that possible?]. suara.com, 2 October. www.suara.com/health/2020/10/02/140300/kemenkes-sebut-kasus-pasung-meningkat-selama-pandemi-covid-19-kok-bisa

WHO (World Health Organization). 2018. *Mental Health Atlas 2017*. Geneva: WHO. www.who.int/publications/i/item/9789241514019

WHO (World Health Organization). 2021. *Mental Health Atlas 2020*. Geneva: WHO. www.who.int/publications-detail-redirect/9789240036703

WHO (World Health Organization). 2022. 'Suicide rate estimates, age-standardized—Estimates by country'. Global Health Observatory data repository. Accessed 3 May 2022. https://apps.who.int/gho/data/node.main.MHSUICIDEASDR?lang=en

12 Dengue control in Yogyakarta, Indonesia: Lessons learned from public health innovation using *Wolbachia*-infected *Aedes aegypti* mosquitoes

Adi Utarini

The global burden of dengue

Dengue, a systemic viral infection transmitted from person to person by the *Aedes* mosquitoes, presents a persistent and escalating problem in many parts of the world. Globally, the dengue infection has been predicted to reach 100 million cases in more than 110 countries, and the incidence rate, death and disability-adjusted life years (DALYs) lost have all increased during the past two decades (Zeng et al. 2021). Although dengue transmission occurs mainly in tropical regions, it has been highest in Asia (Simmons et al. 2012), where more than 75% of the world's population infected with dengue live. Eight countries in the Southeast Asian region are classified as hyperendemic areas, including Indonesia (Murray et al. 2013). Recent studies indicate that dengue has the highest DALYs[1] lost in Southeast Asia compared to other neglected tropical diseases such as schistosomiasis, leprosy, trachoma, hookworm and ascariasis (Shepard et al. 2013).

---

1 Disability-adjusted life year (DALY) is a metric used to measure the decline in quality of life due to premature death and morbidity or diseases attack including dengue (Murray and Lopez 1997; Swain et al. 2019).

In addition to the morbidity and mortality, evidence shows that dengue significantly impacts the economic burden. A systematic review estimated the global cost of dengue illness was US$8.89 billion annually, consisting of 46% non-fatal cases admitted to hospital, 33.6% non-fatal ambulatory patients, 8.5% non-fatal non-medical cases and 11.9% fatal cases (Shepard et al. 2016). Asian countries experienced productivity losses of US$6.7–$1,445.9 for inpatients and US$3.8–$1,332 for outpatients per dengue episode. The cost of productivity losses associated with fatal dengue episodes in Asia is around US$12,035–$1,453,237 (Hung et al. 2020).

Dengue also affects quality of life, mainly psychological and social functions. From the quality of life perspective, dengue infection causes discomfort and nervousness. During the acute phase of the disease, the physical symptoms of dengue have several effects on personal mobility and social activities that persist into the late-acute stage of the disease. The most common symptoms sometimes last beyond the period of fever. These disorders often worsen, especially in those who do not seek treatment (Elson et al. 2020).

Environmental conditions and community behaviour can also affect the development of dengue, which affects the prevalence of dengue year-long. All age groups are vulnerable to this disease. It has become even more challenging because urbanisation, population growth, increased international travel, weak infrastructure and poor sanitation contribute to dengue transmission (Buhler et al. 2019; Ramadona et al. 2019). Other risk factors such as climate change, deforestation and the COVID-19 pandemic have contributed to the persistence of dengue in Indonesia. Changes in temperature indices both on land and at sea, and increased air passenger travel, correlate with dengue fever's burden (Yang et al. 2021). The COVID-19 pandemic has significantly impacted infectious diseases such as dengue fever outbreaks, especially in resource-limited countries with endemic dengue fever and intense COVID-19 transmission.

This chapter describes the ten-year journey and lessons learned from building evidence for the efficacy of public health innovation applying *Wolbachia*-infected *Aedes aegypti* to reduce the incidence of dengue in Yogyakarta, Indonesia, a collaboration between Universitas Gadjah Mada, the Tahija Foundation, Indonesia, and Monash University, Australia.

An old but persistent problem in Indonesia

'I have three children; all were hospitalised due to dengue. One died.'
(A family in Yogyakarta.)

Globally, dengue is considered as a neglected tropical disease together with other diseases such as leprosy, rabies and soil-transmitted helminthiases

(WHO 2020). In Indonesia, the Ministry of Health Regulation No. 1501/2010 'Communicable diseases that can cause outbreak and its effort to control the outbreak' classifies dengue as a potential disease that can cause an outbreak. This disease has continued to threaten many people since *A. aegypti* was first reported in Jakarta and Surabaya in 1968, and dengue haemorrhagic fever was diagnosed with 41.3% (24 deaths out of 58 cases) mortality (Karyanti and Hadinegoro 2009). Thereafter the incidence of dengue has escalated, with several peaks, and has spread to all provinces; nearly all districts have reported dengue cases.

Of the tropical countries in Asia, Indonesia is estimated to have the highest disease burden due to dengue. The incidence of dengue over the past 45 years has increased rapidly, with the highest incidence rate shifting from young children to older age groups. Generally, the pattern of dengue cases is inversely related to the mortality rate, but also, underlying this aggregated trend, heterogeneous temporal and spatial patterns have emerged (Ramadona et al. 2016). In 2021, Indonesia reported 71,044 dengue cases; an incidence rate dramatically decreased from 78.85 per 100,000 population to 26.12 per 100,000 population (Makrufardi et al. 2021; MoH 2022). Possibly the decrease was associated with reduced reporting during the COVID-19 pandemic. Dengue has an endemic–epidemic nature with epidemic cycles between 6 and 8 years (Harapan et al. 2019), but this pattern varies at the district and city level. Dengue outbreaks are reported annually; five districts reported dengue outbreaks in 2020 (MoH 2021).

The four dengue virus serotypes—DENV1, DENV2, DENV3 and DENV4—circulate in Indonesia with a predominance of dynamic serotypes according to time and location (Sasmono et al. 2018). In terms of DALYs, the burden of dengue is equivalent to other infectious diseases such as upper respiratory tract infections and hepatitis B, and almost equal to tuberculosis (Guzman et al. 2010; Halasa et al. 2012; Murray et al. 2013; Shepard et al. 2016). Overall, the burden is due to non-severe cases that do not seek treatment. Even though the disease is widespread throughout the country, the estimated burden is highly concentrated in a small number of large cities, including Jakarta, Bandung and Denpasar. About 90% of dengue cases occurred in 15.3% of land areas in 2015 (O'Reilly et al. 2019). In 2017, Indonesia had an estimated 7.535 million dengue episodes with a national aggregate cost of US$681.26 million (Wilastonegoro et al. 2020), a cost 73% higher than previously estimated (ibid.). Effective dengue control is desperately needed.

For more than 50 years, dengue control interventions in Indonesia have largely relied on a combination of vector control, health education and community participation. Various vector control strategies such as larvicide, fogging, reducing mosquito breeding sites by draining, covering and burying water containers, larvae monitoring (known as *juru pemantau jentik* or *jumantik*), eradication of mosquito nests (known as *pemberantasan sarang nyamuk* or PSN), communication for behavioural impact, and one house–one larvae monitoring observer initiatives (known as *gerakan* 1 *rumah* 1 *jumantik* or G1R1J) have not been adequate to control mosquito populations.

Vector control interventions face implementation challenges. For example, only 31.2% of households did PSN in 2018, with variations among provinces from around 16.2% to 43.6%. Practice in urban areas (32.7%) was slightly better than in rural areas (29.4%) (MoH 2018). Lower achievements were suspected in the implementation of vector control in educational institutions and workplaces. Evidence from a systematic review indicates that although interventions to control dengue mosquito vectors with various approaches can be effective, their association with reducing dengue cases are not fully understood (Buhler et al. 2019). Other challenges in dengue control include dengue case management, hospital-based surveillance data, low community participation, data reporting and recording, and low commitment of stakeholders leading to inadequate financing. These factors contribute to less-effective implementation of dengue control.

Responding to these challenges, the Ministry of Health developed the National Strategy for Dengue Control 2021–2025 in Indonesia (MoH 2021), supported by the World Health Organization (WHO). The following strategies have been identified: (1) strengthening effective, safe and sustainable vector management; (2) increasing access and quality of dengue management; (3) strengthening comprehensive dengue surveillance and responsive outbreak management; (4) increasing sustainable community involvement; (5) strengthening government commitments, program management policies and partnerships; and (6) research, inventions and innovations as the basis for evidence-based policy and program management (MoH 2021).

The context: Yogyakarta Special Region, Java Island, Indonesia

Yogyakarta City is a medium-sized, densely populated and rapidly developing urban area, spread over 32.5 km^2 with an average population density of 14,000 persons per km^2. Yogyakarta City is in the province of Yogyakarta Special Region, and well known as a student city and tourist destination in Indonesia. As a city with good public services and health status, it consists of 14 subdistricts and 45 village administrations. The city has more than 400,000 people, and health services are provided by 11 public hospitals, 11 specialist hospitals and 18 primary health care centres (*puskesmas*). In addition to Yogyakarta City there are four other districts in Yogyakarta Special Region—Sleman, Bantul, Gunungkidul and Kulonprogo.

The health system in Yogyakarta is three-tiered, from the provincial health office to the district health office to *puskesmas*. Responsibility for planning, managing and allocating funds for public health services lies primarily with the district government, coordinated and supervised at the provincial level. The district health office is responsible for managing disease prevention and control programs, and supervises public and private hospitals, while *puskesmas* implement the programs and provide services to the community.

From 2006 to 2016, there were 9,418 cases of dengue haemorrhagic fever detected in Yogyakarta City, an average of 856 cases per year (211 per 100,000 population). The annual pattern of dengue varies. For example, in 2012, the annual number of cases was 360 (91 per 100,000 population), while in 2016 the reported cases reached 1,705 (412 per 100,000 population). The peak incidence of dengue tends to occur during the first six months of each year, although the timing of the seasonal peak varies somewhat from year to year. During the peak month, between 49 and 251 hospitalised cases of dengue fever were notified. At the same time, the monthly incidence of dengue was 12–59 per 100,000 population. The median age of all dengue cases was 11 years with the interquartile range 6–20 years, which remained broadly consistent during 2006–2014. Sixty-eight per cent of children aged 1–10 years were confirmed with dengue infection (Indriani et al. 2018). Despite high morbidity, access to health care services was widespread and the mortality rate was low. The four DENV serotypes have been found in Yogyakarta, with DENV2 (25%) the dominant serotype circulating, followed by DENV1 (22%) and DENV3 (17%) (ibid.). The surveillance system monitors dengue at the district level because early diagnosis tests are not evenly distributed across primary care facilities.

Climatic factors such as temperature and rainfall in Yogyakarta are also associated with the incidence of dengue fever and its transmission. The lowest average monthly rainfall occurs in August (17 millimetres), while the highest average monthly rainfall occurs in December (357 millimetres). Changes in precipitation and air temperature are related to the number of dengue cases, which fluctuate between November (lowest incidence) and March (highest incidence) (Ramadona et al. 2016).

Demographic factors such as population growth and unplanned urbanisation are enablers that contribute to the spread of dengue fever. Ramadona et al. (2019) found that population mobility in Yogyakarta is a crucial driving factor for the movement of dengue incident clusters. As Yogyakarta is a major tourist destination in Indonesia, tourism may also have a significant role in spreading dengue. Mapping the spread of the dengue virus at Yogyakarta Adisucipto Airport found that the airport has a high risk as a breeding ground for *Aedes* mosquitoes, especially for the DENV2 and DENV3 serotypes. To measure the proportion of ovitraps containing *Aedes* eggs or immature mosquitoes, an ovitrap index is used (Sasmita et al. 2021). A high ovitrap index indicates that the area tends to have a higher risk of dengue outbreaks (Satoto et al. 2018).

Dengue surveillance data in Indonesia relies on hospital-based reporting, and reporting of suspected and confirmed cases from all health facilities is mandatory. Ideally, hospitals must report within 24 hours to both the *puskesmas*, which is then obliged to conduct epidemiological investigations surrounding the house of the infected case, and the district government for public health intervention and raising community awareness. In reality, however, delayed hospital reporting and responses to these reports cause challenges to slowing or stopping disease transmission (Indriani et al. 2018; Sulistyawati et al. 2020).

The World Mosquito Program Yogyakarta

Wolbachia-infected *Aedes aegypti*

Wolbachia is a genus of bacteria discovered in 1924, but work on *Wolbachia* and dengue did not start until the 1980s, pioneered by Professor Scott L. O'Neill (WMP 2022a). By 1992, *Wolbachia* were known to be extremely common bacteria occurring naturally in 50% of insect species, including some mosquitoes, fruit flies, moths, dragonflies and butterflies (WMP 2022b). *Wolbachia* live inside insect cells and pass from one generation to the next through the female host to her offspring. Normally, *A. aegypti* mosquitoes do not carry *Wolbachia*; however, many other mosquitoes do, such as *Culex quinquefasciatus* and *Aedes albopictus* (Jeyaprakash and Hoy 2000; Rovik et al. 2022; Weinert et al. 2007; Werren 1997).

Following years of experiments, in 1994 *Wolbachia* was successfully isolated from *Drosophila melanogaster* (fruit fly) and transferred into *A. aegypti* eggs through embryonic microinjection (WMP 2022a). Laboratory studies have shown that *Wolbachia* in *A. aegypti* has several mechanisms that work synergistically to inhibit the dengue virus replication in the mosquito body so that the virus cannot be transmitted from person to person (Moreira et al. 2009). Also, *Wolbachia* infection in *Aedes* and *Anopheles* mosquitoes has been shown to interfere with replicating various pathogens, including viruses, filarial nematodes, bacteria and malaria parasites. This evidence in the laboratory setting bodes well for the long-term stability of the effect of *Wolbachia*-based biocontrols on dengue virus serotypes (Ye et al. 2015). *Wolbachia* does not alter or affect the genetic characteristics of mosquitoes, therefore this is not considered as a genetically modified organism. Further results of a risk analysis conducted by the Australian Commonwealth Scientific and Industrial Research Organisation in 2010 showed that *Wolbachia* technology is safe for humans, animals and the environment (Murphy et al. 2010). Given that *Wolbachia* in *A. aegypti* can spread from one generation to the next as in *D. melanogaster*, this method has the potential to be self-sustaining. If *Wolbachia*-infected *A. aegypti* can be introduced, deployed and sustained in the natural habitat, this innovation can lead to a promising new strategy to help control the spread of dengue (WMP 2022b).

The study phases

The World Mosquito Program (WMP) Yogyakarta (formerly known as the Eliminate Dengue Project Yogyakarta) started in 2011. The program has four phases (Figure 12.1). The first three phases (year 2011 up to August 2020) were considered as the research phase to build evidence to demonstrate the efficacy of *Wolbachia A. aegypti* technology. From late 2020 the nature of research activity slowly transformed into an implementation phase characterised by a greater ownership by the local government, particularly the district health office, and active involvement of the communities for deploying *Wolbachia A. aegypti*, supervised by the WMP Yogyakarta team.

Phase 1 of the study (October 2011 – September 2013) aimed to demonstrate the safety and feasibility of *Wolbachia*-infected *A. aegypti* (referred interchangeably as *Wolbachia* mosquitoes). Key activities included building laboratory facilities, particularly for the diagnostic unit laboratory and entomology laboratory, improving research staff capacity and setting up the research team. After importing the wMel strain of *Wolbachia* mosquito eggs from Australia, a wild insect survey to identify the presence of *Wolbachia* in wild insects in Yogyakarta and genetic similarities between *Wolbachia* from the two different hosts (i.e. *D. melanogaster* and Yogyakarta *A. aegypti*) was conducted to respond to community safety concerns. The results showed that 44.9% of identified insect species were positive for *Wolbachia*, which aligns with data from other countries (Kumalawati et al. 2020) and genetic similarities found (Rovik et al. 2022). In parallel to the above activities, baseline assessments on community understanding regarding dengue and its vector, and dengue epidemiology patterns, were carried out to gain in-depth understanding, and to select potential areas for the pilot release in Phase 2. Through extensive meetings and face-to-face interactions, communities and stakeholders were informed about *Wolbachia* and its mechanisms to reduce dengue. Knowledge transfer to improve capacity of the research

Figure 12.1 The study phases of the World Mosquito Program Yogyakarta to apply *Wolbachia*-infected *A. aegypti* to control dengue in Yogyakarta Special Region

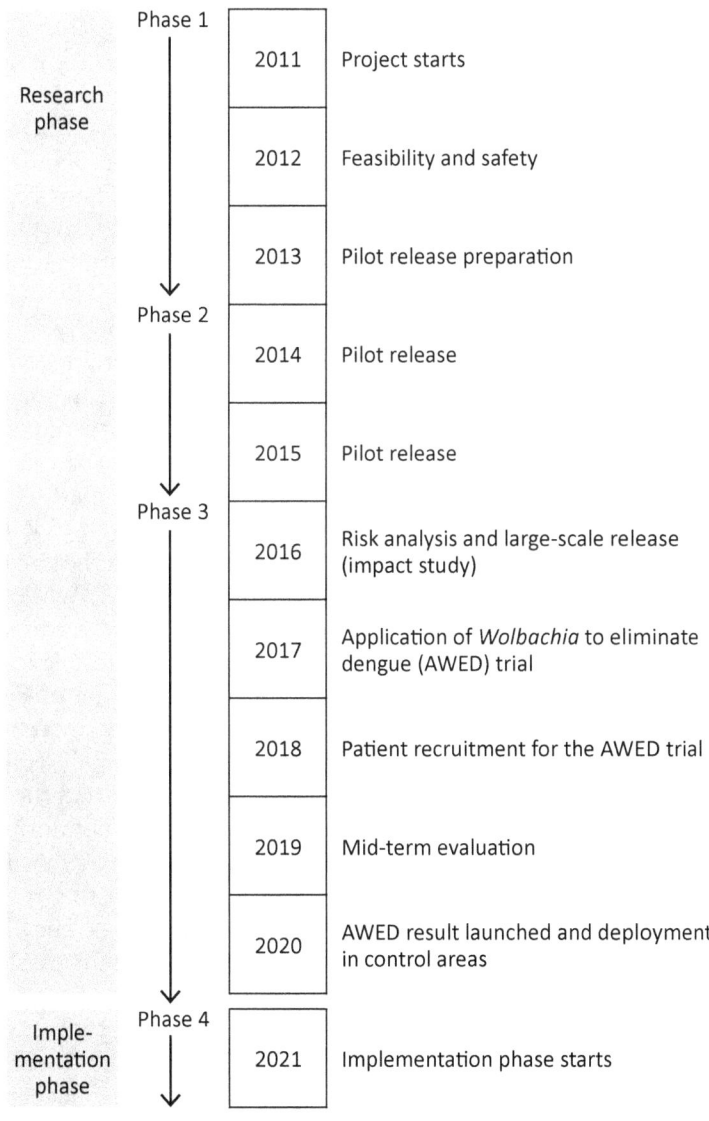

team was carried out through training in Indonesia and Australia, as well as embedding Australian researchers in Yogyakarta during Phases 1 and 2 of the study. Field visits from the WMP Global project leader and senior researchers enhanced the training and supervision process during these phases.

Phase 2 (October 2013 – December 2015) aimed to identify the ability of *Wolbachia*-infected *A. aegypti* mosquitoes to survive in natural populations and to suppress replication of the dengue virus in the local *Wolbachia*-infected *A. aegypti* mosquitoes. Pilot releases of *Wolbachia* mosquitoes were conducted in four hamlets with a total population of about 9,000, namely Nogotirto and Kronggahan hamlets of Gamping subdistrict (Sleman district), and Jomblangan and Singosaren hamlets of Banguntapan subdistrict (Bantul district). The deployment methods differed. The adult release method was used in residential areas of Sleman by releasing 40 adult mosquitoes (males and females) in each release point using a 25 m^2 grid. The releases were conducted over a period of 20 weeks (January to June 2014). In Bantul, we applied the egg-release method using small buckets (November 2014 to May 2015). The eggs were placed in buckets filled with water and fed with fish pellets. Each bucket contained 80–120 eggs and buckets were placed about 25–50 metres apart. The eggs, food and water were changed every fortnight 12 times until *Wolbachia* reached more than 60% in three subsequent observations. The two release methods showed positive results where the prevalence of *Wolbachia* (the number of *A. aegypti* mosquitoes testing positive for *Wolbachia* divided by the total number tested) approached more than 80% within six months of release (Tantowijoyo et al. 2020). Long-term monitoring of each site demonstrated sustainability of *Wolbachia* frequency in their natural habitat over a three-year period. The vector competence analysis showed that, in the natural habitat, *Wolbachia*-infected *A. aegypti* had the ability to block dengue virus replication. In addition, safety monitoring was conducted through detecting horizontal transmission to other insects and vertical transmission to humans by serologically testing the study team members who regularly fed the *Wolbachia* mosquitoes. The findings confirmed absence of both horizontal and vertical transmissions of *Wolbachia* (Utarini 2020).

Phase 3 (2016–2020) aimed to assess the risk and impact of a large-scale release of *Wolbachia*-infected *A. aegypti* on reducing the incidence of dengue in Yogyakarta City. Regarding safety of the *Wolbachia* technology, risk assessment analysis was done independently by 24 experts with various expertise from multiple institutions in Indonesia, coordinated by the Ministry of Research, Technology and Higher Education and the Health Research and Development Agency of the Ministry of Health.

A risk analysis framework developed by the Australian Office of the Gene Technology Regulator was applied and the results concluded that the possible adverse effects of the release of *Wolbachia*-infected *A. aegypti* were negligible and that, therefore, *Wolbachia* is safe for humans, animals and the environment (MRTHE 2017; WMP 2022b).

Two study designs were used to study the impact of *Wolbachia* technology. The first was a quasi-experimental trial using controlled interrupted time series analysis with intervention areas in seven urban villages and control areas in three urban villages in Yogyakarta City. After successful introduction of *Wolbachia* into the natural mosquito population, monitoring of the dengue surveillance data for 30 months showed a 76% reduction in dengue incidence associated with the *Wolbachia* intervention (Indriani et al. 2020). A second study (applying *Wolbachia* to eliminate dengue, or AWED trial) was initiated about six months later—a cluster randomised controlled trial with public randomisation to establish 12 intervention clusters and 12 control clusters. Both study designs used the egg-release method for deploying *Wolbachia* in the intervention areas. These clusters in the AWED trial did not necessarily represent administrative areas but served as a physical and geographical border to prevent the spread of mosquitoes to other regions. The 24 clusters were located in 35 subdistricts of Yogyakarta City and two villages in Bantul district (Anders et al. 2018). The findings from the AWED trial provided strong evidence that *Wolbachia*-infected *A. aegypti* effectively reduced 77.1% of virologically confirmed dengue in the intervention area compared to the control area (Utarini et al. 2021). Based on this evidence together with previous evidence from Yogyakarta City and results from other countries applying the same *Wolbachia* method (Australia, Vietnam and Brazil), the WHO Vector Control Advisory Group concluded that *Wolbachia* intervention demonstrates public health value against dengue and recommended that the WHO initiate the guideline development process to formulate a recommendation on the deployment of *Wolbachia* intervention for dengue control (WHO 2021).

Having the above evidence, the final phase (Phase 4, 2020–2022) aimed to scale up the benefit of *Wolbachia* technology for the community and explored the implementation model of *Wolbachia* intervention to be applied within the dengue control program at the district level. Deployment of *Wolbachia* in the control areas of Phase 3 was completed. The implementation model was developed and implemented in Sleman and Bantul districts, with the intention of exploring an operational and cost-effective model and implementation partners when scaling up the intervention to other dengue endemic sites in Indonesia. In both districts, the local government (via the district health offices) was the primary implementor, with an addition of a local faith-based non-government organisation involved, Muslimat Nahdlatul Ulama, in Bantul district.

Building public acceptance and trust

Releasing *Wolbachia*-infected *A. aegypti* mosquitoes in the community and its success in reducing dengue incidence could have not been achieved without high community acceptance of the technology. Prior to the start of WMP Yogyakarta, both the community and the dengue control programmers understood that the dengue virus is transmitted by *Aedes* mosquitoes, and prevention of mosquito bites and reduction of mosquito breeding sites were the main public health interventions. Without a thorough understanding of *Wolbachia*, *Wolbachia*-infected *A. aegypti* mosquitoes and how the deployment works to reduce dengue infection, the action of releasing mosquitoes could be perceived as contradictory to existing community perceptions and dengue control program practices. Therefore, information and education to instil a high amount of trust in the public (and the stakeholders) was a prerequisite before the actual release of mosquitoes in the community.

Public acceptance of *Wolbachia* technology is a key to successful public health intervention. Gaining public trust was obtained from the start of the program before releasing the mosquitoes, to enable piloting of the intervention and, further, to demonstrate the impact of the technology. Given the importance of community engagement in this program, our efforts to increase community awareness were embedded into the process of building community participation and ownership.

A public acceptance model (PAM) was used by WMP as the basis for obtaining community support for research activities. The PAM was based on a set of public participation principles in community engagement—respectful, inclusive, transparent, responsive and honest—and four key components (raising awareness, a quantitative survey, an issue management system and a community reference group) (O'Neill et al. 2019).

In WMP Yogyakarta, a modified component of PAM was used to gain public acceptance and trust. It consists of five key components: community mapping, community reference groups, community meetings, public campaign and social media, and stakeholder inquiry systems. These strategies are essential because implementation of public health innovation is sensitive to mistrust, low levels of participation, and insufficient uptake of study findings in communities (Tan et al. 2022). Considering the strengths, weaknesses and practical aspects of science communication methods and social marketing, various communication and engagement methods were used. These included community newsletters, a website, print and online broadcast media, social media, community events, communication to engage government stakeholders, formal external partnering and third-party promotion. Our science communication focused on how to increase local community partnership and ownership through continuous dissemination of research processes and results in parallel to the research activities.

Strategies and objectives of community engagement, and communication methods, differed in implementing the five components throughout the program phases. For illustration, during Phase 2 of the program where individual consent and community consent at the smallest community level were applied in Sleman and Bantul, respectively, relatively small populations were involved (less than 9,000 people across the four villages). Community engagement strategies relied heavily on household surveys and group discussions with women health cadres and others for mapping acceptance, presence of the project team in face-to-face meetings with stakeholders and community members, and consultation with the existing community reference group for making important decisions and problem-solving. Community engagement activities were predominated by community meetings and community events with limited public campaigns and use of media. This approach was then shifted as the program moved to a large-scale release at the city level with a population of about 450,000. Extensive use was made of print and online media, radio and television, while face-to-face meetings were limited during Phase 3 of the program, when community consent was given at a higher community level (*kelurahan*). In addition, building community trust and transparency were enhanced through organised community visits to WMP laboratories (diagnostic and entomology laboratories) and increasing the presence of WMP Yogyakarta in public, such as through mobile propaganda using bicycles, a short movie competition, wall painting and WMP Yogyakarta visits and support to empowered communities (Figure 12.2). The saying 'seeing is believing' was practised to deepen community understanding about *Aedes* mosquitoes and *Wolbachia* (Utarini 2016). All these community engagement strategies were implemented along with a community stakeholder inquiry system and daily monitoring of community responses to address any community concerns.

Stakeholder engagement

Using *Wolbachia* technology, implementation of a new vector control method in Indonesia is inevitable because the method has been shown to reduce dengue incidence in Yogyakarta by 77.1%, and a

Figure 12.2 Photos posted on social media illustrating WMP Yogyakarta activities in Yogyakarta City

(1) A field entomology staff explains the egg-release container to community members in Suryatmajan, 2017; (2) A community member in Sorosutan passes the *Wolbachia* mural in his village containing messages to take care of the environment, 2016; (3) A mini-laboratory of WMP Yogyakarta to educate primary schoolchildren at Demakijo 2 Primary School about *Wolbachia A. aegypti* mosquitoes, 2018; (4) The egg-release container placed at the Yogyakarta City municipality office, 2017; (5) Propaganda on bicycles to disseminate *Wolbachia* technology to the public during the celebration of National Health Day in Yogyakarta City.

recommendation has been made for the WHO to develop guidelines for country implementation. Given the importance of safe, responsible and ethical vector control (for humans and ecosystems), Schairer et al. (2019) stated that more information and input from stakeholders at the national and local levels is required. Engagement strategies should be developed according to their purpose, that is, to enquire, to inform and to influence.

Since the beginning of the program, the importance of stakeholder engagement has been well recognised in the process of building evidence of *Wolbachia* technology from its development, piloting, large-scale deployment and implementation to reduce dengue. As the body of evidence grows, stakeholder engagement becomes more emphasised and the need for a multistakeholder approach at national and subnational (provincial and district) levels is crucial if the technology is to be scaled up at local and national levels (Figure 12.3). Stakeholders play different roles in each program phase. For example, when initiating the program, the role of the Ministry of Agriculture at the national and provincial levels was dominant, while the Ministry of Research, Technology and Higher Education played a significant role in Phase 3 of the program. Ministry of Health involvement at all levels has been crucial throughout all the program phases. In a country like Indonesia where health is decentralised to the district level, commitment from the district head or mayor as well as multisectoral approaches at the district government level are critical.

The purpose of stakeholder engagement was shifted from regulatory (obtaining ethical approval and permissions to conduct the study), towards informational (to provide research updates and obtain support throughout the study), influencing political decisions (for funding and further implementation in other sites) and setting good governance (for the government as implementation partner). Throughout the program phases of WMP Yogyakarta, stakeholder engagement has been a dynamic process with various communication materials produced such as briefings, periodic meetings, policy briefs, video testimonies and newspaper articles written by stakeholders. Having large numbers of stakeholders involved, an effective system for managing communication and communication risks is required.

Lessons learned

This chapter describes ten years of complex research for the initiation, development, piloting and proof of efficacy of *Wolbachia*-infected *A. aegypti* technology in Yogyakarta. The evidence from this research serves as the starting point for Indonesia (and other countries) to develop a national road map to implement a new vector control strategy, complementary to the existing dengue control program. Failure to scale up *Wolbachia* technology would inhibit community access to and benefits from this technology. Consequently, more people will continue suffering or even dying from dengue.

Both technical and non-technical challenges need to be anticipated. Finding the right regulatory pathways and mechanisms as well as much doorknocking at different government levels throughout the research phase requires effective leadership, governance and teamwork. The research process entails a spirit of innovation. Community consent, independent risk analysis, early engagement with media and stakeholders, communication of risks and public randomisation are among the activities that need to be undertaken in this process.

Figure 12.3 Mapping of government stakeholders in the World Mosquito Program Yogyakarta

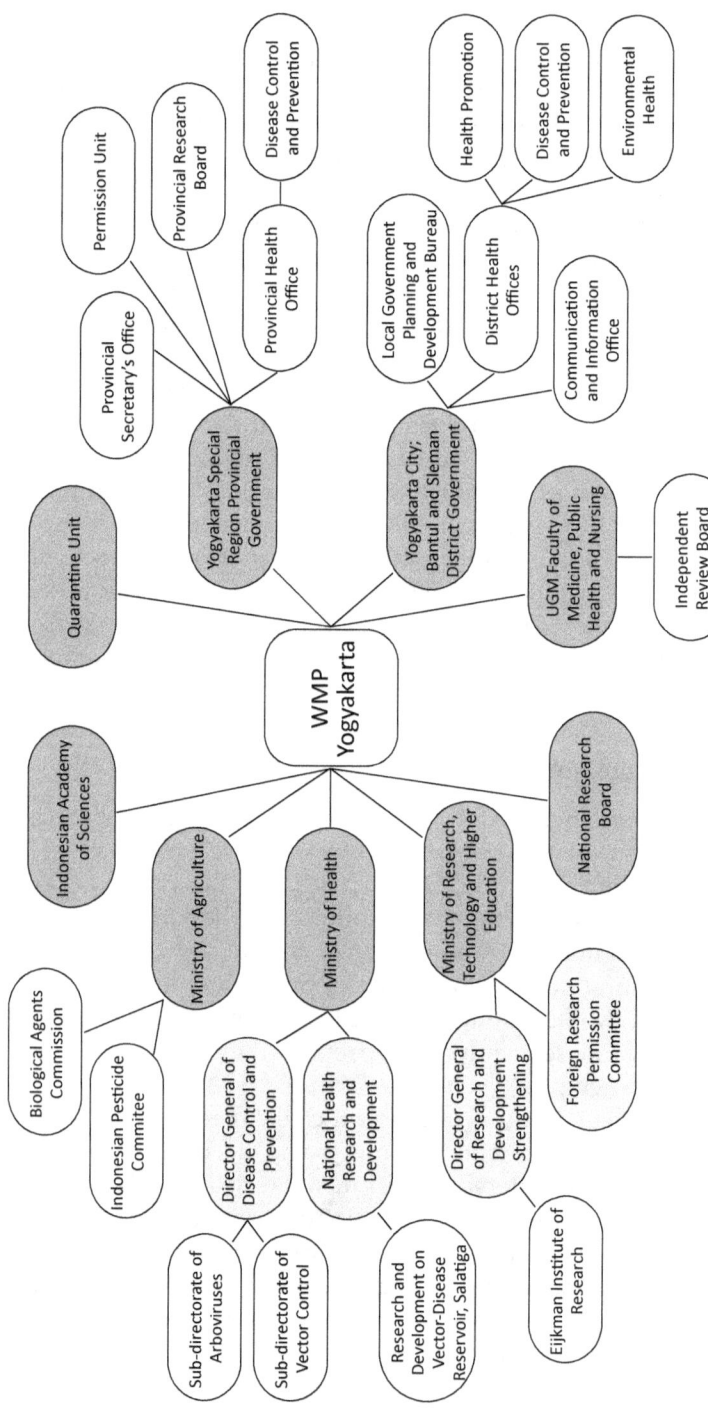

This case study is an example of a real, long-term multidisciplinary collaboration. From a management perspective, multiple years of research involving 80–100 research staff is required to prove this *Wolbachia* technology. Supported by WMP Global, the WMP Yogyakarta multidisciplinary team has built competencies over time to conduct the research, with close collaborative work and high dependence on each team leader to achieve optimum performance. This type of breakthrough research demands multiple years of funding, which is still a luxury for Indonesian researchers. The nature of risks and uncertainties in this research further necessitates good management practices in organising and conducting the research.

If *Wolbachia* technology is to be scaled up in Indonesia, several conditions should be considered: the main vector for dengue transmission in the area is *A. aegypti*; cost efficiencies will increase if the technology is applied in densely populated areas endemic for dengue; government stakeholders and communities approve the release of *Wolbachia*-infected *A. aegypti* mosquitoes; and support is provided by adequate levels of funding, availability of implementation partners, a generic but adaptable implementation model and sufficient production of *Wolbachia*-infected *A. aegypti* mosquitoes.

Finally, we hope that the Indonesian government is willing to lead the national implementation of *Wolbachia* technology as an example of evidence-based public health policy for the benefit of the Indonesian people. The experiences gained in Yogyakarta support the national implementation through providing a model and opportunities for other provinces and districts to learn in a living laboratory for *Wolbachia* technology.

Acknowledgements

The work presented in this chapter is taken from the World Mosquito Program Yogyakarta research project. We thank the Tahija Foundation, Indonesia, for providing financial and managerial support for the World Mosquito Program Yogyakarta; and Monash University/the World Mosquito Program, who provided technical support to the World Mosquito Program Yogyakarta. The support from local communities; district and provincial governments; the Ministry of Health; the Ministry of Research, Technology and Higher Education and its superseding agency, the National Research and Innovation Agency; and the Indonesian Academy of Sciences has been greatly appreciated during the ten-year journey of this research. Also, thanks to Perigrinus H. Sebong, Equatori Prabowo, Achmad A. Tamrin and Citra Indriani for compiling the materials and references for this chapter.

References

Anders, Katherine L., Citra Indriani, Riris Andono Ahmad, Warsito Tantowijoyo, Eggi Arguni, et al. 2018. 'The AWED trial (Applying *Wolbachia* to Eliminate Dengue) to assess the efficacy of *Wolbachia*-infected mosquito deployments to reduce dengue incidence in Yogyakarta, Indonesia: Study protocol for a cluster randomised controlled trial'. *Trials* 19(1): 302. doi.org/10.1186/s13063-018-2670-z

Buhler, Claudia, Volker Winkler, Silvia Runge-Ranzinger, Ross Boyce and Olaf Horstick. 2019. 'Environmental methods for dengue vector control – A systematic review and meta-analysis'. *PLOS Neglected Tropical Diseases* 13(7): e0007420. doi.org/10.1371/journal.pntd.0007420

Elson, William H., Amy R. Riley-Powell, Amy C. Morrison, Esther E. Gotlieb, Erik J. Groessl, et al. 2020. 'Measuring health related quality of life for dengue patients in Iquitos, Peru'. *PLOS Neglected Tropical Diseases* 14(7): e0008477. doi.org/10.1371/journal.pntd.0008477

Guzman, Maria G., Scott B. Halstead, Harvey Artsob, Philippe Buchy, Jeremy Farrar, et al. 2010. 'Dengue: A continuing global threat'. *Nature Reviews Microbiology* 8(Suppl. 12): S7–16. doi.org/10.1038/nrmicro2460

Halasa, Yara A., Donald S. Shepard and Wu Zeng. 2012. 'Economic cost of dengue in Puerto Rico'. *American Journal of Tropical Medicine and Hygiene* 86(5): 745–52. doi.org/10.4269/ajtmh.2012.11-0784

Harapan, Harapan, Alice Michie, Mudatsir Mudatsir, R. Tedjo Sasmono and Allison Imrie. 2019. 'Epidemiology of dengue hemorrhagic fever in Indonesia: Analysis of five decades data from the National Disease Surveillance'. *BMC Research Notes* 12(1): 350. doi.org/10.1186/s13104-019-4379-9

Hung, Trinh Manh, Donald S. Shepard, Alison A. Bettis, Huyen Anh Nguyen, Angela McBride, et al. 2020. 'Productivity costs from a dengue episode in Asia: A systematic literature review'. *BMC Infectious Diseases* 20(1): 393. doi.org/10.1186/s12879-020-05109-0

Indriani, Citra, Riris A. Ahmad, Bayu S. Wiratama, Eggi Arguni, Endah Supriyati, et al. 2018. 'Baseline characterization of dengue epidemiology in Yogyakarta City, Indonesia, before a randomized controlled trial of *Wolbachia* for arboviral disease control'. *American Journal of Tropical Medicine and Hygiene* 99(5): 1299–307. doi.org/10.4269/ajtmh.18-0315

Indriani, Citra, Warsito Tantowijoyo, Edwige Rancès, Bekti Andari, Equatori Prabowo, et al. 2020. 'Reduced dengue incidence following deployments of *Wolbachia*-infected *Aedes aegypti* in Yogyakarta, Indonesia: A quasi-experimental trial using controlled interrupted time series analysis'. *Gates Open Research* 4: 50. doi.org/10.12688/gatesopenres.13122.1

Jeyaprakash, A. and M.A. Hoy. 2000. 'Long PCR improves *Wolbachia* DNA amplification: WSP sequences found in 76% of sixty-three arthropod species'. *Insect Molecular Biology* 9(4): 393–405. doi.org/10.1046/j.1365-2583.2000.00203.x

Karyanti, Mulya Rahma and Sri Rezeki Hadinegoro. 2009. 'Perubahan epidemiologi demam berdarah dengue di Indonesia' [Changes in the epidemiology of dengue haemorrhagic fever in Indonesia]. *Sari Pediatri* 10(6): 424–32. doi.org/10.14238/sp10.6.2009.424-32

Kumalawati, Dian Aruni, Endah Supriyati, Mifta Pratiwi Rachman, Rizky Oktriani, Irianti Kurniasari, et al. 2020. 'Wolbachia infection prevalence as common insects' endosymbiont in the rural area of Yogyakarta, Indonesia'. Biodiversitas 21(12). doi.org/10.13057/biodiv/d211216

Makrufardi, Firdian, Paulin Surya Phillabertha, Erri Larene Safika and Sungkono. 2021. 'Factors associated with dengue prevention behaviour in riverbank area: A cross-sectional study'. Annals of Medicine and Surgery (London) 66: 102450. doi.org/10.1016/j.amsu.2021.102450

MoH (Ministry of Health). 2018. Basic Health Research 2018. Jakarta: MoH.

MoH (Ministry of Health). 2021. Strategi Nasional Penanggulangan Dengue 2021–2025 [The National Strategy for Dengue Control 2021–2025]. Jakarta: MoH.

MoH (Ministry of Health). 2022. Indonesia Dengue Situation Report 2022. Jakarta: MoH. https://ptvz.kemkes.go.id/berita/situasi-dengue-dbd-di-indonesia-pada-minggu-ke-6-tahun-2022

Moreira, Luciano A., Iñaki Iturbe-Ormaetxe, Jason A. Jeffery, Guangjin Lu, Alyssa T. Pyke, et al. 2009. 'A Wolbachia symbiont in Aedes aegypti limits infection with dengue, chikungunya, and plasmodium'. Cell 139(7): 1268–78. doi.org/10.1016/j.cell.2009.11.042

MRTHE (Ministry of Research, Technology and Higher Education). 2017. Kajian Risiko terhadap Pelepasan Nyamuk A. aegypti ber-Wolbachia [Risk assessment on the release of Wolbachia-infected A. aegypti mosquitoes]. Jakarta: MRTHE.

Murphy, B., C. Jansen, J. Murray and P. De Barro. 2010. Risk Analysis on the Australian Release of Aedes aegypti (L.) (Diptera: Culicidae) Containing Wolbachia. Indooroopilly: CSIRO.

Murray, C.J. and A.D. Lopez. 1997. 'Global mortality, disability, and the contribution of risk factors: Global Burden of Disease Study'. The Lancet 349(9063): 1436–42. doi.org/10.1016/S0140-6736(96)07495-8

Murray, Natasha E.A., Mikkel B. Quam and Annelies Wilder-Smith. 2013. 'Epidemiology of dengue: Past, present and future prospects'. Journal of Clinical Epidemiology 5: 299–309. doi.org/10.2147/CLEP.S34440

O'Neill, Scott L., Peter A. Ryan, Andrew P. Turley, Geoff Wilson, Kate Retzki, et al. 2019. 'Scaled deployment of Wolbachia to protect the community from dengue and other Aedes transmitted arboviruses'. Gates Open Research 2: 36. doi.org/10.12688/gatesopenres.12844.3

O'Reilly, Kathleen M., Emilie Hendrickx, Dinar D. Kharisma, Nandyan N. Wilastonegoro, Lauren B. Carringon, et al. 2019. 'Estimating the burden of dengue and the impact of release of wMel Wolbachia-infected mosquitoes in Indonesia: A modelling study'. BMC Medicine 17(1): 172. doi.org/10.1186/s12916-019-1396-4

Ramadona, Aditya Lia, Lutfan Lazuardi, Yien Ling Hii, Åsa Holmner, Hari Kusnanto and Joacim Rocklöv. 2016. 'Prediction of dengue outbreaks based on disease surveillance and meteorological data'. PLOS ONE 11(3): e0152688. doi.org/10.1371/journal.pone.0152688

Ramadona, Aditya Lia, Yesim Tozan, Lutfan Lazuardi and Joacim Rocklöv. 2019. 'A combination of incidence data and mobility proxies from social media predicts the intra-urban spread of dengue in Yogyakarta, Indonesia'. PLOS Neglected Tropical Diseases 13(4): e0007298. doi.org/10.1371/journal.pntd.0007298

Rovik, Anwar, Edwin Widyanto Daniwijaya, Endah Supriyati, Ayu Rahayu, Dian Aruni Kumalawati, et al. 2022. 'Wolbachia genetic similarity in different insect host species: *Drosophila melanogaster* and Yogyakarta's (Indonesia) *Aedes aegypti* as a novel host'. *Biodiversitas* 23(5): 2321–28. doi.org/10.13057/biodiv/d230510

Sasmita, Hadian Iman, Kok-Boon Neoh, Sri Yusmalinar, Tjandra Anggraeni, Niann-Tai Chang, et al. 2021. 'Ovitrap surveillance of dengue vector mosquitoes in Bandung City, West Java Province, Indonesia'. *PLOS Neglected Tropical Diseases* 15(10): e0009896. doi.org/10.1371/journal.pntd.0009896

Sasmono, R. Tedjo, Anne-Frieda Taurel, Ari Prayitno, Hermin Sitompul, Benediktus Yohan, et al. 2018. 'Dengue virus serotype distribution based on serological evidence in pediatric urban population in Indonesia'. *PLOS Neglected Tropical Diseases* 12(6): e0006616. doi.org/10.1371/journal.pntd.0006616

Satoto, Tri Baskoro Tunggul, Antok Listyantanto, Suzana Dewi Agustjahjani, Hari Kusnanto Josef and Barandi S. Widartono. 2018. 'Vertical transmission of dengue virus in the Yogyakarta airport area'. *Environmental Health and Preventive Medicine* 23(1): 22. doi.org/10.1186/s12199-018-0711-6

Schairer, Cynthia E., Riley Taitingfong, Omar S. Akbari and Cinnamon S. Bloss. 2019. 'A typology of community and stakeholder engagement based on documented examples in the field of novel vector control'. *PLOS Neglected Tropical Diseases* 13(11): e0007863. doi.org/10.1371/journal.pntd.0007863

Shepard, Donald S., Eduardo A. Undurraga and Yara A. Halasa. 2013. 'Economic and disease burden of dengue in Southeast Asia'. *PLOS Neglected Tropical Diseases* 7(2): e2055. doi.org/10.1371/journal.pntd.0002055

Shepard, Donald S., Eduardo A. Undurraga, Yara A. Halasa and Jeffrey D. Stanaway. 2016. 'The global economic burden of dengue: A systematic analysis'. *Lancet Infectious Diseases* 16(8): 935–41. doi.org/10.1016/S1473-3099(16)00146-8

Simmons, Cameron P., Jeremy J. Farrar, Nguyen van Vinh Chau and Bridget Wills. 2012. 'Dengue'. *New England Journal of Medicine* 366(15): 1423–32. doi.org/10.1056/NEJMra1110265

Sulistyawati, Sulistyawati, Maria Nilsson, Marlita Putri Ekasari, Surahma Asti Mulasari, Tri Wahyuni Sukesi, et al. 2020. 'Untapped potential: A qualitative study of a hospital-based dengue surveillance system'. *American Journal of Tropical Medicine and Hygiene* 103(1): 120–31. doi.org/10.4269/ajtmh.19-0719

Swain, Subhashisa, Minakshi Bhatt, Sanghamitra Pati and Ricardo J. Soares Magalhaes. 2019. 'Distribution of and associated factors for dengue burden in the state of Odisha, India during 2010–2016'. *Infectious Diseases of Poverty* 8(1): 31. doi.org/10.1186/s40249-019-0541-9

Tan, Rayner K.J., Dan Wu, Suzanne Day, Yang Zhao, Heidi J. Larson, et al. 2022. 'Digital approaches to enhancing community engagement in clinical trials'. *npj Digital Medicine* 5(1): 37. doi.org/10.1038/s41746-022-00581-1

Tantowijoyo, Warsito, Bekti Andari, Eggi Arguni, Nida Budiwati, Indah Nurhayati, et al. 2020. 'Stable establishment of wMel *Wolbachia* in *Aedes aegypti* populations in Yogyakarta, Indonesia'. *PLOS Neglected Tropical Diseases* 14(4): e0008157. doi.org/10.1371/journal.pntd.0008157

Utarini, Adi. 2016. 'How we convinced people to trust a new innovative approach to eliminate dengue'. *The Conversation*, 21 June. https://theconversation.com/how-we-convinced-people-to-trust-a-new-innovative-approach-to-eliminate-dengue-56692

Utarini, Adi, ed. 2020. *Aplikasi* Wolbachia *Dalam Eliminasi Dengue: Laporan Akhir Penelitian World Mosquito Program Yogyakarta* [Wolbachia application in dengue elimination: Final research report of the World Mosquito Program Yogyakarta]. Yogyakarta: Pusat Kedokteran Tropis, Fakultas Kedokteran, Kesehatan Masyarakat dan Keperawatan UGM.

Utarini, Adi, Citra Indriani, Riris A. Ahmad, Warsito Tantowijoyo, Eggi Arguni, et al. 2021. 'Efficacy of *Wolbachia*-infected mosquito deployments for the control of dengue'. *New England Journal of Medicine* 384(23): 2177–86. doi.org/10.1056/NEJMoa2030243

Weinert, Lucy A., Matthew C. Tinsley, Matilda Temperley and Francis M. Jiggins. 2007. 'Are we underestimating the diversity and incidence of insect bacterial symbionts? A case study in ladybird beetles'. *Biology Letters* 3(6): 678–81. doi.org/10.1098/rsbl.2007.0373

Werren, J.H. 1997. 'Biology of *Wolbachia*'. *Annual Review of Entomology* 42: 587–609. doi.org/10.1146/annurev.ento.42.1.587

WHO (World Health Organization). 2020. *Ending the Neglect to Attain the Sustainable Development Goals: A Roadmap for Neglected Tropical Disease 2021–2030*. Geneva: WHO.

WHO (World Health Organization). 2021. Thirteenth Meeting of the WHO Vector Control Advisory Group. Geneva: WHO. www.who.int/publications/i/item/9789240021792

Wilastonegoro, Nandyan N., Dinar D. Kharisma, Ida S. Laksono, Yara A. Halasa-Rappel, Oliver J. Brady and Donald S. Shepard. 2020. 'Cost of dengue illness in Indonesia across hospital, ambulatory, and not medically attended settings'. *American Journal of Tropical Medicine and Hygiene* 103(5): 2029–39. doi.org/10.4269/ajtmh.19-0855

WMP (World Mosquito Program). 2022a. 'Our story'. www.worldmosquitoprogram.org/en/about-us/our-story

WMP (World Mosquito Program) 2022b. 'How our *Wolbachia* methods work'. www.worldmosquitoprogram.org/en/work/wolbachia-method/how-it-works

Yang, Xiaorong, Mikkel B.M. Quam, Tongchao Zhang and Shaowei Sang. 2021. 'Global burden for dengue and the evolving pattern in the past 30 years'. *Journal of Travel Medicine* 28(8): 146. doi.org/10.1093/jtm/taab146

Ye, Yixin H., Alison M. Carrasco, Francesca D. Frentiu, Stephen F. Chenoweth, Nigel W. Beebe, et al. 2015. '*Wolbachia* reduces the transmission potential of dengue-infected *Aedes aegypti*'. *PLOS Neglected Tropical Diseases* 9(6): e0003894. doi.org/10.1371/journal.pntd.0003894

Zeng, Zhilin, Juan Zhan, Liyuan Chen, Huilong Chen and Sheng Cheng. 2021. 'Global, regional, and national dengue burden from 1990 to 2017: A systematic analysis based on the Global Burden of Disease Study 2017'. *EClinicalMedicine* 6(32): 100712. doi.org/10.1016/j.eclinm.2020.100712

Index

A

Adminduk (Administrasi Kependudukan), 60
Aedes aegypti (mosquito), 11, 223, 227–237
aged and ageing, 180n11, 183, 185, 190
   COVID-19 mortality, 115
Alma Ata declaration, 41
amlodipine, 92, 102, 103, 104
amoxicillin, 97, 104
anaesthesiologists, 75
anatomical pathologists, 78
antenatal care, 18, 136, 137–138, 139, 149, 153, 156–157
   see also maternal health
'anti-communist' killings, 3
Arya, Bima, 48
ascariasis, 222
Asian financial crisis, 20, 42, 44, 45
Askes health insurance scheme, 5, 44
assistive devices, 26, 186
Australia
   dengue control, 231
   foreign health investment, 82, 83
Australian aid program, 173
Australian Office of the Gene Technology Regulator, 231
avian influenza, 49, 50

B

Bali: maternal mortality, 151
Balinese culture, 118, 127
Bandung: dengue, 224
Banglitbangkes, 209, 218
Bantul district, 226, 230, 231, 232, 233, 236
Bidan Desa (midwife training), 149
Bipolar Care Indonesia, 204, 211–212
birth certificates, 189
blindness, 186
blood pressure, 84, 92, 153
   see also hypertension
BP Jamsostek, 45
BPJS-K (Healthcare and Social Security Agency)
   administers JKN, 5–6, 27, 44, 73, 89
   costs management, 90
   COVID-19 expenses, 20
   establishment, 45
   information systems, 26
   membership, 5–6, 84
   non-medical expenses, 23
   payment delays, 95
   premiums, 33, 52, 89
   private hospitals, 23, 81, 85
   role, 34
   see also JKN (National Health Insurance)
BPNT (non-cash food subsidies), 194
BPS (Statistics Indonesia): 2020 Census, 59–70
Brazil
   dengue control, 231
   health expenditure, 22
British Virgin Islands: foreign health investment, 83

Brunei: maternal mortality, 151
bubonic plague, 214

C

Cambodia: maternal mortality, 9
cancer, 4, 6, 22, 71
cancer surgeons, 24, 25, 75
cardiovascular disease, 4, 6, 22, 71
censuses
   2010 Population Census, 176, 179, 197–200
   2020 Population Census, 7–8, 59–70, 218
   British administration, 57–58
   COVID-19 disruptions, 7, 57, 60–62, 69
   data availability, 57
   Dutch administration, 58
   history, 57–59
   importance, 7, 56
   Indonesian administration, 59
   Post Enumeration Survey, 69
children
   in census counts, 57
   child health, 4, 9
   child labour, 192, 193
   child marriage, 189
   COVID-19 health disruptions, 18
   disability prevalence, 175
   growth monitoring, 138–139, 140
   health insurance, 189–191
   in households with disability, 192–193
   immunisation, 22, 28, 34, 136, 138–139
   smoking, 46
   stunting, 4, 21, 28, 140
China
   fertility rates, 65
   foreign health investment, 82, 83
   health expenditure, 22
cholesterol, 84
chronic health conditions, 115, 116
   see also by name of condition; non-communicable diseases
cigarette smoking, 22, 34, 46–48, 84
cigarette taxes, 34, 89

ciprofloxacin, 92
Cipta Kerja (omnibus law), 83
clinical pathologists, 75
Community Health Insurance, 44
conditional cash transfers (PKH), 194
constitution amendments, R2H, 37
contraception, 136, 153
Council of Indonesian Ulama (MUI), 48
COVID-19
   amplifies health inequities, 113, 114–117, 133
   cases, Indonesia, 3, 18, 19, 132–133, 213
   cases, worldwide, 132
   census disruptions, 7, 57, 60–62, 69
   deaths, Indonesia, 3, 18, 19, 115, 133, 213
   deaths, worldwide, 132
   dengue impacts, 223
   economic impacts, 17, 18, 29, 30, 33
   emergence, 2, 60
   epicentre, 3, 50, 133
   government expenditure, 20
   government management, 50, 51–52
   health services disruptions, 9, 12, 18, 89, 134, 139–140, 143, 207
   health system pressures, 6–7, 132, 133
   income pressures, 134
   lockdown policies, 18, 20, 22, 50, 52, 116, 134, 213
   mental health, 11, 213–214
   Our World in Data repository, 135
   pregnancy rates, 136–137
   and smoking, 46
   vaccinations, 29, 30, 52, 132

D

decentralisation of health system, 6, 28, 72, 73, 76, 141
demonstrations (activism), 46
dengue
   cases, Indonesia, 224, 226
   cases, worldwide, 222
   control strategies, 11, 224–225
   disease burden, Indonesia, 4, 224

disease burden, worldwide, 222–223
economic burden, 223, 224
mortality, Indonesia, 224
reporting system, 227
risk factors, 223, 226–227
seasonality, 226
surveillance system, 226, 227
symptoms, 223
see also World Mosquito Program Yogyakarta
Denpasar: dengue, 224
dentists, 23, 75, 79
depressive disorders, 205, 209–210
Desa Siaga Sehat Jiwa (mental health programming), 216, 217
diabetes, 4, 22, 71, 84
diphtheria, 49
Directorate of Mental Health and Illegal Drugs, 205, 217
disability
  access to services, 187–191
  assistive devices, 186
  causes, 183–185
  data sources, 10, 176–178, 195, 197–200
  definition, 172–176
  and education, 187–188, 192
  and employment, 188, 189
  environmental barriers, 173–174
  eradicating discrimination, 173
  family impacts, 191–194
  health status for PWD, 189–190
  household expenditure, 192–193
  measuring, 173–176
  prevalence, 10, 173, 178–183
  prevention and support, 194–195
  and schools, 187–188, 192
  types, 183, 184
disadvantaged communities
  health services access, 115, 116, 117–118
  see also disability; rural and remote access to services; transgender people
diseases, see by *name of disease*; infectious diseases; non-communicable diseases

District Health Information Software database, 134–135
doctors, 23, 75, 79, 140, 141, 142, 206
Drosophila melanogaster (fruit fly), 227, 228

E

East Java: oncologists, 24
East Nusa Tenggara
  hospitals, 23, 33
  malaria, 22
  maternal health, 10, 157–159, 162–169
  maternal mortality, 150, 151, 159
Ebola, 134, 143
economic growth, 26, 29–30
elderly population, see aged and ageing
Eliminate Dengue Project Yogyakarta, see World Mosquito Program Yogyakarta
Emotional Health for All, 212
environmental health officers, 79
epidemiologic transition, 1–2

F

Family Card (Kartu Keluarga), 62
family planning services, 18, 68, 150
Fathalla, Mahmoud, 148
fertility rates, 63–65
Framework Convention on Tobacco Control, 47
fuel subsidy cuts, 44, 45
furosemide, 98

G

General Directorate of Health Workforce, 76
general practitioners (GPs), see doctors
generic medicines, 91–92
geographical isolation and health services, see rural and remote access to health services
Global Burden of Disease Study, 4
Google searches, 214
Gorontalo: maternal mortality, 151

government debt, 20, 21, 30
government revenue, 20
  see also tax revenue
GP Farmasi, 93
gross domestic product (GDP), 20, 21, 26, 27
gynaecologists, 75

H

haemorrhage, 153
Haloperidol, 202
Healthcare and Social Insurance Agency, *see* BPJS-K (Healthcare and Social Security Agency)
health data
  disability, 176–178, 195, 197–200
  mental health, 208–211
  quality and quantity, 26, 57, 141
  see also censuses
health expenditure, 5, 20, 26, 30, 31, 81–82, 141, 143, 208
health facilities
  maternity, 149–150, 157–161, 166–167
  numbers and distribution, 5, 73–74
  private investment, 23
  quality, 166–167
  status pre COVID-19, 22–23
  Yogyakarta, 225–226
  see also hospitals; *puskesmas*; rural and remote access to services
health indicators, 1, 21–22, 84
health insurance
  history, 43–46
  see also JKN (National Health Insurance)
Health Insurance for Poor Communities (Askeskin), 44
health policy
  fiscal packages, 21, 22
  influencers, 39–41
  marginalised people, 119, 121–122, 126
  medicine procurement, 91–92
  organised labour and farmers' influence, 41

politicians' influence, 7, 40–41, 45, 48
popular and populist influence, 38, 41, 42, 43, 48, 51–52
power relations, 38, 51–52
predatory elites' influence, 7, 38–51
private investment, 18, 33–34
progressives' influence, 7, 38, 40, 41, 42, 45, 48, 51–52
rural–urban inequities, 71–72, 78, 84, 85
technocrats' influence, 7, 38, 39, 41, 42, 45, 48, 51–52
uneven reform, 38, 43, 51–52
WHO requirements, 40
  see also International Health Regulations
Health Safety Net for Poor Families (JPS-Gakin), 44
health security, 49–50, 52
health services
  acceptability, 113
  affordability, 113
  availability, 113
  emergency responsiveness, 143
  medicines, 95–99
  moral pathology, 119, 126
  preventive services, 23, 27, 34
  risk discourse, 119, 126, 127
  utilisation, 121
health services access
  COVID-19 amplifies inequities, 113, 114–117
  as human right, 113
  inequities, 2–3, 9, 11–12, 89, 113–128, 140–141, 158
  intersectionality analysis, 9, 114, 117, 123–127
  to medical specialists, 71–85
  mental health, 10–11, 210–211
  people with disability, 187–191
  power asymmetries, 125
  see also rural and remote access to health services
health system
  digitisation, 33
  financing, 26–28, 31

foreign investment, 82–84, 85
governance, 72–73, 76–78, 141, 144
private investment, 8, 23, 81–82, 84, 85
referral system, 72–73
resilience, 31
stakeholders, 76–78
transformation, 17, 30–34
vulnerabilities, 5–8
see also BPJS-K (Healthcare and Social Security Agency); JKN (National Health Insurance)
health transition, 1–4, 11–12
health workers
    diverted to COVID-19 response, 140
    foreign nationals, 84
    human resources, 23–25, 31
    maternal care, 157–161, 162, 166, 167
    medicine procurement, 99
    mental health, 205–206, 208, 209, 212, 213, 215
    numbers and distribution, 5, 6, 79, 140–141
    production of specialists, 75, 78–79, 84
    see also by name of health professional, e.g. medical specialists; nurses
hearing aids, 186
heart disease, 4, 6, 22, 71
helminthiases, 223
hepatitis B, 224
HIV/AIDS
    emergence, 2, 49
    health services, 9, 114, 118–121, 125
    stigma and discrimination, 119, 127
hookworm, 222
hospitals
    distribution and access, 23, 31
    foreign investment, 82–84, 85
    insurance claims, 28
    mental health care, 205, 206
    numbers, 24, 33, 74
    private hospitals, 79–82
    public hospitals, 79–82, 85
    teaching hospitals, 75, 78
    types, 75

human resources for health, *see* health workers
hypertension, 22
    see also blood pressure

I

Ibunda mental health service, 212
identity cards, 215
immunisation, 22, 28, 34, 136, 138–139
India: maternal mortality, 9
Indonesia Demographic and Health Survey, 150, 151
Indonesia Family Life Survey, 178, 179, 197–200, 210
Indonesian Cigarette Manufacturers Association, 47
Indonesian Democratic Party of Struggle (PDI-P), 88
Indonesian Medical Association, 40, 76
Indonesian Medical Council, 77
Indonesian Press Council, 212
Indonesian Psychiatric Association, 213
Indonesian Public Health Association, 40
Indonesian Schizophrenia Support Community, 211
infant mortality, 1, 133, 143, 150
infectious diseases, 2, 3, 4, 6, 20, 21, 49
    see also by name of disease
INN generic medicines, 92
International Classification of Functioning, Disability and Health, 174
International Health Regulations, 49–50
interns, 75, 78
intersectionality analysis of health services, 9, 114, 117, 123–127
Into the Light Indonesia, 212

J

Jakarta
  dengue, 224
  hospital beds, 23
  maternal mortality, 151
  oncologists, 24
Jakarta Health Card (KJS), 46, 88
Jaminan pension, 194
Jamkesda (Local Health Insurance for the Poor), 5
Jamkesmas (National Health Insurance for the Poor and Near Poor), 5, 44, 159
Jampersal (Maternity Health Insurance), 159
Jamsostek (Workers' Social Insurance scheme), 5, 44, 45
Japan
  fertility rates, 65
  foreign health investment, 83
Java: maternal mortality, 151
JKN (National Health Insurance)
  benefits, 6, 24, 34
  deficits, 6, 27–28, 52, 89–90, 105–106
  establishment, 5–6, 23, 26–27, 44–46, 73–74, 88–89, 114, 189
  health system structure, 91
  medicine policy and prices, 8, 89–90, 106
  mental health cover, 204, 206, 208, 211, 215
  private hospitals, 81
  use by people with disability, 188, 189–191
  see also BPJS-K (Healthcare and Social Security Agency)

K

kader jiwa (mental health advocates), 206, 207, 209, 217
Kartu Keluarga (Family Card), 62
Kebumen mental health model, 214–216, 217
kidney disease, 4, 6
Kopigawa (mental health support group), 216

L

legislation
  Law No. 9/1960 on Basic Health, 88
  Law No. 3/1966 on Mental Health, 207
  Law No. 4/1984 on Infectious Disease Outbreaks, 20
  Law No. 23/1992 on Health, 42
  Law No. 40/2004 on a National Social Security System, 45
  Law No. 36/2009 on Health, 37, 46, 47, 48
  Law No. 18/2014 on Mental Health, 207
  Law No. 8/2016 on Disability, 10, 173, 195
  Law No. 15/2018 on Health Insurance, 215
  Law No. 2/2020 on State Financial Policy and Financial System Stability for Handling the COVID-19 Pandemic, 20
  Law No. 11/2020 on Job Creation, 83
  Medical Practice Law No. 29/2004, 79
  Ministry of Finance Regulation No. 7/2021 on Regional Fiscal Capacity, 28
  Ministry of Health Regulation No. 1501/2010 on Communicable Diseases, 224
  Ministry of Health Regulation No. 54/2017, 207
  Ministry of Health Regulation No. 30/2019 on Hospital Classification and Licensing, 75
  Ministry of Health Regulation No. 13/2022 about the Strategic Plan of the Ministry of Health 2020–2024, 17, 30
  omnibus law (Cipta Kerja), 83
  Presidential Regulation No. 44/2016 on Lists of Business Fields, 82, 83
  Presidential Regulation No. 39/2019, 59

Presidential Regulation No. 54/2020, 61
Presidential Regulation No. 10/2021 on Investment Sectors, 83
Presidential Regulation No. 47/2021 on Administration of the Hospital Sector, 84
leprosy, 22, 222, 223
life expectancy, 1, 3, 4, 68–69

M

Mahar, Dr, 216
malaria, 21–22, 34, 227
Malaysia
  doctors, 140
  foreign health investment, 83
  health expenditure, 22, 141
  maternal mortality, 9, 151
  neonatal mortality, 133
  nurses, 140
Maluku: hospitals, 33
marginalised people
  health services access, 115, 116, 117, 124, 126
  health services advocacy, 125
  see also transgender people
maternal health
  antenatal care, 18, 136, 137–138, 139, 149, 153, 156–157
  community involvement, 168, 169
  COVID-19 disruptions, 9, 18, 139–140
  definition, 148
  facility births, 136, 137–138, 139
  government programs, 149–150, see also Revolusi KIA
  health facilities, 149–150, 157–161, 166–167
  improvements to, 4
  postnatal care, 136, 138, 139
  services quality, 169
  Sustainable Development Goals, 149
  three delays model, 164–169
  workforce, 157–161, 162, 166, 167
maternal mortality
  causes of deaths, 153, 154–155
  COVID-19 impacts, 143

factors influencing, 151–153
Indonesia, 9–10, 21, 28, 133, 149, 150–153, 159
Southeast Asia, 151
WHO definition, 150–151
Mbah Marsiyo mental health home, 202, 214–216
measles, 49
medical devices, 26
medical schools, 75, 77, 78, 84
Medical Specialist Association, 76
medical specialist colleges, 77
medical specialists, 8, 24, 71–85
medicines
  auction system, 92, 93
  branded generics, 91–92, 102, 103
  civil service management, 99
  e-catalogue, 92–96
  expiry dates, 97
  health care providers, 95–99
  imports, 26
  INN generics, 92, 95, 102, 103
  maximum retail price, 91–92, 93, 96
  mental health, 202, 211
  patient preferences, 103–104
  policies and regulation, 6, 8, 91–92, 106
  price controls history, 91–92
  prices, 8, 89–90, 102–104, 105
  producers and distributors, 93–95
  profits, maximising, 100–102, 105
  quality, 105
  sales incentives, 100–101
  transport costs, 94
  unethical prescriptions, 98–99, 100–101
men
  disability incidence, 185
  smoking, 46
mental health
  access to services, 10–11, 210–211
  budget allocation, 208
  case study: Ahmed, 202, 214, 216
  case study: Aisyah, 203–204, 216–217
  COVID-19 exacerbates, 11, 213–214
  data sources, 208–210, 217, 218

diagnostic assessment tools, 209–210
disease burden, 201
Google searches, 214
legislation, 207, 218
medication costs, 211
online support systems, 217
reform priorities, 218
rehabilitation, 216
reporting systems, 208–210
stigma, 203, 204, 210, 211, 217
treatment pathways, 206–207
Mental Health Atlas, WHO, 208, 218
mental health care system, 205–207, 217–218
mental health organisations, 204, 211–213
Mexico: health expenditure, 22
midwives, 79, 101, 140, 141, 149
see also traditional birth attendants
Millennium Development Goals, 149
Mini International Neuropsychiatric Interview (MINI), 209–210
Ministry of Administrative and Bureaucratic Reform, 76
Ministry of Agriculture, 235
Ministry of Education, Culture, Research and Technology, 76
Ministry of Finance, 34, 76
Ministry of Health, 26, 72, 235
Ministry of Internal Affairs, 76
Ministry of Research, Technology and Higher Education, 235
Ministry of Social Welfare, 208
MNCH (maternal, neonatal and child health), see children; infant mortality; maternal health
moonlighting, 80
mortality rates, see COVID-19; maternal mortality; infant mortality
mosquitoes, 11, 223, 227–237
Muhammadiyah, 48

N

Nahdlatul Ulama, 48, 232
National Center for Mental Health, 207, 217
National Civil Service Agency, 76
National Economic Recovery Program, 20, 30
National Health Insurance, see JKN (National Health Insurance)
National Health Strategy 2021–2024, 31
National Strategy for Dengue Control 2021–2025, 225
neglected tropical diseases, see dengue
neonatal care, 136, 138, 139
neonatal mortality, 1, 133, 143, 150
neonatologists, 75
Netherlands: foreign health investment, 83
neurosurgeons, 75
New Order
  fall of, 37, 38, 42, 51
  health insurance, 43–44
  health policies, 4, 7, 41–42
  health security, 49
  tobacco control, 46
Nilam, Jessica, 212
non-cash food subsidies (BPNT), 194
non-communicable diseases, 2, 3, 4, 6, 22, 28, 33, 71, 84
  see also cigarette smoking
nurses, 23, 79, 101, 140
  mental health, 205, 209, 213, 215
nutrition, 4
nutrition indicators, 150
nutritionists, 79

O

obesity, 84
obstetricians, 75
older adults, see aged and ageing
omnibus law (Cipta Kerja), 83
Omran, Abdel, 2
oncologists, 24, 25, 75
One Data (Satu Data), 59, 62, 63
O'Neill, Scott L., 227

Onie, Sandersan, 212
Our World in Data repository, 135
ovitrap index, 227

P

paediatricians, 75
Panti Sosial Dosaraso (residential care facility), 216
Papua
  doctors, 141
  hospitals, 33
  malaria, 22
paracetamol, 93
pasung (shackling), 202, 203, 207, 209, 214, 215
pathologists, 75, 78
patriarchal family structure, 165
pertussis (whooping cough), 49
Pharmaceutical Manufacturers Association, 93
pharmacies, *see* medicines
Philippines
  doctors, 140
  health expenditure, 5, 22, 141
  maternal mortality, 9, 151
  nurses, 140
physicians, *see* doctors
PKH (conditional cash transfers), 194
polio, 49
population age structure, 64–66
population growth rates, 63
population, Indonesia, 63
  see also censuses
postnatal care, 136, 138, 139
posyandu, 150
poverty
  and access to health services, 116
  and disability, 191–192
preconditions for health, 42, 43
pregnancy rates during COVID-19, 136–137
primary health care, 31, 72–73
'productivist' model of social welfare, 43–44
prosthetics, 186
psychiatrists, 205, 209, 212, 215
psychological distress, 205, 210

psychologists, 205, 209, 212, 213
PT Asabri, 45
PT Askes, 45
PT Jamsostek, 45
PT Taspen, 45
public health
  development of, 56–57
  MMR as indicator, 133, 150, 151
public health officers, 79
public health professionals, 23
Public Procurement Policy Board (LKPP), 92, 95
pulmonary disease, 71
puskesmas
  dengue management, 227
  health system role, 23, 31, 73
  maternal health care, 162
  mental health care, 205, 206, 207, 214–215
  numbers and distribution, 75, 141, 150

R

R2H (right to health), 37–52
  definition, 37n1
  government failures, 38
  preconditions for health, 42, 43
  see also health policy
rabies, 223
radiologists, 75
Raffles, Thomas Stamford, 56, 57
Rahasia Gadis (A Girl's Secret), 212
reading glasses, 186
recession, 20
rehabilitation specialists, 78
Revolusi KIA, 162–163, 166, 168
right to health (R2H), *see* R2H (right to health)
Riliv mental health service, 212
Riskesdas, 179–180, 202–203, 210
Rumah Tunggu (maternity waiting house program), 157–158, 162
rural and remote access to health services, 5, 23, 28, 71, 72–74, 78, 84–85, 115, 140–141, 157, 166, 168, 210

S

Safe Motherhood Initiative, 148, 149
Sakernas, 177–178, 179, 197–200
SARS, 49
Satu Data (One Data), 59, 62, 63
schistosomiasis, 222
schizophrenia, 211
screening programs, 33
Selaras Jiwa (mental health support group), 216
Self-Report Questionnaire 20, 210
Seychelles: foreign health investment, 83
shackling, *see pasung* (shackling)
Sian, Tshui, 214, 216
Siauw, Benny Prawira, 212
Sierra Leone: Ebola, 143
Simkeswa reporting system, 208
Singapore
    fertility rates, 65
    foreign health investment, 82, 83
    neonatal mortality, 133
Slamat, Mas, 216
Sleman district, 226, 230, 231, 233, 236
Smart Indonesia Program (PIP), 187
smoking, 22, 34, 46–48, 84
social determinants of health framework, 125
Social Safety Net – Health scheme (JPS-BK), 44
social security, 44–45, 193–194
    see also JKN (National Health Insurance)
social welfare 'productivist' model, 43–44
social workers, 205, 208
socioeconomic determinants of health services, 116
spectacles, 186
State Revenue and Expenditure Budget, 20
Statistics Indonesia (BPS) census, 59–70
structural determinants of health services, 125, 126
stunting, 4, 21, 28, 140
Suharto (former president), 37
Suharyanto (head of BPS), 61
suicide, 204–205, 209, 212, 214, 216–217
Sukarnoputri, Megawati, 88
Supartini, Ninik, 216
Supas (intercensal survey), 151
surgeons, 75, 78
survivorship (life expectancy), 1, 3, 4, 68–69
Susenas, 89, 176–177, 178–179, 183, 197–200
Sustainable Development Goals, 149
Swaperiksa, 213

T

tagana (mental health volunteers), 215, 217
tax revenue, 20, 26, 27, 30, 33, 34
teaching hospitals, 75, 78
telemedicine, 33, 143
tetanus, 49
Thabrany, Hasbullah, 45
Thailand
    doctors, 140
    fertility rates, 65
    health expenditure, 5, 22, 141
    maternal mortality, 9, 151
three delays model (maternal health), 164–168
tobacco companies, 47–48
tobacco control, 46–48
tobacco-related diseases, 46
trachoma, 222
trade unions, 46
traditional birth attendants, 149, 157–162
    see also midwives
transgender people, 114, 122, 123, 126
    case study: Asana, 118–126
    case study: Vivi, 120–124
tuberculosis, 21, 34, 49, 224

U

Ubah Stigma mental health service, 212
United Nations Convention on the Rights of Persons with Disabilities, 10, 173
universal health care, WHO definition, 27
universal health cover, *see* JKN (National Health Insurance)
upper respiratory tract infections, 224
urban access to health services, 28, 71, 72–74, 84, 115, 140–141, 158
Utomo, Bagus, 211

V

vaccinations, COVID-19, 29, 30, 52, 132
veterans' pension, 194
Vietnam
    dengue control, 231
    doctors, 140
    health expenditure, 5, 22
    maternal mortality, 9, 151
Village Potential (Potensi Desa), 89
vitamin A supplements, 18

W

Washington Group on Disability Statistics, 175–176, 177
West Kalimantan: oncologists, 24
West Papua: malaria, 22
wheelchair use, 174
White Cigarette Producers Association (GAPRINDO), 47
whooping cough (pertussis), 49
Widodo, Joko (Jokowi), 12, 45–46, 59, 88
Winasa, I Gede, 45
Wolbachia bacteria, 11, 223, 227–237
women
    caregiver role, 192, 193
    decision-making by, 164–166, 169
    disability incidence, 185
    disability and marriage, 189
    health support groups, 212
    smoking, 46
    valuing, 148
    see also maternal health
World Bipolar Day, 212
World Health Organization
    dengue control, 231
    MMR definition, 150–151
    right to health, 40
World Mosquito Program Yogyakarta
    community engagement, 232–234
    lessons learned, 235, 237
    overview, 11, 227–228
    risk assessment, 230–231
    stakeholder engagement, 233–235, 236
    study designs, 231
    study phases, 228

Y

Yogyakarta
    city status, 225–226
    maternal mortality, 150
Yudhoyono, Susilo Bambang, 45

INDONESIA UPDATE SERIES

1989
Indonesia Assessment 1988 (Regional Development)
Edited by Hal Hill and Jamie Mackie

1990
Indonesia Assessment 1990 (Ownership)
Edited by Hal Hill and Terry Hull

1991
Indonesia Assessment 1991 (Education)
Edited by Hal Hill

1992
Indonesia Assessment 1992: Political Perspectives on the 1990s
Edited by Harold A. Crouch and Hal Hill

1993
Indonesia Assessment 1993: Labour: Sharing in the Benefits of Growth?
Edited by Chris Manning and Joan Hardjono

1994
Indonesia Assessment 1994: Finance as a Key Sector in Indonesia's Development
Edited by Ross McLeod

1996
Indonesia Assessment 1995: Development in Eastern Indonesia
Edited by Colin Barlow and Joan Hardjono

1997
Indonesia Assessment: Population and Human Resources
Edited by Gavin W. Jones and Terence H. Hull

1998
Indonesia's Technological Challenge
Edited by Hal Hill and Thee Kian Wie

1999
Post-Soeharto Indonesia: Renewal or Chaos?
Edited by Geoff Forrester

2000
Indonesia in Transition: Social Aspects of Reformasi and Crisis
Edited by Chris Manning and Peter van Diermen

2001
Indonesia Today: Challenges of History
Edited by Grayson J. Lloyd and Shannon L. Smith

2002
Women in Indonesia: Gender, Equity and Development
Edited by Kathryn Robinson and Sharon Bessell

2003
Local Power and Politics in Indonesia: Decentralisation and Democratisation
Edited by Edward Aspinall and Greg Fealy

2004
Business in Indonesia: New Challenges, Old Problems
Edited by M. Chatib Basri and Pierre van der Eng

2005
The Politics and Economics of Indonesia's Natural Resources
Edited by Budy P. Resosudarmo

2006
Different Societies, Shared Futures: Australia, Indonesia and the Region
Edited by John Monfries

2007
Indonesia: Democracy and the Promise of Good Governance
Edited by Ross H. McLeod and Andrew MacIntyre

2008
Expressing Islam: Religious Life and Politics in Indonesia
Edited by Greg Fealy and Sally White

2009
Indonesia beyond the Water's Edge: Managing an Archipelagic State
Edited by Robert Cribb and Michele Ford

2010
Problems of Democratisation in Indonesia: Elections, Institutions and Society
Edited by Edward Aspinall and Marcus Mietzner

2011
Employment, Living Standards and Poverty in Contemporary Indonesia
Edited by Chris Manning and Sudarno Sumarto

2012
Indonesia Rising: The Repositioning of Asia's Third Giant
Edited by Anthony Reid

2013
Education in Indonesia
Edited by Daniel Suryadarma and Gavin W. Jones

2014
Regional Dynamics in a Decentralized Indonesia
Edited by Hal Hill

2015
The Yudhoyono Presidency: Indonesia's Decade of Stability and Stagnation
Edited by Edward Aspinall, Marcus Mietzner and Dirk Tomsa

2016
Land and Development in Indonesia: Searching for the People's Sovereignty
Edited by John F. McCarthy and Kathryn Robinson

2017
Digital Indonesia: Connectivity and Divergence
Edited by Edwin Jurriëns and Ross Tapsell

2018
Indonesia in the New World: Globalisation, Nationalism and Sovereignty
Edited by Arianto A. Patunru, Mari Pangestu and M. Chatib Basri

2019
Contentious Belonging: The Place of Minorities in Indonesia
Edited by Greg Fealy and Ronit Ricci

2020
Democracy in Indonesia: From Stagnation to Regression?
Edited by Thomas Power and Eve Warburton

2022
In Sickness and in Health: Diagnosing Indonesia
Edited by Firman Witoelar and Ariane Utomo

www.ingramcontent.com/pod-product-compliance
Lightning Source LLC
Chambersburg PA
CBHW072131290426
44111CB00012B/1856